Here's what the Reviewers are Saying About *Object-Oriented Programming with ActionScript*:

"*Object-Oriented Programming with ActionScript* is a thorough and inspirational technical book written by highly talented and well-respected authors and Flash community members. A great contribution to Flash development and a valuable reference tool for any serious Flash developer."
—**Aria Danika**, *Senior Moderator Flashkit.com,*
Co-founder www.openedsource.net

"*Object-Oriented Programming with ActionScript* is an essential book for any developer that builds Flash applications. Authored by the most qualified and well-respected ActionScript programmers in the world, this book will certainly emerge as the ultimate resource on the subject."
—**Jobe Makar**, *President,* http://www.electrotank.com

"The Flash community has more than its fair share of creative, intelligent, visionary talent. The fact that Macromedia Flash brings together the technical and the artistic mind so well ensures this to be true. Even amongst these peers though, both Branden and Sam stand out as a couple of the best teachers and practitioners of the art and science of Flash. In this book you will discover some of the formal programming background and common sense that have helped raise them to these heights."
—**Peter Santangeli**, *Vice President, Flash MX Engineering,*
Macromedia, Inc.

"Branden Hall and Samuel Wan have taken an advanced topic and reduced it to an understandable level with an approach chock full of concise and practical real-world examples."
—**Michael Grundvig**, *Senior Application Developer,*
http://www.electrotank.com

"Object-Oriented programming in Flash provides Flash application developers with a good overview of the i~~~~~~~ ~~~~~~
Contains valuable insights from a highly ~~~~~
of authors."
—**Colin Moock**, *Moock.org*

D1416539

Object-Oriented Programming with ActionScript

Contents At a Glance

Object-Oriented Programming with ActionScript

Branden Hall and Samuel Wan

www.newriders.com

201 West 103rd Street, Indianapolis, Indiana 46290

An Imprint of Pearson Education

Boston • Indianapolis • London • Munich • New York • San Francisco

Object-Oriented Programming with ActionScript

Copyright © 2003 by New Riders Publishing

FIRST EDITION: September, 2002

International Standard Book Number: 0-7357-1183-6

Library of Congress Catalog Card Number: 200210637

06 05 04 03 02   7 6 5 4 3 2 1

Interpretation of the printing code: The rightmost double-digit number is the year of the book's printing; the rightmost single-digit number is the number of the book's printing. For example, the printing code 02-1 shows that the first printing of the book occurred in 2002.

Printed in the United States of America

Trademarks

Warning and Disclaimer

Publisher
David Dwyer

Associate Publisher
Stephanie Wall

Executive Editor
Steve Weiss

Production Manager
Gina Kanouse

Managing Editor
Sarah Kearns

Acquisitions Editor
Deborah Hittel-Shoaf

Development Editor
Jennifer Eberhardt

Project Editor
Michael Thurston

Copy Editor
Linda Seifert

Indexer
Chris Morris

Product Marketing Manager
Tammy Detrich

Publicity Manager
Susan Nixon

Manufacturing Coordinator
Jim Conway

Book Designer
Louisa Adair

Cover Designer
Brainstorm Design, Inc.

Cover Production
Aren Howell

Proofreader
Benjamin Lawson

Composition
Wil Cruz

Table of Contents

About the Authors

Branden Hall is a senior developer for Fig Leaf Software in Washington D.C. He spends most of his time developing, consulting with clients, and supporting the highly popular Flash mailing list that he founded, Flashcoders. He also spends a lot of time speaking at industry events such as the Flash Forward conferences and Macromedia's Devcon. When he's not working, Branden enjoys numerous hobbies including building vintage video game machines and mountain biking. Branden lives in Hyattsville, Maryland with his amazing wife Patti and a growing family of cats.

Samuel Wan has worked in many roles as an independent contractor, book author, and instructor in the area of interactive web development. He holds a graduate degree in human-computer interaction from the University of Michigan School of Information. Samuel has contributed to several publications on Flash design and interactive programming, and has spoken at many web industry conferences in the United States and Europe.

About the Contributing Authors

Andreas Heim is from the small town of Hattenhofen, close to Stuttgart, in Germany, a center of German car engineering. Originally intending to become a professional soccer player, his education took him into the area of media studies and programming. After creating an interactive CD-ROM, his focus shifted from film and video to interactive media. His school required him to complete a six-month internship, which brought him to  Smashing Ideas where being a soccer-playing-and-beer-drinking German intern was highly respected. He had so much fun in Seattle that he extended his stay to one year, before deciding to stay permanently. Andreas currently works on all kinds of cutting edge digital media projects, including bringing Flash to devices, while enjoying his time outside of work, snowboarding and playing soccer. He is also a Macromedia Advisory Board member.

Nigel Pegg, an incurable generalist, approaches Flash development with a varied experience in multimedia design and computing science. Having completed his CS degree while working at various web design shops, Nigel got out of school looking for some way to apply his schooling and server-side expertise to his passion and experience with tools like Macromedia Flash and Director. While working at multimedia development shop redengine.com, Nigel built dragspace.com, a wild experiment in Flash 4 programming, and ended up with a job at Macromedia helping lead a team in the development of Flash MX's UI Components.

About the Technical Reviewers

These reviewers contributed their considerable hands-on expertise to the entire development. As the book was being written, these dedicated professionals reviewed all the material for technical content, organization, and flow. Their feedback was critical to ensuring that *Object-Oriented Programming with ActionScript* fits our readers' need for the highest-quality technical information. Andreas Heim was also a technical reviewer for this book (see his bio on the previous page).

Patricia Geneva Lee, or Patricia G. L. Hall, is a happily married newlywed who is still getting used to dealing with her name and its recent evolution. She is a web applications developer, having worked on building and maintaining web sites, content management systems, and corporate intranets since 1998.

Patti has earned Bachelor of Arts degrees in English literature and French language and literature and has completed three years of graduate study in public relations. Luckily, she doesn't spend much time thinking about the dichotomy of her past education and present profession.

Dave Yang is an independent developer and founder of Quantumwave Interactive Inc. (http://quantumwave.com/), a web and multimedia development firm based in Toronto. He is also the technical director and lead developer for companies in both Canada and the U.S.

Dave's background comes from diverse fields including computer mathematics, programming, design, and computer graphics. He develops projects using various technologies such as Flash, ColdFusion, JSP, ASP, XML, and Director. Some of his projects include database-driven games and web sites, CD-ROMs and kiosks, and educational and commercial software for organizations such as the Art Gallery of Ontario, Discovery Channel, Disney, Kraft, McDonald's, and the NBA.

Dave's articles on object-oriented programming, software methodologies, techniques, and developments are widely used by other developers in the Flash community.

Cortlandt Winters got his BA in filmmaking and dramatic literature in 1989 from Vassar College and entered the computer field soon after with a desire to create interactive film and animation. Since video capabilites on popular systems were still immature, he focused on programming language design and natural language parsers in the meantime and obtained a formal MS in computer science while popular systems improved. He has  now spent the past eight years creating multimedia educational software for the SUNY Research Foundation and General Dynamics. He has used both system level languages and scripting languages extensively. The laundry list includes C, C++, Prolog, Toolbook, Java, Javascript, XSLT, and Flash. In late 2001 he encountered Python and has been transfixed on it since. He is currently developing a system for collaborative storytelling with JavaCC, Jrun, and Flash—finally.

Acknowledgments

Branden Hall

I would like to thank first off and foremost my co-author Sam and everyone else involved in the creation of this book. Everyone kicked me in the butt when I needed it and helped make this book something that I am very proud of. Next, my wife Patti deserves a big heap of thanks for nagging me when I needed it and putting up with way too many late nights and groggy mornings. (I am not a happy person to be around before 9 a.m.) I also want to thank my parents. They always instilled in me that I could do anything I put my mind to and always supported me and my efforts even when I didn't really deserve it. Finally, thanks to everyone at Fig Leaf who has been there for me, especially Jody Keating and the senior staff.

Samuel Wan

I would like to thank the people at New Riders Publishing for the opportunity to write a book we've always felt was missing from the existing repertoire of ActionScript texts. New Riders understands the growing sophistication of Flash users, and gave us a chance to address a fundamental shift towards problem-solving applications of Flash technology.

Flash development requires skills from many disciplines, and my growth is the result of many generous people, especially my parents. In human-computer interaction, Professors Mirel, Venoit, Bartlett, Olson, Radev, Furnas, and other faculty at the School of Information have provided conceptual foundations that will last beyond the life span of any technology I can hope to master. Many friends and teachers have opened doors along the way, or learned side-by-side with me since the beginning (listed chronologically): Bill Rudman, Clay Smith, Grace Halim, Jessica Speigel, Aaron Adams, Were-Here.com, David Emberton, Scott Hamlin, Eric Wittman, Jim Heid, Manuel Clement, Lynda Weinman, Margaret Carlson, Jim Caldwell, Dave Yang, Robert Penner, Nigel Pegg, Andreas Heim, and many more. I definitely wouldn't have made it this far without Hoi Yin Lo in my life. Most of all, I must thank the whirlwind of ingenuity that is Branden Hall; the impact of his contributions to the Flash industry are widely respected and appreciated.

Tell Us What You Think

As the reader of this book, you are the most important critic and commentator. We value your opinion and want to know what we're doing right, what we could do better, what areas you'd like to see us publish in, and any other words of wisdom you're willing to pass our way.

As the Executive Editor for New Riders Publishing, I welcome your comments. You can fax, email, or write me directly to let me know what you did or didn't like about this book—as well as what we can do to make our books stronger.

Please note that I cannot help you with technical problems related to the topic of this book, and that due to the high volume of mail I receive, I might not be able to reply to every message.

When you write, please be sure to include this book's title and author as well as your name and phone or fax number. I will carefully review your comments and share them with the author and editors who worked on the book.

Fax: 317-581-4663
Email: steve.weiss@newriders.com
Mail: Steve Weiss
          Executive Editor
          New Riders Publishing
          201 West 103rd Street
          Indianapolis, IN 46290 USA

Introduction

Over the past few years, Flash has undergone an incredible transformation from a cool animation tool to an extremely powerful platform for writing complex and compelling web applications. The most compelling changes have come with the newest version of Flash, Flash MX.

Suddenly, with Flash MX, it's possible to toss out many of the old and confusing HTML front ends for web apps and swap them out with a totally Flash solution. This possibility is born from two major features of Flash MX: huge improvements to ActionScript and the new component system.

Unfortunately, although these possibilities are out there, it's not going to be easy for most Flash developers to get there. This is because this type of development goes beyond simple scripting and into the land of real, object-oriented programming— a place where few Flash developers have traveled.

That's where this book comes in; it's a code warrior's trail guide. A book that steps beyond basics and the idle theory and shows you how to approach building cutting-edge code with ActionScript.

We've stepped in all the puddles, fallen down all the ravines, and found most of the shortcuts, so follow us and you're bound to get where you want to be as Flash developer.

Who Should Read This Book?

This is a book for people who already know Flash. If you've dabbled in ActionScript enough to know your `if` statements from your `while` loops, this book is for you. Even if the term "object-oriented" doesn't mean a thing to you yet, as long as you're comfortable with coding ActionScript this book will be very valuable for you.

This book is also for developers who are already developing applications with Flash but feel that they don't necessarily know the best way of going about their work. A large portion of this book is devoted to best practices, so even seasoned developers will be able to get something out of this book.

Chapter 1, "Starting Off on the Right Foot," also goes into more detail about who will benefit from this book.

Who This Book Is Not For

This book is not for people who have never coded in ActionScript before or people who aren't familiar with the Flash interface. If you don't like to program, and aren't interested in code, this book isn't going to do anything for you.

If you don't know ActionScript well enough yet to really get into this book, we'd highly recommend our sister book, Phillip Kerman's *ActionScripting in Flash MX*, also from New Riders. Phil's book will take you from variables all the way to the point where you're ready to tackle this book.

Overview

This book is divided into three main parts: object-oriented programming, components, and advanced topics.

Part I, "OOP and ActionScript," takes you from square one, describing what OOP is, and what problems it solves. It continues through topics such as design patterns and how to use OOP in the real world, and finishes up with a complete walkthrough of the creation of an object-oriented game—from design to completion.

Part II, "Components," is devoted entirely to components and begins with an in-depth explanation and how to use them. It then travels deep into component architecture so that you know how to customize them for your own use. Finally, you learn to create your own components, using such advanced topics as live preview and custom user interfaces.

Part III, "High-Level ActionScript," covers advanced topics and runs the gamut of Flash and programming knowledge. From server-side interaction, to data structures and utilization of Flash's object structure, it's all in there. These chapters are the result of years of experience developing with Flash and about as close as you're going to get to direct brain-dump from us!

Conventions

This book follows a few typographical conventions you should probably know about:

- A new term is set in *italic* the first time it is introduced.
- Program text, functions, variables, and other "computer language" are set in a fixed-pitch font, for example:

```
this.createEmptyMovieClip()
```

And Now...

And now, you're ready to step into the world of object-oriented programming with ActionScript...

I

OOP and ActionScript

1

Starting Off on the Right Foot

By Samuel Wan

THIS BOOK IS ABOUT PROBLEM SOLVING from the ActionScript programmer's perspective: defining the quickest and smartest way to get things done with Macromedia Flash MX.

Flash developers' skills have become more sophisticated over the past few years. As people find innovative new ways to use Flash, the technology has also evolved to keep up with our ever-growing needs. The race is constant and breathtaking—Flash experts learn the latest ActionScript techniques, and then push the techniques to their limits. Macromedia responds by improving the technology and adding new tools. Then, users take the newest version of Flash and push the limits even further. This thrilling race toward the future often leaves behind a void for those who recently started learning Flash. It's an information void on acquiring the ActionScript knowledge that more experienced users have gathered over time.

What's Next for Flash Developers?

There are zillions of tutorials online, bookstores full of wonderful introductions to Flash, and a community of developers who share their knowledge enthusiastically! However, a growing number of people have gone through all the beginner and intermediate material. They've read the books, finished the tutorials, and even completed a few cool projects with ActionScript. If you've reached this level of experience with Flash, then you've probably realized a few things:

1. The most compelling projects are highly interactive, and they rely on lots of ActionScript to drive the interface logic.

2. A smarter approach is necessary for building complex interfaces. Simply "writing code" without some sense of planning can lead to repeated errors and wasted effort.

3. Strategies for advanced ActionScript are scattered throughout the web, or simply not documented at all. This loose distribution of knowledge makes it difficult to learn, adapt, and keep up with important discoveries.

Solid ActionScript skills are crucial to the design of complex interfaces. With the release of powerful new features in Flash MX, Macromedia has positioned the technology as a rich client for web applications. Earlier trends focused on animation and navigation. The new direction for the web places a stronger emphasis on complex interfaces and applications to get interfaces to do useful things and to solve problems. For ActionScript programmers, the difference between simple navigation and complex Flash applications is the quality of code required to pull off a successful project. With Flash applications, you're trying to accommodate the user's interaction with different levels of information, making sure events are handled in the correct sequence, displaying the appropriate data, and juggling data between different parts of the interface.

There are countless web applications you can build with Flash MX, maybe even a few that nobody's imagined yet. We could teach you how to build a few Flash applications, but then you'd only learn how to build a few Flash applications. Instead, we're more interested in explaining core concepts of advanced ActionScript that are crucial to any complex Flash project. You will find that time invested in learning deeper ActionScript patterns will pay off as your Flash projects grow in size and importance.

For Intermediate ActionScript Users

If you have some experience with ActionScript, and you're looking for some direction on further improving your skills, then this book was written for you. Making the journey from intermediate to expert can feel lonely because there are few resources out there for advanced ActionScript programmers. You can find a lot of good tutorials on specific techniques, but the really important stuff—fundamental concepts for problem solving with ActionScript—never surface in the Flash community. This book doesn't describe every advanced technique in ActionScript; rather, it provides a foundation of essential concepts you'll need to understand if you want to develop complex Flash projects quickly and efficiently.

> If you're still learning basic ActionScript (if you don't know the difference between if and while statements, and for loops are still a bit confusing to you), we would highly recommend Phillip Kerman's excellent introduction to ActionScript, *ActionScripting in Flash MX*.

If you've been working in ActionScript for a long time, you've probably started seeing recurring patterns in your daily work, and probably wish that you wouldn't have to solve the same problem every time a new project comes along. Sure, you can always cut-and-paste external ActionScript files, but they always seem to require some tweaking to fit comfortably with each new project. We'll go into detail on how to use Flash MX efficiently in three ways:

1. **Object-Oriented Programming (OOP)**—It's more than a catchy phrase. OOP offers a way to design code to save you a lot of time and effort. The first one-third of this book helps you establish a solid understanding of object-oriented programming in the ActionScript language: what OOP is about, what OOP is good for, and how to apply OOP strategies when designing your code. If you're not completely sure how OOP applies to ActionScript, Part I, "OOP and ActionScript," is essential reading before you go any further!

2. **Flash MX Components**—Components are re-usable, self-contained user interface elements with customizable appearance and behavior. Flash MX components are to Flash 5 smart clips as the Industrial Revolution was to the Dark Ages. If you approach a user interface problem that you've encountered again and again, it's time to build a component and solve this problem once and for all. We've dedicated Part II, "Components," toward the explanation of components.

We start with a basic introduction to components, discuss how to combine different components into a powerful interface, and then lead to more powerful ways to exploit the component architecture in Flash MX. This book explains how to link different components into a full interface with ActionScript, and also goes into great detail on how to plan, design, and build a useful component.

> Note: One of the contributing authors, Nigel Pegg, helped define the standards for components at Macromedia, and also built many of the original Flash MX components.

3. **Advanced ActionScript Techniques**—Even though we won't cover the entire range of ActionScript techniques, Flash MX has some new features you'll have to master if you're going to use the technology effectively. Part III, "High-Level ActionScript," provides insights into specific topics we feel are most essential to Flash development. Besides OOP and components, we discuss:

   - Debugging
   - Text field manipulation
   - Hidden powers of the new movieclip object
   - Flash-server integration
   - Data structures in ActionScript

For Intrigued Programmers

The power of ActionScript and the richness of Flash interfaces have also caught the attention of traditional programmers. We're seeing growing numbers of people experienced in Java, C++, and other multimedia languages such as Director Lingo, making their way into the Macromedia world of Flash. If you would like to translate your programming skills into ActionScript, you might find the whole Flash architecture a bit…weird. Don't worry, we know exactly how you feel.

   To people with experience in other languages, ActionScript might look familiar but behave strangely at the same time because it's essentially JavaScript syntax (ECMA-262) running within a timeline-based animation technology. Concepts such as OOP, event-handling, and modular programming are key ingredients in Flash MX, but they work a bit differently for two reasons:

1. ActionScript (JavaScript, ECMA-262, and so on) is a loosely typed, object-based language. As a result, programming in ActionScript can either be a frustrating process, or a heavenly experience in free expression. It all depends on whether you try to force other language paradigms onto ActionScript, or whether you adapt to the free-flowing character of the language. This book introduces object-oriented programming from the ActionScript perspective, and helps you orient your previous knowledge of programming within the ActionScript framework.

2. The Flash MX authoring environment integrates drawing, animation, and programming tools into a single workflow. What this means is that you can build the graphics for interface elements and edit the code for these UI elements—all within the same environment. The catch is knowing how to organize your graphics and code. This book introduces some strategies for abstracting the interface from the logic to make your projects easier to manage and more re-usable. We'll also describe advanced techniques for user interface programming that take advantage of unique features in Flash MX.

Getting Started the Right Way

The chapters following this first chapter cover OOP, and chapters further on in the book discuss components, and then advanced ActionScript techniques. Along the way, you'll be presented with ideas and then shown examples on how to apply the ideas with short, practical examples. Because this book involves the reader's participation in actually writing and testing code, it's a good idea to start off with some advice on how to use the authoring tool in an efficient manner.

Developing good work habits always pays off in the long run. Consider the variety of tasks you perform in Flash MX: switching between window panels, editing code, testing code, adding graphics and text, and so on. It's important to learn how to perform these tasks naturally and smoothly. Once you're comfortable with the environment, you can spend less time wrestling with the authoring tool and more time concentrating on the project at hand. The rest of this chapter provides helpful tips on using the Flash MX authoring environment from a programmer's perspective.

Tip #1: Get Comfortable!

ActionScript programming involves a lot of switching back and forth between several main areas:

- **Timeline**—Layers of linear frames that contain animation, sound, and keyframe ActionScript.
- **Stage**—The main area for editing graphics and animation.
- **Property Inspector**—A context-sensitive panel that gives you access to properties of whatever object you're working on (lines, shapes, movieclips, textfields, keyframes, and so on).
- **Actions panel**—The main text editor for writing ActionScript code.
- **Library and Components panels**—The Library panel contains all your graphics. You need constant access as you define linkages for symbols that you want to expose to ActionScript from the library. The Components panel allows you to build interfaces by dragging individual UI components onto the stage. It's also possible to build nonvisual components that define code rather than graphics in a Flash project.

If you work with ActionScript all the time, the first thing you can do to make your life easier is to rearrange the Panel Layout in the Flash MX authoring tool. The people involved with this book spend every day working in the Flash MX environment, so we really value an authoring environment that's easy to use. Although we have slightly different styles, we found some common suggestions for making the Flash MX environment a more comfortable space.

Floating Actions Panel

First of all, check out the Panel Sets option in the Windows pull-down menu. Figure 1.1 shows a list of preset layouts in the Panel Sets menu, including layouts for programmers/developers at different resolutions. The layout in Figure 1.1 is already configured with the "Developer" Panel Set. This layout is okay, but not ideal.

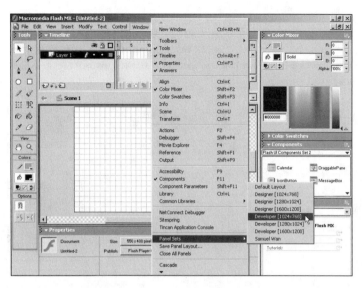

Figure 1.1 The Developer layout model.

We recommend that you choose the Developer Panel Set, and then adjust it to fit your needs. First, drag the Actions panel out of its docking position by using your mouse on the left-side "grip" in the panel's title bar. Drag the panel to the upper-left corner of the screen to create a floating panel. Then, pull on the lower-right corner of the panel to expand it over the Timeline and stage area. Be sure the Actions panel doesn't cover the Property Inspector though, you'll be switching between the Actions panel and Property Inspector quite frequently! You can collapse the Actions Toolbox and open the pop-up menu to set the Actions panel to Expert Mode. Figure 1.2 shows the final position for the Actions panel.

It's important to give the Actions panel lots of space so that you can read all your code at a glance. To jump between the Actions panel and everything else, you can easily toggle the Actions panel on and off by using the F9 hotkey. You can save this layout by choosing the Save Panel Layout command in the Windows pull-down menu, and then providing a name for the layout. Next time you want to revert to this layout, just select it from the Panel Sets menu.

One of our tech editors, Dave Yang, suggests the Andale Mono font for the Actions panel. This font has some useful features that make code easier to read. For example, it features more distinctive differences between the lower-case "l" and the number "1" characters, as well as the letter "O" and the number "0". You can download the free font from Microsoft at: `http://www.microsoft.com/typography/downloads/andale32.exe`.

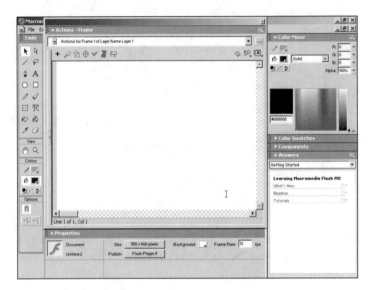

Figure 1.2   Recommended position for the Actions panel.

Floating Reference Panel

Next, you should probably adjust the Reference panel. During the process of writing code, you'll often need to look up ActionScript documentation in the Reference panel, so try to keep it somewhere easily accessible. One approach is to drag it out of the bottom docking area and expand it on top of the Actions panel as shown in Figure 1.3. This allows you to open and close the Reference panel any time you need to look up some information about a particular ActionScript command. Developers with dual monitors often position the Actions panel and Reference panel in the second monitor, while others like to dock the Reference panel to a floating Actions panel. Again, the point is to provide as much space as possible for reading text. You can toggle the Reference panel on and off by using the Shift+F1 hotkey.

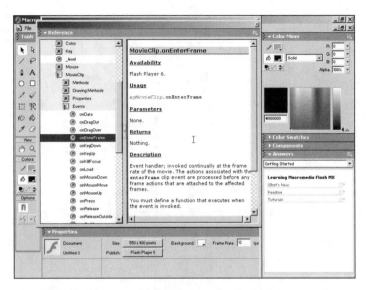

Figure 1.3 Recommended position for the Reference panel.

Minimalist Layout and Hotkeys

This is just a personal preference, but the most space-efficient layout combines the use of hotkeys and floating panels to make your workflow as efficient as possible. It's not recommended for everyone, but give it a try and see if you're more comfortable with it.

- Make the Timeline shorter by choosing the "short" option in the Timeline's upper-right pop-up menu.
- Remove clutter by only docking the Components (F11 key) and Library panels (Ctrl+L).
- Get rid of the Tools panel entirely and rely on hotkeys to toggle between different tools (see Figure 1.4).

I've included a copy of the minimalist Layout panel set for this introductory chapter. You can try the layout by saving a copy into the Configuration/Panel Sets folder and restarting the Flash MX editor. Figure 1.4 shows all the hotkeys for the tools. The most frequently used hotkeys discussed in this book are bolded.

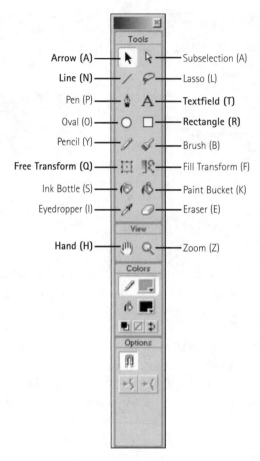

Figure 1.4 Hotkeys for tools.

You can also define your own hotkeys by selecting the Keyboard Shortcuts option in the Edit pull-down menu.

Andreas Heim has another tip for calibrating the Info panel. By default, the Property Inspector shows you the coordinates of the upper-left corner of an object, not the registration point used for Action-Script. Unless they are identical, this can lead to confusion. To avoid that, open the Info panel, set the measure point to the registration point in the 9-point-grid, and the Property Inspector will show the same coordinates.

Tip #2: Use the Actions Panel To Your Advantage

Now let's take a look at the Actions panel more closely. The process of writing code actually involves several main tasks, and you can use the Actions panel to make those tasks more efficient.

Assigning Code

The first main step in writing code is to assign your code to a target. For example, you can select a keyframe, movieclip, or button by clicking with the mouse and then pressing F9 to open the Actions panel. Once you've opened the Actions panel for a target, there's a handy feature to keep the Actions panel focused on that target, no matter what else you click with the mouse: just press the Pin icon in the upper-right corner of the screen. Now, you can drag items around the stage with your mouse and the Actions panel will still stay focused on the same piece of code.

Looking Up Code

With all the new commands in ActionScript, it's easy to forget how to use a specific command! Fortunately, the Actions panel provides lots of tips and references to help you write your code.

Figure 1.5 shows two lists of ActionScript commands, in case you forget which command to use. There's a collapsible Actions toolbox in the left part of the panel, and an expanding pull-down menu that you can access by clicking on the + icon. If you select an action in the Actions toolbox, you can press the Reference panel icon in the upper-right corner to open the documentation for that particular action. Give it a try. The Reference panel is a great tool for exploring the ActionScript language!

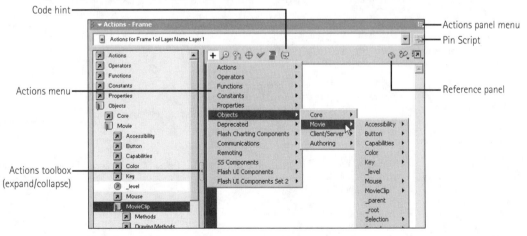

Figure 1.5 The Actions panel.

Code Hinting

After a while, you'll become familiar enough with ActionScript to know which command you want to use. But what if you can't remember the exact parameters for an ActionScript method? Flash MX has a code-hinting feature that pops up a small hint about what you should use in a method argument (see Figure 1.6). For example, try typing the following line of code into the Actions panel:

```
this.createEmptyMovieClip(
```

Figure 1.6 Automatic code hinting.

What if you're using an object but don't remember the specific name of a method? No problem. Code hints are also provided for object methods and properties, if you follow a certain naming convention. By adding an underscore character and a two-letter abbreviation of the object type, you can get a pop-up listbox of all the possible methods for that object.

For example, let's say that you want to change the depth of a movieclip, but you've forgotten the specific name of that method in the MovieClip class. If you name the movieclip "myclip_mc." with a period at the end, the Actions panel will recognize the "_mc." suffix as an abbreviation for the MovieClip class. Then, you'll see a list of all the methods and properties available for movieclips.

Try typing the following code into the Actions panel to see how code hinting works (see Figure 1.7):

```
myclip_mc.
```

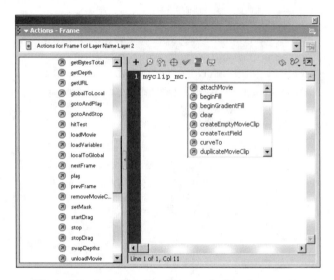

Figure 1.7 Code hint for object methods and properties.

Code Hinting Defined In XML Files

Flash MX relies on several XML files to define code hints. You'll find these files in the <flashmx install dir>\First Run\ActionsPanel\ folder of the Flash MX directory. Even if you're not familiar with XML, the files are easy to read and tell you a lot about each object.

The first file, ActionsPanel.xml, defines all the objects, methods, properties, and relevant information such as tips, method parameters, and the lowest version of Flash that supports that action. The second file, ASCodeHints.xml, defines all the patterns that trigger code hints in the Actions panel. Looking in this file, you'll see that variable names with the suffix "_sound." triggers code hints for sound objects, "_txt." triggers code hints for textfields, and so on.

Macromedia components also support code-hinting. The XML files for components are stored in the folder at <flashmx install dir>\First Run\ ActionsPanel\CustomActions\. For example, variable references to components with the suffix "_lb." trigger code hints for List Box, and the suffix "_sb." triggers code hints for Scroll Bar.

You can either modify the XML documents in the main folder or create your own to customize color coding. You can also define your own menu entries based on the syntax and structure in the UI component's XML files.

In later chapters, we'll go over the XML code hint mechanism in more detail when we describe how to build complex Flash components. We just wanted to make the point that you can use code hints to find methods as easily as looking them up in the Reference panel.

> If you make unwanted changes to the ASCodeHints.xml file and forget how to revert to the original code hints, simply delete the ASCodeHints.xml file (or any of the XML files in FlashMX/Configuration/ ActionsPanel/), close the Flash MX editor, and re-open the Flash MX editor. An original copy of the deleted XML file will reappear again in the ActionsPanel folder.

Editing and Testing Code

When you're editing and testing your ActionScript code, the Actions panel provides some features to help you make sense of the code.

The syntax-coloring feature colors different parts of the code to indicate whether the code is a keyword, identifier, string, or comment. The default colors are okay, but we recommend the following color scheme for easier reading (see Figure 1.8):

- Keywords and Identifiers = #0000FF
- Comments = #CC0000
- Strings = #009933

Some expert programmers also use an alternative scheme with comment colors set to the same gray used in Dreamweaver, a hex value of #848284. This way the comments won't distract from the actual code. It also frees up the color red, which can be used to highlight literal numbers for easier debugging.

You can access the color settings by opening the Actions panel pop-up menu (labeled in Figure 1.5) and then choosing the Preferences option.

The Actions panel pop-up menu also has an option for viewing line numbers. It's a good idea to turn on line numbers for the next feature: syntax checking! Syntax checking lets you check your script for errors before compiling the whole movie. Large movies may take up to several minutes to compile, so syntax checking can save you a lot of time. Best of all, you can check your syntax simply by pressing Ctrl+T. If your code contains any errors, a pop-up window will appear, pointing you to error messages in the Output window. These error messages contain information about the line of code that caused the error, so turning on the line number feature can really come in handy when you're testing your code.

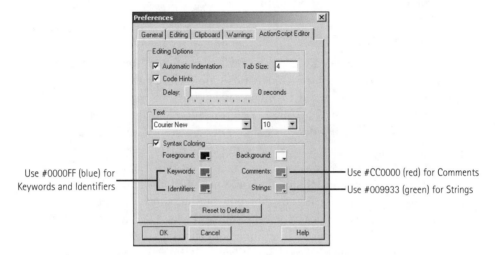

Use #0000FF (blue) for Keywords and Identifiers

Use #CC0000 (red) for Comments

Use #009933 (green) for Strings

Figure 1.8 Recommended syntax coloring.

Tip #3: Place Code Inside Keyframes

ActionScript code can only exist in three places:

- Keyframes on the Timeline
- Movieclip events
- Button events

In Flash 5, movieclip and button events could only be defined by choosing the movieclip or button, and then opening the Actions panel. Because the code was linked to individual instances of a movieclip, there was no "a" icon in the keyframe to indicate that code was stored in the movieclip instance. Forgetting where you stored event-handling code in Flash 5 often meant searching through different movieclips and buttons on the stage.

In Flash MX, all events can be defined dynamically, so there's no need to write ActionScript on top of movieclip and button instances. In fact, it's a good idea to write *all* your code inside keyframes for the sake of keeping your ActionScript organized and easy to navigate. Most importantly, good object-oriented programming lets you re-use the same chunks of ActionScript without having bits and pieces of code scattered throughout the movie.

If you've got a big module of code that can be re-used across multiple projects, you might consider storing the code in an external text file. You can import external ActionScript code using the `#include` pragma. The following example imports the ActionScript from an external text file into a Flash keyframe:

```
#include "myexternalcode.as"
```

Be sure you don't end the command with a semicolon, and leave an extra line after the `#include` command. Most ActionScript programmers use the suffix ".as" to denote a text file that contains ActionScript code.

Storing your code externally makes re-use much easier. In Flash MX, you can use external .as files to contain onClipEvent events. More significant is the fact that you can also define entire component classes with `#initclip`/ `#endinitclip` pragmas inside a single external .as file. Editing ActionScript with external text editors presents some major disadvantages because you don't have immediate access to the code-hinting and Reference panel features. However, many text editors for Windows and Mac OS support ActionScript definitions. What follows are the most popular editors and URLs for downloading an editor's ActionScript syntax definition files (some are more complete than others):

- Dreamweaver (has full highlighting support)
- BBEdit—`http://www.mcom8.com/flash5actionscript.as.sit.bin`
- EditPlus (a favorite among ActionScripters)— `http://www.editplus.com/others.html`
- Textpad—`http://www.textpad.com/add-ons/syna2g.html`
- Ultraedit—`http://www.textpad.com/add-ons/syna2g.html`

Conclusion

We hope this introduction has given you a sense of what you'll find in the book and has helped you develop a more efficient workflow in the Flash MX editor. Remember, if you ever need to look up information quickly, just use the code hints and the Reference panel!

2

OOP in Flash: A Tale of Different Angles

By Branden J. Hall

Shattering Perceptions

My dad, being the hands-on type of guy that he is (he works in construction) often taught me and my younger brother life's lessons in some interesting ways. One day when I was about 12, he came home with a large sheet of glass, probably about 1/2 inch thick, that he had gotten from a job site. He leaned the sheet up against our back fence, then he handed me a sledgehammer and told me to try to break the glass. So, I mustered up all the strength a 12-year old could muster and took a swing at the face of the glass. The head of the hammer hit, the glass flexed, and I was thrown about four feet backward!

As I was dusting myself off, Dad handed my 8-year-old brother a normal hammer, and told him to hit the glass as hard as he could on its edge. What followed was really, well, neat. The whole glass was almost instantly covered in cracks and then fell apart into little shards that were all nearly the same size.

It turns out that it was a special type of tempered glass used in skyscrapers so that pissed off programmers couldn't accidentally send themselves to an untimely demise while banging their heads on it. It's nearly impossible to break the glass head-on, but a decent whack on its edge and it's reduced to shards.

Dad's goal was to teach us a little bit about his work, and to show us something cool. But to this day I remember another lesson: Approaching a problem from a different angle can make a world of difference.

Introduction

Approaching the problem of programming from a different angle is what object-oriented programming (OOP) is all about.

In this chapter you're going to cover a lot of ground. Starting from the basics of what OOP is and why it came to be, you're going to delve deep into OOP principles and how to apply those in ActionScript. Through all of this, keep one thing in mind: Object-oriented programming is primarily a mental tool. Just making a program in an object-oriented manner in no way means that it will be efficient, will be easy to understand, or will even work. That's why this chapter, like the rest of this book, focuses on concepts rather than syntax. Understanding the concepts of OOP is most important when you are planning your code rather than when you are actually coding.

A Historical Perspective

Traditionally, programming has been done in a procedural manner. Do step 1, then do step 2, then step 3, and so on. There may be various loops and branches, but the entire process can be written down on a whiteboard as a simple flow chart (see Figure 2.1).

The problem is that as programs increase in complexity, you simply run out of whiteboard space. Also, many types of programs, such as GUIs, don't really fit into the idea of procedural programming. Imagine trying to map the code of a simple MP3 player to a flow chart and you'll see the problem. Now further imagine trying to coordinate a large team of programmers into coding a system based on that flow chart. Talk about a mess.

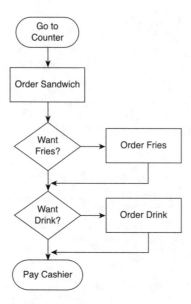

Figure 2.1 The flow of logic in a procedural program.

To sort it all out, you would probably start by decomposing the problem into particular chunks. Say, the code to decompress and play the music, the code to handle playlists, and the code to handle all of the user controls (pause, play, stop, and so on). It's this kind of decomposition that leads directly to object-oriented programming.

It's important to note that you don't have to use an object-oriented language to write object-oriented code, but it does help. Object-oriented languages help you write object-oriented code by providing syntax to help you create and manage objects.

Object of My Desire

So, what is an object? An *object* is an abstract representation of a thing or concept. As such, an object contains both information and behavior (see Figure 2.2). This idea of objects as containers for both data and code is one of the core concepts of object-oriented programming, and you will often hear it referred to as *encapsulation*.

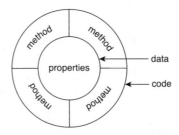

Figure 2.2 Related data and code inside a single container.

The data inside an object is referred to as its *properties*. These properties can be of any data type: a number, a *string* (a collection of characters; for example, "some text" is a string), other objects—you name it. If you had a cat object for example, it might have color, age, and breed properties.

In ActionScript, getting or setting an object's properties is as simple as specifying the object, then a period, then the name of the property.

```
myCat.color = "Gray";
```

However, as you'll learn in a bit, it's considered bad form to directly access an object's properties in this manner.

The code inside an object is referred to as that object's *methods*. Methods are a lot like functions (in fact, in ActionScript they *are* functions). Methods can accept a number of *arguments* (parameters sent to a function) and return a result. An object's methods are what that object can "do." The Cat object, for example, might have meow, eat, and sleep methods (see Figure 2.3).

To access an object's methods, you use dot-syntax just like with an object's properties. However, just like functions, calling a method also requires that you specify the arguments (or lack thereof) that you want to send to it. For example, the following code calls the sleep method of myCat and passes it the value 20, perhaps representing 20 minutes.

```
myCat.sleep(20);
```

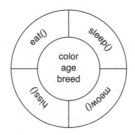

Figure 2.3 A Cat object.

A Classy Affair

Where do objects come from? No, it's not from two grown-up objects that love each other very much—it's from classes.

Classes describe how to build a particular type of object just like a recipe describes how to create a particular dish. Just like with dishes and recipes, you can create any number of unique objects from one class (see Figure 2.4). This is why objects are often referred to as *instances*, because they are an instance of a particular class.

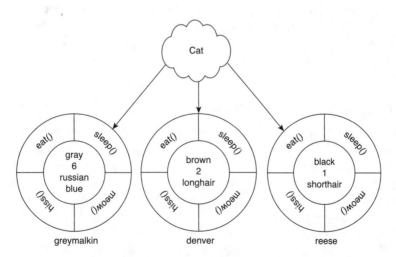

Figure 2.4 Multiple objects can be created from a single class.
(Actual names of my cats are used here.)

A class defines all of the properties that will be inside of all objects created from it. However, it's important to understand that although each object will have these properties, every object is unique and the value of its properties is fully independent from all other objects.

A class also defines all of the methods for all objects created from it. Unlike properties, all of the methods of objects based off of a single class are the same. You can change them, but we'll be discussing that idea, called overwriting, later.

To create an object from a class, use the `new` operator. For example, one of the built-in classes in ActionScript is the `Array` class. To build an object from this class you would type:

```
myArray = new Array();
```

Notice that it looks like you are calling a method with those parentheses. In fact, you are calling a special method called the constructor.

In addition to the methods a class defines for its objects, a class also has to define a constructor method. The *constructor* is a special method that is called when an object is first created. It handles all of the initialization of the new object, which is just "setting up" the object so that it's ready to be used; setting properties, assigning defaults, and so on. Just like all other methods, the constructor can accept arguments. In the case of the constructor, you pass "arguments" when you use the `new` operator. For example, this code would create an array with the elements 1, 2, and `"bob"` in it:

```
myArray = new Array(1, 2, "bob");
```

Prototype-Based Versus Class-Based Languages

One thing you may notice while wandering around inside Flash is that you never actually see the word "class." This is because there are a couple of different ways to implement the idea of "classes," and all ECMAScript-based languages, such as ActionScript, fall under a particular type known as proto-type-based languages. (In comparison, Java and C++ fall into the class-based languages moniker.)

Well, what does this mean? It means that instead of having a special key-word for defining classes, ActionScript allows you to create special objects known as *prototype objects* that act just like classes. If the idea was applied to the real world, prototype-based languages would create new cats by cloning, and class-based languages would create new cats by following a set of directions on how to build a cat.

The fact that ActionScript is a prototype-based language can cause some confusion, particularly when you are creating your own classes. This is because to the untrained eye, the *constructor* method of your class looks just like a plain old function. It is, in fact, a plain old function; you just "agree" to only use it as a constructor function. For example here's the constructor method of a Cat class.

```
function Cat(coat, sex, breed){
    this.coat = coat;
    this.sex = sex;
    this.breed = breed;
    this.isAsleep = false;
}
```

It just looks like a normal ActionScript function. However, there are two things that might tip you off that this function is special. First of all, notice all of the uses of the keyword this. The special keyword this refers to the object in which the code is inside. Hence, by saying this.coat = coat; all objects created from the Cat prototype object have a coat property as soon as they are created.

> It's a fairly common practice to capitalize only class names (and hence constructors) and then start everything else with lowercase. It isn't an official standard, but most programmers do it because it does make spotting classes a bit easier.

Second, notice that the name of the function is capitalized. That function *is* a constructor, so with just the little bit of code, you can now create new instances of the Cat class:

```
myCat = new Cat("gray", "male", "Russian Blue");
```

And of course, if you had another cat you could just create another object:

```
myOtherCat = new Cat("black", "male", "domestic shorthair");
```

Now, here's some information that may seem really strange at first, but here in ActionScript, just by defining the Cat constructor method, you've also created a new object called Cat. Remember, ActionScript is a prototype-based language, and a prototype object is an object that acts like a class. In fact throughout this book you'll see references to the Array class and the Array object. They are, in fact, the same thing so don't get confused by name change.

> Unlike most other OOP languages (such as C++ and Java), ActionScript's objects are perfectly malleable at any time. That is, you can modify just about any object, including prototype objects, anytime you want. You have to do these kinds of modifications to create prototype objects, but in general, direct object manipulation is considered a bad practice from an object-oriented standpoint.

Building Prototype Objects

You now know all about constructors, but there's more to prototype objects than just their constructors. Remember that objects are containers for both data and code. The data part is already covered by the constructor (it declares all the properties), but you don't yet have any methods defined for our prototype object!

If you know the alternate syntax for writing functions (if you don't, be sure to check out the sidebar), you may have an idea on how you could add methods to your object. Perhaps like this:

```
function Cat(color, sex, breed){
   this.color = color;
   this.sex = sex;
   this.breed = breed;
   this.meow = function(){
      trace("Meow!!");
   }
}
```

> Functions can be defined in two forms. The first form, and the one most people know is
>
> ```
> function doSomething(){
> ..
> }
> ```
>
> The second form is a bit odd, and is based on the fact that in ECMAScript-based languages, functions are treated like a data type. That is, the name of a function is just a variable that "points" to it. For example:
>
> ```
> doSomething = function(){
> ..
> }
> ```

Yes, the preceding code would work, and each object created from the `Cat` class would have a method called `meow`; however, there is a problem with this technique. That problem has to do with memory. It turns out that if you add methods in this manner, each object gets a full copy of the method created for it. Although this might not be a problem for a small class like ours, it could quickly become a major issue if you used this technique to create a larger class. Unlike properties, all of the methods of objects based off of the same class are exactly the same. So, why not just define the methods once, and have all of the objects created from the class just refer back to it? Well, that's exactly what the *prototype* property is for!

Every prototype object (remember, in ActionScript it's the same thing as a class) has a special built-in property called `prototype`. This property defines what things should be in all objects built from the class but should just refer back to a single definition. For example:

```
function Cat(color, sex, breed){
    this.color = color;
    this.sex = sex;
    this.breed = breed;
}

Cat.prototype.meow = function(){
    trace("Meow!!");
}
```

Now, not only will all objects created from `Cat` have a `meow` method, but they will also all refer back to a single definition of it.

Extension Cords

The ability to modify objects at any time is rare among object-oriented languages and although it does make it easier to do "bad" OOP, it also makes it much easier to modify or extend objects on-the-fly in Flash.

For example, say you were creating a web application for buying cat toys online and that there were often buy-3-get-1-free type deals. If you stored all of the items that a user has bought in an array, you would probably often have to determine how many of a particular item the user bought. You could extend your instance of `Array` (`shoppingBasket`) like this:

```
shoppingBasket.count = function(name){
    var i = this.length;
    var result = 0;
    while (i—){
        if (this[i] == name){
            ++result;
        }
    }
    return result;
}
```

Another option would be to extend *all* array objects in your movie by adding the count method to the Array class's prototype:

```
Array.prototype.count = function(name){
    var i = this.length;
    var result = 0;
    while (i--){
        if (this[i] == name){
            ++result;
        }
    }
    return result;
}
```

Now, all arrays in your movie, even ones created *before* you created this method, have a new count method. The reason that all array objects in the movie are extending is because of how objects "look up" their methods. Every object in ActionScript has what is known as a *prototype chain* (see Figure 2.5). This "chain" always starts at the actual object and ends at the prototype of the Object class.

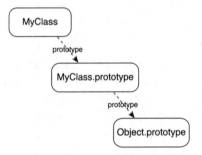

Figure 2.5 The prototype chain.

You may now be asking when should you use the first method of extending and when should you use the second. Think about that problem in the same way the government deals with secrets: need-to-know. That is, if the majority of the arrays in your code need to have the count method, then by all means, extend the Array prototype object. However, if only one or two arrays need the method, then use the first method.

If you extend a single object, but need a second object to have the method as well, you don't have to define the method twice. All you need to do is point the second object's method at the first object, like this:

```
otherBasket.count = shoppingBasket.count;
```

Understanding the Prototype Chain

The Object class is the most basic object you can have, and all other objects are based off of it. Sometimes, if you just need a "container" for data, creating an instance of Object is in order. However, if you need more than one such a container it's a better idea to instead define your own custom class.

The Object class has one unique ability that can, in a few cases, come in handy. Just by adding a method to the Object class's prototype, you've extended every single object in your entire movie. Every array, every movieclip, every single object now has that method.

When you first ask for a property or method of an object, it looks at the object itself to see if the property or method exists there. If it doesn't, then Flash looks at the prototype of the class the object was created from. If Flash still can't find the property or method, it starts looking at the prototype's prototype and so on until it reaches the Object class's prototype.

So, just by adding methods to this "chain," any object that looks in that chain now has access to them. In fact, this concept of a prototype chain is core to the next concept we are going to cover, inheritance.

Inherit a Fortune

Although Flash enables you to modify objects on-the-fly, doing so isn't considered good OOP practice. The preferred method is to use a special process called *inheritance*, which allows you to do this kind of tweaking without actually messing with the original object. The idea behind inheritance is actually pretty simple: One class can *inherit* all of the functionality of another more generic class, and then extend that class with its own methods and properties.

As mentioned earlier, inheritance in ActionScript is achieved by tweaking the prototype chain (see Figure 2.6). You set the prototype of the class you want to do the inheriting (the sub class) to a new instance of the class you are inheriting from (the super class). For example:

```
PastaRecipe.prototype = new Recipe();
```

There is a lot of discussion in the Flash community about the best practices concerning inheritance. This is due to various problems with all of the available methods of inheritance. For this reason I really can't recommend using inheritance unless you are positive it's the only and best way to solve a problem. For more information on this, see Chapter 4, "Practical OOP: Welcome to the Real World."

Now, the prototype of PastaRecipe will be filled with an instance of Recipe, and hence PastaRecipe will have inherited all of Recipe's properties and methods.

It's important that you do inheritance *before* you add any methods to your sub class, because when you do inheritance in this manner you are completely overwriting the prototype of sub class. (See Figure 2.6.)

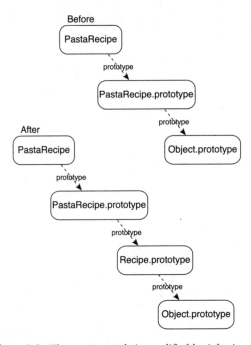

Figure 2.6 The prototype chain modified by inheritance.

That's not where inheritance stops though. In fact, the PastaRecipe class mentioned above wouldn't work properly because its sub class, Recipe, may do some special set-up work inside of its constructor, and you are never actually calling that constructor. This problem isn't isolated to the Recipe class. Nearly all objects have non-trivial constructors, and never calling them can cause all sorts of problems. So, in the case of this example, inside of PastaRecipe class's constructor you need to explicitly call its super class's constructor. It just so happens that Flash MX added an easy way to do just this—and more—the super keyword.

Using *super*

The super keyword allows an object to access its "super" class, or the class that it is inheriting from. This comes in handy in a number of ways, such as to call the super class's constructor. To do so you would simply type:

```
super();
```

You can also pass arguments through super; for example,

```
super("sauce", 20);
```

Note that there is no pathing involved with super. In addition to calling the constructor, you can also call any methods in the super class. Why would you have to call the super class's methods? Well, say you created your own mix method for the PastaRecipe class, but your mix method could still use the ability of the Recipe class's mix method to handle the more "generic" parts of the task. If that were the case you would simply have to add the following inside of PastaRecipe's mix method:

```
super.mix();
```

Use of super in this manner comes in handy when implementing a particular concept of OOP called polymorphism. *Polymorphism* is just a fancy way to say "same interface but different code." The idea is that similar objects should have identical or at least very similar interfaces. This allows you to easily interchange objects built off of those classes.

Polymorphism

What does inheritance have to do with polymorphism? Quite a bit, actually. For example, say you created a Feline class that had a method called hunt. You could then create two sub classes based off of Feline, say HouseCat and Cheetah. Because house cats pounce while cheetahs chase down and tackle, you would have to overwrite the hunt method for both classes so that it reflected how each type of feline hunts. However, the *way* we call the hunt method for both classes remains the same. So any place where you use a HouseCat in your code, you could substitute it for a Cheetah and vice versa.

This may seem a bit abstract at first, but the idea is very powerful. Think about VCRs and DVD players. How they work internally is totally different,. but anyone who has used a VCR remote control can easily handle the basic controls of a DVD player. Play always plays, stop always stops. The polymorphic nature of VCRs and DVD players means that users can ignore the actual implementation of these devices and instead focus on using them.

Actually implementing polymorphism is just a matter of defining two classes that have similar "interfaces" but work differently internally. In fact, you can in some cases just stop there. However, such classes are often related in some way. In the case of VCRs and DVD players, they are both video playback devices. So, if you were creating a simulation of VCRs and DVD players, you would probably want to create a single base class called VideoPlayer that both your VCR and DVD classes inherited from.

Since VideoPlayer is more-or-less just an abstract idea, there isn't too much that it can do by itself. One of the things it can do though, is display status to the TV when a button is pressed. Both VCRs and DVD players need to do this, so why not have their stop methods call back to VideoPlayer? You can in fact do this exact thing by using super like this:

```
// first inherit from VideoPlayer
VCR.prototype = new VideoPlayer();

VCR.prototype.stop = function(){
    // do some VCR specific tasks
    // …
    // then call the stop method of the super class, VideoPlayer
    super.stop();
}
```

Owning a Hammer Versus Building a House

So, now you know all about the OOP tools available to you in ActionScript. However, as the saying goes, just because you have a hammer doesn't mean you know how to build a house. As a matter of fact, there are numerous massive tomes written about writing object-oriented code. However, there are a few concepts and best practices that will help prevent you from writing code that uses object-oriented syntax but is anything but object-oriented.

The most important concept to remember is that OOP is about messages. That is, it's about objects communicating with each other via their methods (see Figure 2.7). Even though it's both possible and easy to directly modify any property of an object, it's best if objects remain black boxes of sorts where the only communication in and out of them is through a defined interface (its methods).

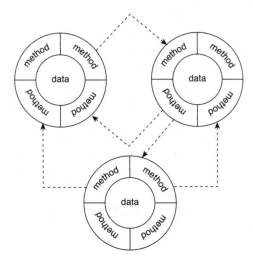

Figure 2.7 Idealized object communication: methods are the only way in and out.

This concept is based on two thoughts. First, by keeping objects as black boxes, it makes it easier to track down problem code to a particular object and hence debug. Second, you can modify the code inside of any class as much as you need to as long as the interface doesn't change (in other words, the input and output for the class's methods).

It's relatively common for beginning programmers to simply map each of the properties in an object to two methods, so-called getter and setter methods. The getter method returns the value of the property while the setter method sets the value of the property. This practice is, in general, a bad idea because it really doesn't do much to hide what's going on inside of the object.

Now, getters and setters aren't a bad idea in themselves, but what's the point of making them methods if all you are doing is directly setting or getting variables? Remember, a major part of object-oriented programming is abstraction. An object's interface (its methods) should make it as simple as possible to utilize and keep its inner workings (and properties) secret. If you find that a class you have defined just contains a collection of getters and setters, you may want to re-think your design. A few getter/setter pairs is fine, but always be aware that over use of them is a nearly sure sign of poor class design.

Because OOP is all about objects communicating with each other, it is vital that you plan your objects and how they will interact before you start to program. By laying out exactly what classes you need to create and defining how objects built from those classes will interact, you will greatly simplify your development effort. Definitely don't skimp on this planning stage. The longer you spend planning your object model, the easier it will be to code and debug. Besides that, by thoroughly planning your code, you can much more easily separate it and assign different classes to different members of your team.

The larger the projects you start building, the more vital you will find this planning stage. In fact, when you do start building bigger applications, you will probably want to start to investigate a language that was created just for planning large object-oriented systems, the Unified Modeling Language (UML).

Conclusion

You've gone a long way in this chapter. You started out learning the basic concepts behind OOP: objects, properties, methods, and classes. After learning how to apply these concepts to ActionScript, you moved on to extending classes and inheritance, and then finished up by learning some more object-oriented theory and best practices.

As you can tell by now, there is quite a bit to object-oriented programming. Like most other fields of study, there's always more to learn about OOP. If you get heavily into OOP, you may want to look into at least two other subjects. First of all, design patterns, which are essentially recipes for solving common problems with OOP. Secondly, you may want to learn about Universal Modeling Language (UML). UML is a visual language for describing object-oriented code. It's very helpful for mapping out your code before you actually start to write it, particularly if you work in a team.

Chapter 3, "Event Wrangling: When To Do What," makes the jump from theory to execution: You'll take a look at some real-life examples of object-oriented programming in ActionScript.

3

Event Wrangling:
When To Do What

By Branden J. Hall

When Bugs Attack

When I was a little kid (probably around five or six), my parents kept an old wooden barrel on the front porch for decoration. It was an authentic barrel, with the metal rings holding it together and everything. I remember distinctly thinking how cool it was and pretending to be a cowboy hiding behind it for cover during a fearsome O.K. Corral-style shootout. Later, this same barrel ended up being quite traumatic for me!

One summer morning, just as my mom and I were about to leave the house on some errand or other, I climbed up on the barrel and plopped down, swinging my legs while I waited for Mom to come out of the house. Suddenly I heard a loud buzzing sound beneath me and started to see dozens and dozens of yellow bugs fly out of a hole on the side of the barrel. I was a bit curious about the critters for about half a second, that is until they started to fly up my shirt and sting me unmercifully. It turns out the barrel was infested by a nasty species of wasp known as yellow jackets.

So, my kid instincts flew into high gear and I leapt off the barrel, flapping my arms like mad and dancing around the porch like a lunatic, bawling my eyes out. My mom, hearing my probably deafening cries, came running out to the front of the house where I was, at this point slammed up against the door continuing to wave my arms and flinging my legs around and screaming like a maniac. She kept yelling at me to ask what was wrong, but because I was so scared I just kept crying. Because she couldn't see the yellow jackets inside of my shirt she was getting more and more distressed and confused. Finally (it was probably about two seconds later, but it seemed like hours at the time!) she grabbed me, yanked my shirt off, shoo'd the yellow jackets away, and carried me inside to put ointment on my dozen or so stings.

The only reason that I ended up getting stung that many times was because I wasn't able to properly communicate to my mom what had happened. Basically, I didn't handle the event properly. Now while you won't need ointment if you improperly handle events in Flash, it definitely can sting trying to sort out the bugs that crop up. (Okay, sorry that was a *really* bad pun!)

Introduction

In this chapter you are going to learn about one of the most core parts of object-oriented programming in Flash, events. Make sure you understand this chapter thoroughly; much of the later chapters rely on the information you will learn here.

You'll start out by learning what an event is in the context of ActionScript. From there, you will learn the different ways you can work with events in Flash MX, including which method is most appropriate for any given situation. Then, some code examples will help you get your feet wet with event-based programming. Finally, you'll dig into how to create your own event sources and how to apply them to your own projects.

What Is an Event?

Application programmers (the folks who make the everyday programs you use for Windows or Macintosh) have long known that the key to graphical user interface (GUI) programming is events. So, what is an event, and why are events so important? To answer that question, take a closer look at GUIs.

A GUI is, at its most base form, a large menu that lets the user choose what he wants to do. The problem is that how the user does this choosing is based on a lot of complex interactions: keys being pressed, keys being released, the mouse moving, a mouse button being pressed—you get the idea. Each one of these interactions is an event. It occurs at a specific time and may have information associated with it. (The key that was pressed, for example.) Now, events aren't limited to forms of user input. Things such as timers, network connections, and file I/O also can create events. Basically, anytime you are working with something external to your code, whether that is the hard disk, the user, or even time, you will be working with events.

Methods of Event Handling

There are two main methods to work with events in Flash MX: callbacks and listeners. Both have their strengths and weaknesses as well as situations for which they are best suited. The most important thing to remember about both methods is that organization and documentation are key to writing maintainable code.

Callbacks

The first method of working with events is known as a *callback*. Callbacks take advantage of the fact that ActionScript is a highly forgiving language. In particular, callbacks execute a function that doesn't exist, and Flash won't generate an error or even complain. Some forms of callbacks also utilize the fact that you can overwrite any variable in Flash at any time, which includes functions.

The quick-and-dirty explanation of a callback is when an event occurs, the object that is the event's source tries to execute a specific function. This may seem a bit confusing, but after you've read a bit more and seen them in action, you'll see that callbacks are pretty simple.

A good example of a callback in action is the XML class. Now, I'm not going to get into the ins and outs of XML quite yet, instead I'll go into how the XML class utilizes callbacks.

When you create an XML object your goal is to load XML formatted data into it from a source that can't deliver the XML instantaneously, such as a hard disk, or more commonly for Flash, an Internet connection. Therefore, your code needs to be able to deal with this latency. An XML object does this by using an event callback.

Specifically, after an XML object has finished loading and parsing data, it runs its `onLoad` method. That is, the act of finishing the loading and parsing of its data is an event, so the XML object does a callback. The interesting thing is, the `onLoad` method doesn't, by default, do anything. After all, how is the object supposed to know what it needs to call when it's done loading and parsing?

So in order to actually handle the event, you give your XML object an
onLoad method and put your own code in it. Just note that you need to do this
before you tell the object load its data, otherwise it's possible that the data will
be loaded before your onLoad method is defined. The code looks like this:

```
myXML = new XML();
myXML.onLoad = function(valid){
        if (valid){
                trace("Loaded good XML!");
        }
}
myXML.load("somexml.xml");
```

An example of event callbacks in use with an XML object.

> You may notice that your onLoad method is receiving a single argument, valid. Arguments passed to
> the callback method like this give more information about the event. This one tells you if the XML that
> was loaded conforms to XML standards; that is, it is well formed (which is the technical term for a valid
> XML document). The argument is also false if Flash can't load the document.

The previous onLoad is obviously pretty trivial. Usually, you would need to do
a bit more than just print a statement to the Output panel. This actually brings
up a bit of a sticky point with callbacks; their scope is that of the event source.
So, if you were to reference this inside of an onLoad method, you would be
referring to the XML object, not the Timeline like you may expect.

```
function doSomething(){
    …

}

myXML = new XML();
myXML.onLoad = function(valid){
   if (valid){
      this.doSomething();      // won't work
   }
}
myXML.load("somexml.xml");
```

An example of the scope issues with callbacks.

The problem is that it's not the event source that usually cares about the event;
it's some other, external object. In the case of XML, it's often the Timeline
that the XML object lives in. So, it might be tempting to just try to use _
parent inside of the onLoad code. However, remember that _parent is only a
property of MovieClips, so it won't work in this case.

Instead, you need to explicitly reference the Timeline. You could do it like this:

```
function doSomething(){
    …
}

myXML = new XML();
myXML.onLoad = function(valid){
   if (valid){
      _root.doSomething();      // will work, but bad form
   }
}
myXML.load("somexml.xml");
```

Working around scope problems with absolute pathing.

The issue with this is that this code is no longer portable. A better solution would be to give the XML object a property that refers to the Timeline where it lives, and then reference that.

```
function doSomething(){
    …
}

myXML = new XML();
myXML._tl = this;
myXML.onLoad = function(valid){
   if (valid){
      this._tl.doSomething();      // will work and good form
   }
}
myXML.load("somexml.xml");
```

Working around scope problems with a new property.

In this case you are giving the XML object a new property, _tl (short for Timeline), which refers to the location of the XML object. Now, this whole segment of code can be placed anywhere in your movie and it will still work.

Components: A Variation on Callbacks

Besides the "usual" type of callbacks, the new components included with Flash MX use a slightly different form of the same idea. Components are special self-contained movieclips, and as such, they have access to a _parent property. So, all the component's callbacks actually exist in the scope of their parent Timeline. This is both a good and a bad thing. It's good because you don't have to do any of the tricks to tell the component what its parent is. This also makes more sense than regular callbacks because events, more often than not, are used as a form of communication between objects. That is, the object that creates the event usually isn't the one listening for the event.

The reason that this variation on callbacks is bad, or at least potentially confusing, is that in order to use such callbacks you just write a function on the component's parent movieclip. As such, there's no easily discernable connection between the two unless you happen to know that the function *is* a callback. This problem is exacerbated by the fact that components allow you to set the name of the function to be run in the Properties Inspector, the Components panel, or with ActionScript. For example, if you had an instance of the push button component named `myButton_pb`, you could set its `Click Handler` parameter in the Properties Inspector or Component panel to `onMyButton`. You could do the same thing but using the code:

```
myButton_pb.setClickHandler("onMyButton");
```

After that you'd just have to define a function named `onMyButton` in your code:

```
onMyButton = function(){
    ...
}
```

A callback function from a component.

If you just saw this function, the only clue you would have that it's a callback would be that its name starts with "on." However, because you can name a component's callback anything you like, that might not always be the case. Because of this it is very important that you comment component callbacks. Components and their callbacks will be covered in more detail in Chapter 6, "Using UI Components."

Listeners

The second method of capturing and working with events is known as listeners. If you come from a Java programming background, listeners may seem very familiar to you, as they are extremely similar to how Java handles events. Otherwise, you'll be happy to know that although listeners are a powerful idea, they are easy to learn and implement.

Listeners, although easy, are definitely more complex than callbacks, but this is because they address the two important shortcomings of callbacks (see Figure 3.1). The first point at which callbacks fall short is they execute in the scope of the object that's the source of the event, not the object that's receiving the event, which would be logical. The second problem with callbacks is that for any given event there can be only one object receiving that event.

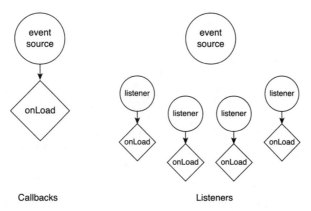

Figure 3.1 The differences between callbacks and listeners.

Magazine subscriptions and listeners work the same. If you want a particular magazine, you subscribe to it and can unsubscribe at any time (at least they say you can). In the magazine there are a lot of articles, but you can choose which articles you want to read and which ones to just ignore. In the world of magazine publishing you would be referred to as a subscriber; in ActionScript, an object that's subscribed in this manner is a listener.

As you already know, objects that support listeners generate events. What might not be clear yet is that these events have specific names (such as onKeyDown and onResize). To "hear" these events, the listeners that are subscribed must have methods with those exact names. This is how listeners can only "listen" to some events coming from an event source to which they are subscribed.

Various objects in Flash MX support listeners, that is, they are event sources and allow other objects to subscribe to those events. Any object that supports listeners has two methods for doing the subscribing and unsubscribing: addListener and removeListener. Both of these methods support a single argument; a reference to the object to be subscribed or unsubscribed. One of the objects that supports listeners is the Mouse object. It supports a number of events, such as onMouseDown and onMouseUp. All the events from the Mouse object are context insensitive. In other words, they fire *any* time the mouse interacts over a Flash movie.

With all this new information in mind, take a look at this example:

```
foo = new Object();
foo.onMouseDown = function(){
    trace("foo heard the mouse was pressed");
}
Mouse.addListener(foo);
```

A listener in action.

Take a close look at this code. First, a new object named foo is created. Then, foo is given a new method called onMouseDown and in this method it does a simple trace. Finally, the addListener method on the Mouse object is called and passed a reference to foo (notice that it's not a string). Hence, foo is now "subscribed" to the Mouse object, so now anytime an event is created by Mouse, foo will be notified. So, if you press the mouse button, foo's onMouseDown method will be run and you'll get the message in your Output panel.

One thing to note is that listeners, like callbacks, can be passed arguments from the event source. However, it's not all that common to see this happening because listeners only "listen" for global events that don't need any clarification.

An important point to remember is that any objects that want to can subscribe to an event source. So, if there was another object, bar, it could subscribe to Mouse as well and capture any events it would like:

```
foo = new Object();
foo.onMouseDown = function(){
    trace("foo heard the mouse was pressed");
}
Mouse.addListener(foo);

bar = new Object();
bar.onMouseUp = function(){
    trace("bar heard the mouse was let go");
}
Mouse.addListener(bar);
```

Multiple listeners subscribed to a single event source.

This kind of multi-subscription just isn't possible with callbacks. In addition, you may have noticed that because of the nature of listeners, the role of the event source and the event listener is clearly delineated, unlike with callbacks. The code that gets triggered when an event occurs is inside the object that's listening, not the object that is the source of the event.

Event Handling Best Practices

Now that you know about the two ways to handle events, you are probably wondering when you should use callbacks and when you should use listeners. You are also probably mulling over how to best utilize event handling in the real world.

Callbacks or Listeners?

For the most part, if you are just utilizing event sources rather than creating your own (which comes later in the chapter), you don't actually have much control over which method to use. Most of Flash MX's built-in classes support either callbacks or listeners; only a handful supports both.

However, there is pattern and reason to which objects support which method of event handling. Classes that provide access to events that occur to the .swf as a whole (that is, `Mouse` and `Key`) support listeners because there's no telling how many objects might want to listen to it for that type of event. On the other hand, classes that would, under normal circumstances, only have a single object listening for their events tend to only support callbacks.

This methodology for choosing a way to handle events is pretty solid, and as such it's a good rule of thumb for your own development. If a class is generating an event that could logically interest a number of objects, use listeners, otherwise callbacks will do the job.

Now, personally, I prefer listeners. They simply aren't as messy as callbacks when it comes to object-oriented code. Listeners simply allow for the clean separation of event source and event subscriber. In fact, I've been known to extend some of the built-in classes so that they support listeners. This kind of monkeying around with internal classes isn't really needed though, it's just my personal idiosyncrasy.

In a bit you are going to learn about how to make your own custom event sources, but for now remember that it's best, when you have direct control of the situation, to support both callbacks and listeners. It just gives you much more flexibility later on.

Events in the Real World

So far you have only seen some trivial examples on how to use events. There are some real world issues that those examples fail to touch on.

Event Doubling

First, all movieclips are full-fledged objects now, and they happen to support a number of callbacks, namely:

onData	onMouseMove
onDragOut	onMouseUp
onDragOver	onPress
onEnterFrame	onRelease
onKeyDown	onReleaseOutside
onKeyUp	onRollOut
onKillFocus	onSetFocus
onLoad	onUnload
onMouseDown	

The event that each of these callbacks is for is pretty self-explanatory. You may notice though, that the names of the callbacks happen to coincide with the name of the listeners that the Mouse and Key classes support. In fact, both types of events fire at the same time and this can cause issues.

For example, the code that follows lives on the first frame of the main Timeline of a movie. It declares an onMouseDown method in the main Timeline and then subscribes the main Timeline as a listener to the Mouse class.

```
this.onMouseDown = function(){
    trace("Mouse was pressed");
}
Mouse.addListener(this);
```

*This **onMouseDown** method actually runs twice for each mouse click!*

The result of this code is that the onMouseDown method runs twice each time the mouse is pressed. Because of this, avoid subscribing movieclips as listeners to either the Mouse or Key classes. Otherwise, you'll run into this same event-doubling issue.

Turning Callbacks On and Off

Most Flash developers who are new to working with events don't take advantage of them to their full potential. To see the difference between code that happens to utilize callbacks and code that really takes advantage of all aspects of callbacks, look at this code, which assumes that there is a movieclip named foo_mc on the stage:

```
foo_mc.onPress = function(){
    this.startDrag();
}
foo_mc.onRelease = function(){
    this.stopDrag();
}
foo_mc.onMouseMove = function(){
    updateAfterEvent();
}
```

A simple, but unoptimized, example of callbacks in action.

Examine what's going on in this code. First, when foo_mc is clicked on, it starts to be dragged. Then, when foo_mc is released, dragging ceases. Finally, anytime the mouse is moved, foo_mc calls the updateAfterEvent function, which forces Flash to redraw the screen, thus making the dragging action appear much smoother than it would under normal circumstances.

The problem with this code is that the onMouseMove code doesn't always need to be called. In fact, the only time it really needs to be called is when you happen to be dragging around foo_mc. This can actually be quite problematic, particularly if your movie has a lot going on at once, because updateAfterEvent is a relatively CPU-intensive operation. So, here's a more optimized version of the code:

```
foo_mc.onPress = function(){
    this.startDrag();
    this.onMouseMove = function(){
        updateAfterEvent();
    }
}
foo_mc.onRelease = function(){
    this.stopDrag();
    this.onMouseMove = undefined;
}
```

A more optimized example of callbacks.

In this code, the onPress callback creates the onMouseMove callback, and the onRelease callback destroys the onMouseMove. Thus, the updateAfterEvent function is only called when it should be, rather than any time the mouse is moved.

Reuse and Readability

When you are working with numerous events in a large project, it can get quite messy, with many functions floating around that start with "on." Because of this, it's best to comment each listener and callback so that you know what type of event handling it is and what exactly is triggering the event. This makes your code that much more readable and reusable.

Also, as in the first XML example of this chapter, be sure your callbacks don't contain absolute references in them. This makes your code much more fragile and exposes you to a number of common bugs. Making a simple reference to the movieclip or object to be targeted external from the actual callback works best for making your code less error prone. See the XML example earlier in the chapter for this strategy in use.

Forging Custom Events

As you start to create your own custom objects, you'll begin to notice places where it would make sense to support events. In this case you have a number of decisions to make: what events should there be, what, if any, data needs to be communicated about each event, and which type of event handling should you use.

First, events themselves should be created only when needed. Not every little change to an object should create an event; instead, think of events like greeting cards. You don't send a card to all your friends and relatives every Tuesday wishing them "Happy Tuesday." Instead, if you send out any cards at all (I'm pretty bad about them myself), it's only for special occasions such as birthdays or other holidays. This all comes back to the concept of object encapsulation; don't expose the internal workings of an object because doing so essentially "locks" your object into working that way, otherwise all the other objects that utilize it will break.

Secondly, if at all possible have your events send information about what has occurred. Both callbacks and listeners support sending arguments when events are generated, so utilize this functionality if it makes sense to. Giving more detail about the event is, if nothing else, very useful for debugging.

Finally, you should, if at all possible, support both callbacks and listeners; it just makes your code more flexible, and a big point of OOP is to make your code as flexible, and hence as reusable, as possible.

Creating callbacks is easy—remember they are just calling a function that may, or may not, exist. As usual, be sure you document what each callback does and what, if any, arguments it passes.

```
Counter = function(max){
    this.max = max;
    this.value = 0;
}
Counter.prototype.increment = function(){
    ++this.value;
    if (this.counter == this.max){
        this.onMax();                // here's the callback
        this.counter = 0;
    }
}
```

A simple class that supports a single callback, onMax.

Creating objects that support listeners is a bit more complicated though. Macromedia, the creator of Flash, happened to make a specific object that adds listener support to any object. However, this object, AsBroadcaster, is undocumented and as such I can't recommend it for actual production use. The good news is that the syntax for AsBroadcaster is pretty logical and with just a bit of code you can create a functional clone of AsBroadcaster written in ActionScript.

AsBroadcaster only really supports one function, initialize, which when passed to an object adds listener support to that object. When this has occurred the object in question now has three new methods, addListener, removeListener, and broadcastMessage. The addListener and removeListener methods are familiar by now, but broadcastMessage might not be. It is what is used to actually send out events to the subscribed listeners. Its syntax is as follows:

```
broadcastMessage(eventName, arg1, arg2, …, argN);
```

where eventName is a string that gives the name of the event (for example, onMouseDown) and the rest of the arguments are any additional data you want to send to the listeners.

Now that you know how AsBroadcaster works, here's the code for your own ActionScript-only version, EventBroadcaster.

```
_global.EventBroadcaster = new Object();

EventBroadcaster.initialize = function(obj){
   obj._listeners = new Array();
   obj.broadcastMessage = this._broadcastMessage;
   obj.addListener = this._addListener;
   obj.removeListener = this._removeListener;
}

EventBroadcaster._broadcastMessage = function(){
   var eventName = arguments.shift();
   var list = this._listeners;
   var max = list.length;
   for (var i=0; i<max; ++i){
      list[i][eventName].apply(list[i], arguments);
   }
}

EventBroadcaster._addListener = function(obj){
   this.removeListener(obj);
   this._listeners.push(obj);
   return (true);
}

EventBroadcaster._removeListener = function(obj){
   var list = this._listeners;
   var i = list.length;
   while (i--){
      if (list[i] == obj){
         list.splice(i, 1);
         return (true);
      }
   }
   return (false);
}
```

The EventBroadcaster object allows you to easily add listeners to any object.

As you can see, whenever addListener is called, the object that was passed to it gets placed into the _listeners array. Then, when broadcastMessage is run, the _listeners array is looped over and all objects stored in it have the name of the method passed to it to run. (Note that the event name is pulled off the argument's array via arguments.shift() and that all other arguments are passed to the objects that are subscribed.)

After this code is in your movie somewhere, all you have to do is to run
EventBroadcaster.initialize on any object that you want to support listeners.
For example, the following is a new version of the Counter object that supports
listeners:

```
Counter = function(max){
    this.max = max;
    this.value = 0;
    EventBroadcaster.initialize(this);
}
Counter.prototype.increment = function(){
    ++this.value;
    if (this.counter == this.max){
        this.onMax();
        this.broadcastMessage("onMax");
        this.value = 0;;
        }
}
```

The **Counter** *class reworked to support listeners via* **EventBroadcaster**.

Be sure you note the use of both initialize and broadcastMessage in the code.
Now any instance of Counter will fully support listeners.

Conclusion

In this chapter you've come quite a long way! You started from the basics of
what events are, continued on to how to work with events, and finally you
learned how to create your own custom events. Remember that events are a
powerful concept that, when combined with well-designed object-oriented
code, give you all the tools you need to create cutting-edge Flash applications.

In Chapter 4, "Practical OOP: Welcome to the Real World," you are going
to take the step from theories behind object-oriented programming to
practical, applied OOP in the real world of Flash development. Hold on,
this is going to be an interesting ride!

4

Practical OOP: Welcome to the Real World

By Branden J. Hall

The Not-So-Great Wall of Baltimore

For around six months of my life I lived in what could charitably be called a bad part of the city of Baltimore, Maryland. I lived in what was once a textile warehouse, four floors above a very seedy "gentlemen's club." It was the kind of place where you had to memorize which stairs didn't exactly hold weight and exactly how to prop up the washing machine so it didn't go galloping across the floor like it was possessed every time it reached the spin cycle. The place was a hole, but it was all I could afford, so it was home.

When I first moved in, I found out that the space wasn't actually divided into rooms. There was only one real wall in the place, thus dividing the space into "the front" and, appropriately enough, "the back." When roommates moved in they were expected to construct their own room out of some of the space. Only one of the rooms that was already there was built in the manner in which you would think of rooms being built, that is, with actual walls. The others rooms were essentially glorified tents.

My dad is a construction worker, so I had at that point observed numerous times the building of new walls. Hell, I had helped Dad do it a few times (although in truth all I really did was hold the box of screws). So, a few days after I moved in, I scrounged together some slightly irregular 2×4s and some battered drywall and set out to create what I thought would end up being the best room in the whole apartment. Oh, how mistaken I was.

After nearly a full day of working on the walls I had some of the most ugly, non-level, and structurally unsound walls I had ever seen. In fact, a few weeks later one of the walls fell on me. The fact of the matter was that I knew the theory behind how to build a wall, but because I had never built one, I had no idea about a lot of the finer details such as how to build them so they don't fall down.

Introduction

Over the past few years I've learned that building object-oriented code with Flash is a lot like building a wall. When a wall fails you get bonked on the head; when code fails though, bosses and clients scream at you. Given the choice, I'd take a bonk on the head any day.

There are a number of reasons why relatively few Flash developers know how to write good OO ActionScript. One of the reasons is that there aren't a lot of resources for learning how to create OO code with a prototype-based language. In fact, Flash is pretty unique in that there's no other mainstream GUI development tool that has a prototype-based language at its core.

Because of this, some of the most successful ActionScript programmers learned some other OO language such as Java or C++ before they came to Flash. Thus they have been able to borrow a lot of the concepts and solutions that those languages utilize and apply them to Flash. This chapter is all about that kind of reappropriation of good ideas in order to turn OO theory into successful OOP based ActionScript.

This chapter is divided into three parts. In the first part, object design, you will learn how to create custom objects that are as flexible and powerful as possible. In the second part you will learn more about object relationships and how you can leverage them successfully. The final part is a collection of hacks and little-known tricks that you can use to solve particular problems that arise out of ActionScript's loose nature.

Object Design

The whole point of object-oriented programming is to make development faster, easier, and more structured. Just because you make your code OO though, doesn't mean you'll reap these benefits. In fact, poorly designed objects can result in the exact opposite of the desired effects.

Rules and Rules-of-Thumb

One of the most important rules dealing with object design is that an object should represent a single thing or idea. It's very common for newcomers to the land of OOP to just group data and code and call it an object. But just as I learned with my walls, using the right parts doesn't result in success if you don't put those pieces together properly.

The inverse, dividing your code into too many objects so that each only represents a fragment of a concept, also results in poor code. Finding the right median can, at times, be difficult, but that's why you should be sure to spend enough time at the beginning of a project designing your objects. If that step of the process isn't done correctly, a domino effect will ensue and getting the project done and debugging it on time will prove to be far more difficult than you initially planned.

Well-designed objects are programs unto their own, and as such they can be individually tested and debugged. If you are finding it difficult to test a particular object due to the way it's interconnected to other objects, you may be suffering from your objects not being properly encapsulated. Be sure that if at all possible you do not directly expose the properties of an object; instead, force the use of methods to modify data inside of the object.

Properties and Methods

Although it is best to discourage direct access to the properties of objects you design, sometimes it seems like directly accessing a property almost makes too much sense. In particular, sometimes an object simply has to hold one particular variable, and at a later time it might be necessary to retrieve the value of that variable.

It almost seems dumb *not* to just let the property be accessed directly, but if you do so you are severely compromising the integrity of your object design. It's the OO equivalent of painting yourself into a corner.

The most obvious solution, using a method to get a value and another to set a value, is a much better solution to the problem (see Figure 4.1). This pair of functions (often called a getter/setter pair) works well because it keeps your object's properties hidden. The only problem is that using such getters and setters is awkward, to say the least.

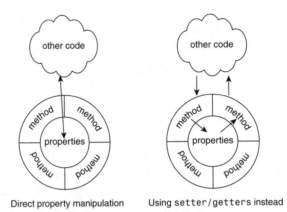

Direct property manipulation   Using setter/getters instead

Figure 4.1   Direct property manipulation versus getter/setters.

Thankfully, in Flash MX, there's a better solution to the problem of property "hiding" than just getter/setter pairs. First, you do create such a pair, but then you can wrap those two functions into a single property so that if that property is read, the getter is called and if it is modified, the setter method is called. For example:

```
foo = new Object();
foo.setType = function(value){
    this.typeValue = value;
}
foo.getType = function(){
    return this.typeValue;
}
foo.addProperty("type", foo.getType, foo.setType);

foo.type = 5;          // call the setter
trace(foo.type);       // call the getter
```

*Using **addProperty** to make the object easy to use yet flexible.*

Now in your code you can have the simplicity of directly manipulating the type property while still maintaining the flexibility of being able to change how the data is both assigned and returned. Notice that the name of the internal variable set is *not* the same as the "façade" property created via addProperty.

Verb's the Word

Another design issue when it comes to properties and methods is naming conventions. I find that you can much more easily distinguish between properties and methods if you give all your methods names that are both verbs and suggest what they do. For example, calcTax and draw are good method names, while book and doIt are not.

Let's say I create a method that would take some data and package it into some standardized form. In this case it might be tempting to name the method that does this package. Instead, it would probably be better to name it createPackage. This method of "verbing" your method really does end up being helpful in the long run!

Privacy Where There Is None

One particular issue with ActionScript (and its parent ECMAScript for that matter) that many Java and C++ programmers bemoan is that there is no explicit way to forcibly hide the methods and properties of an object.

Both Java and C++ allow you to do this, on a property-by-property and method-by-method basis set whether or not the property or method in question is available to code external from the object in which it lives. At first this may seem like the code equivalent of the sneeze guard on salad bars— useful, but generally just make up for a lack of common sense and courtesy. However, permissions systems are important for a number of reasons, such as copyright protection (making sure third parties can use an object—just not know how it works) and security (disallowing objects that deal with sensitive data from accidentally exposing that data). Both of these points are particularly important for companies that sell premade object libraries.

Without such concepts of "private" portions of classes, ActionScript allows any object to inherit from any other and any object to "dig into" and possibly modify any other object in the movie. In addition, with Flash, as with nearly all web technologies, the second it's on the Net the source code is available. There are numerous dissemblers for Flash that will extract the original ActionScript from an .swf. At its core, ActionScript is an interpreted language, so it's just not possible to obfuscate the code to any form that would even be remotely secure.

The standard way to get around these issues is to ignore them. The problem with this approach (or lack there of) is that sometimes, even if it can't be enforced, it would be good to at least be able to denote between public and private parts of an object. The best way I've found to do this is a naming scheme.

In particular, methods and properties that are supposed to be private to the object itself should have some sort of prefix that makes them easily identifiable. Because I try pretty hard not to expose any properties directly, I tend to just add a prefix to methods. My personal favorite is to use a $ or _ (underscore) in front of methods that aren't to be called by external code.

```
TaxMan = function(name){
        this.name = name;
}


TaxMan.prototype.calcTax = function(income){
      if (this.$isScrewed()){
            return income * (99/100);
      }else{
            return income * (1/3);
      }
}


TaxMan.prototype.$isScrewed = function(){
      if (this.name == "Branden Hall"){
            return true;
      }
}
```

"Cooperative" marking of private methods in action.

As you can see, this isn't a comprehensive solution, but it can aid in development and later use of objects.

Scope Issues (Non–Halitosis Related)

One problem that many developers ran into with Flash 5 was that there was not a global place to put code that needed to be accessible from anywhere in the movie while still being portable. This type of code usually consisted of various object definitions that would need to be used throughout a complex application.

The obvious choice, _root, has problems when you are working with loading .swfs into levels because there's a _root for each level. The most common solution to the problem ended up being to stuff the info inside Object. As a built-in class (prototype object, same thing, remember) Object has the benefit of being accessible from anywhere in a movie. In addition, unlike other objects, it's relatively empty to begin with.

When this solution started to become a bit more widespread, the authors of various code libraries realized that name conflicts (that is, two pieces of code creating and using separate variables of the same name in the same scope) would end up becoming a problem sooner rather than later. To deal with this these authors started to put these objects inside namespaces. A *namespace* is, in the case of ActionScript, just an object that's used to hold a related collection of code. For example, code that Sam (my co-author) and I wrote back in the Flash 5 days would use WOAQ (a combination of the beginnings of our usual online nicknames woozle and aquaman). To do this we would have a little bit of code like this at the beginning of our libraries:

```
if (Object.WOAQ == null){
    Object.WOAQ = new Object();
}
```

Flash 5–style namespace creation.

Then we would proceed to stuff all our various objects inside of Object.WOAQ.

In Flash MX we have a new scope, _global, just for creating globally accessible code. Once you put something into _global, you don't actually have to stick the _global in front of any references to it.

```
_global.foo = 5;
trace(foo);
```

*After a, variable is put inside **_global**, you don't have to give its full path.*

While _global is a wonderful new addition to ActionScript, its easy-to-use nature is encouraging its use far beyond the Object hack that was used in Flash 5. This fact, combined with the reality that if you use any components _global will automatically be stuffed with numerous objects, means that name collisions are more possible than ever. Because of this, whenever possible, it's best to stick anything you need to make global into a namespace. This precaution protects your code and prevents the kind of bugs that will make you tear your hair out trying to fix.

```
_global.WOAQ = new Object();
WOAQ.foo = 42;
```

*Using namespaces with **_global**.*

Overall, namespaces are the sort of thing that you don't really care about until they are not there and your code breaks. Save yourself the headache and just use them!

Relationships Between Objects

The design process for applications doesn't end at the individual objects themselves. In fact, that's just the beginning! Often more complicated and convoluted than the objects are the relationships between them.

UML

There are a number of tools out there to assist you in designing OOP-based applications. One of those tools, the Unified Modeling Language (UML), provides a standardized way for visually documenting all aspects of an OO program, from objects' interfaces to object relationships and event use diagrams. If you plan to use Flash MX to build large-scale applications where there will be numerous developers involved, you would be well served to learn about UML.

The only problem with using UML to model a Flash application is that although it is technically language neutral, it has strong leanings toward class-based languages such as Java and C++. You can certainly successfully use UML with ActionScript, you're just going to have to decide which parts of UML to utilize and which parts to ignore.

Inheritance

Inheritance, although a very powerful concept, simply is not used all that often in Flash—at least compared to other OOP languages such as Java. There are a number of reasons for this, but one of those reasons is that it's just too ambiguous and difficult in ActionScript.

This difficulty stems from the fact that there is no standardized way to do inheritance in ECMAScript–based languages, with the notable exception of the most recent specifications utilized by JScript.NET from Microsoft.

"New"-Based Inheritance

The closest thing to a standard method for inheritance is what Macromedia recommends because it works with all implantations of ECMAScript. You first saw this technique in Chapter 2, "OOP in Flash: A Tale of Different Angles," but if you've forgotten about "standard" inheritance, here it is again:

```
SubClassSubClass.prototype = new SuperClassSuperClass();
```

When a line like this is executed, a couple of things occur:

- `SubClassSubClass`'s prototype is cleared out.
- An instance of `SuperClassSuperClass` is created, thus calling `SuperClassSuperClass`'s constructor.
- `SubClassSubClass`'s prototype is filled with that instance.
- All instances of `SubClassSubClass` will now inherit all `SuperClassSuperClass`'s methods.
- A special property of `SubClass`'s prototype object named constructor now incorrectly points to `SuperOClass` (it should point to `SubClass`'s constructor).

Notice not all these results are what you would call desirable. In particular, the biggest issues are the extraneous creation of an instance of `SuperClassSuperClass` and the clearing of `SubClassSubClass`'s prototype.

The fact that this style of inheritance creates an object in doing its job may seem to be a minor annoyance at most (it does waste memory after all), but in fact it can be quite problematic in certain situations. Say you wanted to do reference counting (keeping track of how many instances of a class there are) of `SuperClass`. In this situation, "standard" inheritance would break your count because the act of inheriting automatically calls the `SuperClass`'s constructor.

The other issue, the clearing of the `SubClass`, is less of a problem, but it is still a problem. Because of this issue you are forced to do inheritance directly after you declare the `SubClass`'s constructor. This way there's nothing in `SubClass`'s prototype when it's wiped out.

One important thing to note is that due to the nature of components and how Macromedia recommends building them, none of these problems are an issue within components. So, you should only care about these issues with inheritance if you are creating your own objects and using inheritance to set up those objects into a hierarchy.

"__proto__"-Based Inheritance

The other way to do inheritance, "__proto__"-based inheritance, involves using a sparse document property of all objects in an undocumented and nonrecommended (at least by Macromedia) way.

All objects in ActionScript have a special property named __proto__, which points to the object from which the parent object should look for properties and methods that are not contained directly within the object. Under most normal circumstances, _proto_ points to the prototype property of an object. Macromedia recommends that you only read __proto__ and never set it; however, by setting it in a particular way you can create a cleaner way of doing inheritance.

The actual code to set __proto__ is as follows:

```
SubClass.prototype.__proto__ = SuperClass.prototype;
```

This code says that the prototype property of SubClass should look at the SuperClass's prototype for additional methods and properties. The short of it is that SubClass should inherit from SuperClass.

Because this line of code doesn't create an instance of SuperClass, you don't run into any of the problems that you would using New based inheritance.

There is one small problem with __proto__-based inheritance, though: the new special keyword super fails to work properly at times. The super keyword is always supposed to point at a class's superclass. However, if you use __proto__ inheritance, it won't work if you are trying to point at the superclass's constructor. It will work properly, however, for all other methods of the SuperClass.

The good news about this problem is that it can be fixed. If you set a property named __constructor__ inside SubClass's prototype and point it to SuperClass, everything will work as intended.

```
SubClass.prototype.__constructor__ = SuperClass;
```

As always, with undocumented code be sure you keep in mind that this little gem may disappear in future versions of Flash.

Mopping Up the Mess

I doubt that anyone was able to get through those last two sections without getting a little lost. That's the problem; inheritance in ActionScript is an ugly, messy affair filled with many different speed bumps and traps. No one should have to know that much about the internals of ActionScript to make a rudimentary OOP concept such as inheritance work.

The good news is that after you read this section you *won't* have to know and understand all the ins and outs of inheritance to use it! Specified here is a method, inheritFrom, which is part of the new Function object in Flash MX:

```
Function.prototype.inheritFrom = function(superClass){
    if ($majorVersion == null){
        var v = getVersion();
        _global.$majorVersion = Number(v.substring(v.indexOf(" ")+1,
v.indexOf(",")));
    }
    if ($majorVersion == 6){
```

```
        this.prototype.__constructor__ = superClass;
        ASSetPropFlags(this.prototype,"__constructor__",1);
        this.prototype.__proto__ = superClass.prototype;
    }else{
        this.prototype = new superClass();
    }
}
```

The **inheritFrom** *method makes inheritance a snap.*

Once you have this code in your movie, all you need to do is use it:

```
SubClass.inheritFrom(SuperClass);
```

Now SubClass inherits from SuperClass. The only rule you have to abide by is that this line of code must come before you put anything into SubClass's prototype.

This works because all functions (and hence all classes) now have the inheritFrom method built in to them. This is why the inheritFrom method is placed in Function.prototype. (Remember, functions are objects too!)

For more information on inheritance in Flash MX, as well as previous versions, be sure to check out the web site of one of the illustrious tech editors of this book, Dave Yang (http://www.quantumwave.com).

The basic concept behind inheritFrom is that it automatically detects which version of the Flash plug-in it is being run in, and *only* if it's being run in the Flash 6 plug-in will it use __proto__-based inheritance, otherwise, it will use New-based inheritance.

To do this, it first looks to see if a variable $majorVersion has been declared yet. If it hasn't, then it parses apart the version of the plug-in to pull out what the major version is (that is, Flash 1, 2, 3, 4, 5, 6, 7, and so on). Then, if the major version is 6, it will first fix the __constructor__ property, and then it hides this property using the undocumented and unsupported AsSetPropFlags method (this prevents the property from showing up in for...in loops). For more information on AsSetPropFlags see the Flashcoders wiki at http://chattyfig.figleaf.com/flashcoders-wiki/. Finally, inheritFrom uses __proto__ to do the inheritance.

If $majorVersion is something other than 6 it simply uses plain old New-based inheritance.

Design Patterns

As the old saying goes, there's more than one way to skin a cat. However, why bother trying to create a new technique for exfoliating a kitty if you can learn from an expert feline dermis remover?

The same type of statement can be said for OOP in any and all programming languages. PhDs and other incredibly smart folks have already solved a huge number of the "problems" normally encountered while writing OO-based programs. Why not use their knowledge to get those problems out of the way first and then move on to more unique and specific issues?

The problem with reusing ideas from OOP masters is that few of us have access to those people, and up until the early 1990s there was no standard way to document such code solutions.

In 1995, a book named *Design Patterns: Elements of Reusable Object-Oriented Software* hit the shelves (because it was written by four authors, it's often called the Gang of Four book, or just GoF). It specified a format for documenting software "design patterns" (a term taken from a highly influential book on urban planning and architecture, *A Pattern Language*). It then went on to offer 23 design patterns of its own. Since then, design patterns have been one of the hottest topics in OOP. Numerous authors have written books and papers on patterns and how they affect different parts of the programming industry.

So, what is a design pattern? A *design pattern* is an abstract and language-neutral answer to a common OOP problem. It's a nugget of knowledge that provides a proven solution to a reoccurring problem.

> Should this teaser about the power of patterns have gotten you interested in them, I would highly recommend that you purchase the GoF book and dig right in. Many of the patterns outlined in GoF are directly applicable to ActionScript and will give you a new insight in OOP code design.

There are two patterns that I find myself using quite a bit in my code, so here's a bit more info on the Model-View-Presenter pattern and the Decorator pattern (which is featured in GoF).

Model-View-Presenter

The Model-View-Presenter (MVP) pattern is an improved version of another, older pattern you may have heard of, Model-View-Controller (MVC). The MVP pattern's goal is to make more flexible and reusable GUI-based applications. In particular, it designates that an application (or piece of an application) should be divided into three parts: the model, the view, and the presenter (see Figure 4.2).

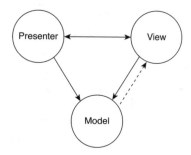

Figure 4.2 The relationships between the model, view, and presenter.

The *model* is a class that handles all the data for the application. However, rather than just making the data directly accessible by the view and presenter, it provides methods to do this. (This keeps the model as flexible as possible.) In addition, it also provides for listeners (see Chapter 3, "Event Wrangling: When To Do What," for more information on listeners) so that the view and presenter can find out when data inside of the model changes. The model provides such listeners so that it doesn't have to be aware in any way of what, if any, views and presenters are connected to it. Models should in no way be aware of any interface issues.

The view is often not a single class, but a collection of components that gives the user a visual interface to work with. The view is allowed to know about the model and presenter it is connected with, but it should only connect up to the model to get data. If it receives user input, it should forward it to presenter.

Finally, presenter is a class that is responsible for taking user input that comes from the view and using it to transform the model as needed. A good example of this is drag-and-drop style input: the view will only tell the presenter of the result of the action, not the full information about the mouse being pressed, dragged, and released. The view is allowed to know about both the model and view it is connected with, and acts as a liaison between the two.

The MVP pattern is a complex one, and it takes time and practice to really be able to utilize MVP to its full power. Luckily, in Chapter 5, "OOP Hands-On: An OOP Application from Start to Finish," you will use MVP to build a completely object-oriented game in Flash MX. In addition, to get a better grasp of how MVP works in the real world, you can look at nearly any standard application and mentally disassemble it into a model, view, and presenter.

For example, think about a simple drawing application—the model holds a data structure specifying where all the lines, curves, and fills are, while the view actually displays the shapes. If the user draws something, the mouse events are captured by the view and passed to the presenter, which turns the events into shapes and inserts the new data into the model. Finally, the model tells the view to update to display the new shape.

The Decorator Pattern

Another pattern which comes in handy quite often in ActionScript development is the Decorator pattern. The goal of the Decorator pattern is to provide many of the same capabilities that proper inheritance provides, but in a more flexible and decoupled manner.

With the Decorator pattern, you can add some abilities to an object, but you don't have to bother with inheritance, and you can also easily add other capabilities later.

You accomplish this by placing an instance of the object you are "decorating" inside your decorator object. You must then code your decorator object so that its interface (that is, its methods) conforms exactly to the interface of the object you are decorating. By doing this, you can trick other objects into thinking they are working with an instance of the original object and not the decorated version. Your decorator object just passes requests to the instance of the regular object inside of it while doing any additional tasks before or after it's done.

Here is an example of a decorator in action. The LoadVarsDebug object decorates the LoadVars object and prints debug statements anytime an instance of it is modified in any way:

```
_global.LoadVarsDebug = function(){
    trace("LoadVars: created new LoadVars object");
    this.conn = new LoadVars();
    this.conn._decorator = this;
    this.conn.onLoad = function(success){
        this._decorator.onLoad(success);
    }
    this.conn._loadedStatus = function(prop, oldVal, newVal){
        trace("LoadVars: set loaded : "+newVal);
    }
    this.conn.watch("loaded", this.conn._loadedStatus);
    this.noRecurse = false;
```

```
   }

LoadVarsDebug.prototype.getBytesLoaded = function(){
   var value = this.conn.getBytesLoaded();
   trace ("LoadVars: getBytesLoaded : "+value);
   return value;
}

LoadVarsDebug.prototype.getBytesTotal = function(){
   var value = this.conn.getBytesTotal();
   trace ("LoadVars: getBytesTotal : "+value);
   return value;
}

LoadVarsDebug.prototype.load = function(url){
   trace ("LoadVars: load : url = "+url);
   return this.conn.load(url);
}

LoadVarsDebug.prototype.send = function(url, target, method){
   trace("LoadVars: send : url = "+url+" : target = "+target+" : method =
   ➥"+method);
   return this.conn.send.apply(this.conn, arguments);
}

LoadVarsDebug.prototype.sendAndLoad = function(url, targetObj, method){
   trace("LoadVars: sendAndLoad : url = "+url+" : targetObj = "+targetObj+" :
   ➥method = "+method);
   return this.conn.send.apply(this.conn, arguments);
}

LoadVarsDebug.prototype.toString = function(){
   if (!this.noRecurse){
      this.noRecurse = true;
      var value = this.conn.toString();
      this.noRecurse = false;
      trace("LoadVars: toString : "+value);
      return value;
   }
}

LoadVarsDebug.prototype._setContentType = function(value){
   trace("LoadVars: set contentType");
   this.conn.contentType = value;
}

LoadVarsDebug.prototype._getContentType = function(){
   var value = this.conn.contentType;
   trace("LoadVars: get contentType : "+value);
   return value;
}
```

continues

```
LoadVarsDebug.prototype._setLoaded = function(value){
    this.conn.loaded = value;
}

LoadVarsDebug.prototype._getLoaded = function(){
    var value = this.conn.loaded;
    trace("LoadVars: get loaded : "+value);
    return value;
}

LoadVarsDebug.prototype.addProperty("contentType",
➥LoadVarsDebug.prototype._getContentType,
➥LoadVarsDebug.prototype._setContentType);
LoadVarsDebug.prototype.addProperty("loaded", LoadVarsDebug.prototype._getLoaded,
➥LoadVarsDebug.prototype._setLoaded);
```

A Decorator pattern for the **LoadVars** *object.*

As you can see, every method of the LoadVarsDebug object just forwards the "request" to the actual LoadVars object it holds inside of itself.

One of the nicest things about decorators is that, because the interface to the object doesn't change at all, you can decorate an object multiple times by decorating the decorators.

Flair Pattern

The Flair pattern is one you won't find in any books (well, excluding this one, obviously). That's because it's a pattern that Sam and I developed while writing this book. The motivation for writing this pattern is similar to that of the decorator. That is, we wanted to design a way to add functionality to objects. However, we wanted our system to be able to add and remove said functionality at any time. This type of idea simply wouldn't mesh with how most OOP languages work, but in ActionScript it's actually remarkably easy.

First, a flair object is a static object that has methods directly attached to it. To keep these objects straight, it's best to store them in their own family namespace based on the type of object you are "flairing." For example, if you were building a flair to add automatic highlighting to TextField objects:

```
if(TextFlair == null){
_global.TextFlair = new Object();
}
TextFlair.HighlightFlair = new Object();
```

Starting to build a flair.

Now that the actual object is built, the next step is to add methods to it. All flair objects need to have at least two methods, snapOn (to apply the flair to an object) and snapOff (to remove it from an object).

Now, it's pretty obvious that in order for a flair to work, its snapOn method needs to add code to the objects it is "flairing." This could potentially cause a problem though; what if you try to apply two flairs to an object and some of the properties or methods they add conflict? Well, to be blunt, all sorts of things would break. To prevent that, flair objects are only allowed to add a single property to the object they are enhancing, and that property should be a dollar sign ($) followed by the name of the flair object. This property is an object. The flair can then add any methods it would like to that property.

Similarly, the snapOn method essentially has to remove any listeners from that property and then remove the property itself. Here's the full code for the HighlightFlair flair:

```
if(TextFlair == null){
   _global.TextFlair = new Object();
}

TextFlair.HighlightFlair = new Object();

TextFlair.HighlightFlair.snapOn = function(obj, normalColor, hiColor){
   obj.$highlightFlair = new Object();
   obj.$highlightFlair.normalColor = normalColor;
   obj.$highlightFlair.hiColor = hiColor;
   obj.$highlightFlair._obj = obj;
   obj.$highlightFlair.onSetFocus = this.onSetFocus;
   Selection.addListener(obj.$highlightFlair);
   obj.$highlightFlair.onSetFocus();
}

TextFlair.HighlightFlair.snapOff = function(obj){
   Selection.removeListener(obj.$highlightFlair);
   delete obj.$highlightFlair;
}

TextFlair.HighlightFlair.onSetFocus = function(){
   trace(Selection.getFocus());
   if (eval(Selection.getFocus()) == this._obj){
      this._obj.backgroundColor = this.hiColor;
   }else{
      this._obj.backgroundColor = this.normalColor;
   }
}

TextFlair.HighlightFlair.snapOn(foo_txt, 0x999999, 0x99ff99);
```

The *HighlightFlair* flair.

After you have a `flair` object, using it is quite simple; you just have to snap it on! This snippet assumes you have a textfield named `foo_txt`.

```
TextFlair.HighlightFlair.snapOn(foo_txt, 0x999999, 0x88ff88);
```

Now the `foo_txt` textfield automatically changes colors anytime it is selected.

Features, Hacks, and What ActionScript Isn't

Due to the flexible nature of ActionScript, developers who are used to more restrictive languages, such as Java and C++, often feel a bit overwhelmed with the "wiggle room" that ActionScript gives you. Because of this, ActionScript and other ECMAScript-based languages are often seen as not object-oriented or as toy languages. This is, of course, far from the truth. The flexible nature of ActionScript actually lets you add your own features as you see fit.

Resolve

After looking at the `LoadVarsDebug` example of the Decorator pattern earlier in this chapter, you may have thought how nice it would be if you could just find out if a particular object didn't contain the method or property you were trying to access. This way you could, in that case, forward that request onto the object you were decorating.

It turns out that with an undocumented (but utilized by Macromedia in its Flash Remoting libraries) method you can do just that. It just so happens that every object in ActionScript supports a special method named `__resolve` (note the two underscores) that gets called if you try to access a property in the object that doesn't exist. It also happens to get passed the name of the nonexistent property (remember, methods are just properties of an object that are of type `Function`).

Once `__resolve` gets called, you have a couple of options for what you want to do. In the case of custom classes you create, you may want to simply trace out an error, like this:

```
SomeClass.prototype.__resolve = function(propName){
    trace("Sorry, "+propName+" does not exist.");
}
```

A simple use of `__resolve`.

If your __resolve function returns something, that something is now the value of the missing property. This comes in handy if you want to do something with the arguments passed to a method that doesn't exist. For example, the getBytesLoaded, getBytesTotal, load, send, and sendAndLoad methods of the LoadVarsDebug class defined previously could be totally replaced by this simple __resolve:

```
LoadVarsDebug.prototype.__resolve = function(propName){
    var f = function(){
        var value = this.conn[propName].apply(this.conn, arguments);
        trace ("LoadVars: "+propName+" : "+value.toString());
        return value;
    }
    return f;
}
```

Using __resolve to call methods.

> You've seen it mentioned before that functions are fully fledged objects in Flash MX, and sending them back as a return type from a method is one of the results of this change.
>
> The ability to think of functions as just another object type is an extremely powerful idea that can come in handy in many different sticky situations. In addition, it gives you some powerful new tools, namely function.apply and function.call, which allow you to do some interesting tricks with functions and their scope.

Other design patterns you may read about, such as proxy and façade, should also utilize __resolve to ease their development time and effort.

Implementing Interfaces

One of the nicest features of Java, at least from an object-oriented point of view, is interfaces and the implements keyword. An *interface* is simply a class that defines a set of methods that any class that conforms to it must specify. The implements keyword is used to then "sign a contract" between a class and an interface. This contract says that the class must specify all the methods named in the interface.

You see, interfaces are classes that are known as *abstract*. This means that although they define the names, arguments, and return types for a set of methods, they don't actually specify the code for those methods. The reason this is so powerful is because in Java, any class can implement multiple interfaces. In other words, you can snap new functionality onto Java classes one piece at a time (you just have to define how that functionality works yourself).

The problem with trying to apply this idea to ActionScript is that because of its loose nature you can't specify any such contract between classes. Also, things that you have to use interfaces for in Java, such as listeners, just work in ActionScript without any need for additional functionality. Finally, ActionScript has no real concept of abstractness built in. Despite all this, the core concept of adding functionality in a piecemeal fashion is still very desirable.

One simple way to make this core concept work in ActionScript is to go against how Java interfaces work and instead make an object that contains actual functional code in it.

After you have this collection of code, you can copy it into any object you'd like, including the prototype property of a custom class, like this:

```
Function.prototype.implement = function (obj){
    for (var i in obj){
        this.prototype[i] = obj[i];
    }
}

// define a set of functionality
HelloBehavior = new Object();
HelloBehavior.sayHello = function(){
    trace("hello!");
}
HelloBehavior.sayGoodbye = function(){
    trace("goodbye!");
}

// create a custom class and apply to it the behavior
MyClass = function(name){
    this.name = name
}
MyClass.implement(HelloBehavior);

// create an instance of myClass to test it
testObj = new MyClass("bob");
testObj.sayHello();
```

Faking an interface/behavior in ActionScript.

As you can see, MyClass implements HelloBehavior so now testObj, an instance of MyClass, has access both sayHello and sayGoodbye method.

Although this technically is quite different from actual Java interfaces, the concept of adding functionality in a piecemeal fashion is there.

Conclusion

As you are probably beginning to see, there is far more to ActionScript development than meets the eye. Now that you have a better idea about what goes into OO ActionScript development for real-world applications, you won't end up having a project of yours fall down as unceremoniously as my wall did. One important fact that has not yet been mentioned is probably the most important of them all—never stop learning, because often the best tool, whether it is mental or real, is one you haven't heard of yet and more often than not, someone else has already solved a problem you are facing. Never underestimate the power of reuse. Utilizing existing ideas and code will help you write better code faster.

5

OOP Hands-On:
An OOP Application
From Start to Finish

By Branden J. Hall

A Truly "Hands-On" Experience

As you may have already noticed, the lessons that stick with me the most tend to be the ones that I learned at expense of my health and general well being. I am the type of person that learns best from experience to say the least and because of this next story I have a habit of steering clear of metal chains...

I think I was about 11 years old when my family went on a trip to Busch Gardens theme park in Virginia. Being a kid, I wanted to go on everything, but being 11, I was still a little too afraid of the roller coasters to give those a shot. So, as one of our first stops, my parents took my brother and I to one of those rides where you sit in a big plastic log as it travels through what looks like a sawmill. The highlight of the ride was supposed to be this big drop at the end just barely saving you and your "log" from getting sawn in half, but the highlight for me was a bit more exciting than that!

Like most modern amusement rides, this log ride had a long winding set of barriers set up at the entrance where everyone queued up. The problem was that some of those barriers consisted of wood posts with chains running between them. Actually, that's not quite right, the chains were only attached to the posts at the end, the middle posts just had holes through them that the chain went through. Being a kid, I started to fidget with the chain while we were waiting. My dad kept telling me to stop, but I didn't. Big mistake.

Somehow I managed to get my pinky finger stuck in one of the chain links and just at that exact moment someone at the front of the line *stood* on the chain, thus dragging me by my pinky quite quickly to what appeared to be the dismemberment of said pinky. Luckily Dad saw this coming (I think with me as a child there was *always* something coming) and dashed over to grab the chain before I was dragged into the post. He then yanked on it to give me some slack to free myself (which had the amusing affect of making the man at the front of the line go flying) and soon, with the exception of a slightly bruised pinky, everything was fine.

Do I mess with chain barriers anymore? My pinky starts to throb if I ever get close to one!

Introduction

There's something to be said about hands-on experience. By actually sitting down and getting your hands dirty (or nearly yanked off in my case) you learn lessons far faster and deeper than you ever could just by reading a book.

In this chapter you'll walk-through the process of specifying, architecting, and developing a small object-oriented game, called KeyStone, based on the Model-View-Presenter design pattern.

The Game: KeyStone

The game you are going to create, KeyStone, is a sort of reverse Tetris, where users are presented with a full screen of colored cells, and their goal is to try to remove all the cells (see Figure 5.1). The only rule is that they may only remove a cell if it has at least one neighbor that's the same color. If a cell is clicked on and it satisfies that rule, then the game will remove all the squares in that particular "island" of color. The game then makes the cells above this new "hole" fall down into place.

You can probably get a better idea about how the game works by grabbing the finished FLA off the book's web site (keystone-final.fla in the Chapter 5 zip file) and giving it a try yourself. Once you are comfortable with the rules, keep on reading.

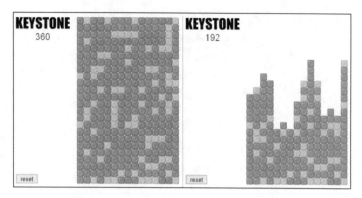

Figure 5.1 KeyStone in action—at the beginning of a game and in the middle of one.

Model-View-Presenter

In the previous chapter you learned about the Model-View-Presenter pattern and how its goal is to cleanly separate user input processing, data, and interface. There are some additional details about MVP that you need to now understand.

As you know, the model is the data for the program, the presenter handles the input, and the view handles the user interface. There are actually some specific rules on how these objects can interact to stick with MVP.

First, the view and presenter are allowed to fully manipulate each other via each other's methods. Both the view and presenter may also access methods of the model. The model on the other hand is not allowed to know at all about the presenter and view. It may not directly access either of them, instead, it broadcasts events when the data inside of it changes. The view (and only the view) can subscribe to these events in order to know how it should update itself (see Figure 5.2).

The purpose of these rules is to keep the model, view, and presenter as separate as possible so that they can be swapped out easily. By following these rules you can later very easily change how the user plays the game or what the game looks like without ever having to touch the code inside of the model.

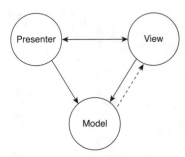

Figure 5.2 The Model-View-Presenter relationship.

Architecting the Game

In other programming languages you would be essentially forced into making the model, presenter, and view their own class. In this case though, you'll just make classes for the model and presenter. The view will just be represented by various methods in the main Timeline. Now that that's out of the way, start designing the model.

The Model

First off, you want to keep the model as flexible as possible. It shouldn't have any values hard-coded into it if at all possible. With that in mind, it's pretty obvious that the model for this game is going to have to store a 2D array of the values for the game board. (For more information about 2D arrays and other data structures see Chapter 11, "Debugging: Annoying Bugs and Where To Find Them.") The actual range of values that should be stored in this array should also be flexible.

With all this in mind, it's clear that the constructor for the model needs to accept three arguments: width, height, and range of values for the cells (see the following table).

The model then needs to support two methods for interacting with it, one for resetting the model and the other for clearing a single square (see the following table). It's a simple leap of logic that the method that clears squares will be passed the x- and y-coordinates of the square to remove.

Now, because models are only supposed to communicate with the other objects via events, the model also needs to support listeners and a couple of events. The EventBroadcaster class defined back in Chapter 3, "Event Wrangling: When To Do What," will handle the listeners. The two actual events that the model needs to send are when the model's data is updated or when the user "wins" by removing all the cells.

In the case of the model's data updating, you could always just send back with the event the data on the entire grid of cells. This, however, would be very inefficient and downright slow if your game was going to use a large number of cells. A better idea would be to only send out a list of the cells that had been updated. In addition, it would probably be a good idea to pass back how many cells the user has left to remove.

In the case of the user winning, no real data needs to be sent back.

The actual names of both events should be as unique as possible to avoid potential name collision issues later. (Imagine the mess if an object subscribes to two different event sources that generate events under the same names!) A good choice for KeyStone would be to use its initials in the name of the event, for example, `onKSUpdate` and `onKSWin` (see the following table).

So, at this point this is the shape of the model's interface:

Constructor	`width, height, numTypes`
Methods	`reset()`
	`remove(x, y)`
Events	`onKSUpdate(cells, numLeft)`
	`onKSWin()`

Note that while there isn't a method to just get the state of the game at any time (the state of all the cells and of the number of cells left) it would be perfectly legitimate to make one. The only reason that there isn't one is because it would only need to be called when the game board was reset, and that happens so rarely (relatively) that it's simply easier to force a call to `onKSUpdate`.

The View

Thinking about the view as an object may seem a bit strange at first; after all, *everything* is part of the "view" in Flash. This is why the view object in this case doesn't have to be an actual object. Sure, you could build it as one in case you wanted to create multiple games all at once, but how common is that need?

So, instead of designing an actual class for the view, you're just going to define its various methods on the main Timeline of your movie. After all, the main Timeline is an instance of the `MovieClip` object, so technically, your code is encapsulated in an object.

You already know that the view is going to have to have two methods, `onKSUpdate` and `onKSWin`, which will be called automatically from the model. In addition, the view will also need to have another method to capture the event generated by the actual reset button (which will be a simple push button component).

The view also will have to have two other methods. The first one, which is probably the least obvious, is one that will be copied into each one of the actual "cell" movieclips onPress callback. It's best to define this method here in the view and then just copy it in, because otherwise you'd just end up making a couple hundred copies of the whole function, which isn't very memory efficient.

The last method in the view is the initializer. It's the code that actually builds the physical grid of cell movieclips, places them in the right spot, and adds code to them. This code is encapsulated into its own function so that the code is as portable and reusable as possible. Because you have an init method you can reset the whole game anytime you'd like!

The Presenter

In the case of this game, the presenter really doesn't have to do much. In fact, although it is going to be a class, it barely merits even being that. The only reason to bother with the presenter is for the sake of flexibility. Remember, the goal of the presenter is to abstract the manipulation of the model from the input received by the view. With the code built in this manner it would be relatively trivial to create a computer-controlled player, a self-running demo, or perhaps even support remote players!

The presenter needs to be aware of the model and view, so those should be passed to it in the constructor. Then the only method that the presenter needs to support is one to handle the removal of cells from the grid. This is because there is a case when the user can click all they want on the view, but the model shouldn't be changed. This is when the view is in the process of animating the cells disappearing and falling into place.

Assembling the Pieces

Now, if this were a project you were building on your own, this is the point where you read, re-read, and re-read again the specification that you just wrote. If pieces of it don't make sense you'll need to redesign them. Remember, object design, like any kind of design, is an iterative process. If you can get most of your change to your code done in the planning stage, you'll end up saving yourself a lot of work and unnecessary code.

Obviously, the most "reusable" part of this game is the model that handles all its data and core logic. As such, the model is a good place to start coding.

Building the Model

First is the model's constructor. As stated previously, it needs to accept a width, a height, and a value representing the maximum number of types to be represented. From this data it needs to build a 2D array to store the information about each cell. To facilitate quick data access, each cell will be an object that stores the location of the cell, a unique ID, and the type of the cell.

```
_global.KeyStoneModel = function(width, height, numOptions){
    this.width = width;
    this.height = height;
    this.numOptions = numOptions;
    this.board = new Array();
    var temp;

    // create the gameboard
    for (var i=0; i<height; ++i){
        this.board[i] = new Array();
        for (j=0; j<width; ++j){
            temp = new Object();
            temp.id = i*this.height + j;
            temp.x = j;
            temp.y = i;
            this.board[i][j] = temp;
        }
    }
    // make this an event source
    EventBroadcaster.initialize(this);
}
```

The model's constructor.

As you can see the "meat" of this code consists of a loop within a loop that creates a two-dimensional array of objects.

The `reset` method of the model is similarly simple. All it has to do is to loop through the array of cells, set each one of their types to a random value, and then pass back an object that references all the cells (because all of them have updated).

```
// reset the cells to a random type
KeyStoneModel.prototype.reset = function(){
    var i, j, type;
    var updates = new Object();
    this.totalLeft = this.height * this.width;
    for (i=0; i<this.height; ++i){
        for (j=0; j<this.width; ++j){
```

continues

```
        type =  Math.floor(Math.random()*this.numOptions);
        updates[this.board[i][j].id] = ({x:j, y:i, type:type});
        this.board[i][j].type = type;
      }
    }
    this.broadcastMessage("onKSUpdate", updates, this.totalLeft);
}
```

The model's reset method.

Finally, for the model at least, is the `remove` method. This is by far the
most complex code in the entire game. It also illustrates the power of
OO programming.

The `remove` method needs to do what is known as a recursive search to find
all of the neighbor cells that match the clicked cell's type. (For more information on recursion, see Chapter 16, "Useful Code and Handy Ideas.") All you
need to know for now is that the `remove` method and its `removeHelper` method
handle all the finding, removing, and "settling" of the cells. When it sends out
the list of cells that have been updated, it happens to place some additional
info in the cells that were removed. This is done so that in the view we can
make the clicked-on cells fade away before the cells above them fall into place.

The beauty of the `remove` method is not in its complexity, instead it's in
the simplicity of its interface. You know what it expects and what it spits out,
you don't have to care how it actually does the work (although the code is
commented so that you can sort it out).

```
KeyStoneModel.prototype.remove = function(x, y){

    // internal method to handle recursively finding matches
    removeHelper = function(x, y, type){
        // same idea repeated four times (one per direction)
        // check to see if the cell is the type we need
        var total = 0;
        if (board[y+1][x].type == type){

            // mark the cell as dead
            board[y+1][x].type = null;

            // mark this cell to be updated
            updates[board[y+1][x].id]= {x:x, y:y+1, type:null, removed:true};

            // increment total
            ++total;

            // see if this is a new low for the column
            // if so, place it in the cols object
```

```
        if (cols[x] == null ¦¦ y+1 > cols[x]){
           cols[x] = y+1;
        }

        // check all of this cells neighbors
        total += removeHelper(x, y+1, type);
    }
  if (board[y-1][x].type == type){
     board[y-1][x].type = null;
     updates[board[y-1][x].id]= {x:x, y:y-1, type:null, removed:true};
     ++total;
     if (cols[x] == null ¦¦ y-1 > cols[x]){
        cols[x] = y-1;
     }
     total += removeHelper(x, y-1, type);
  }
  if (board[y][x+1].type == type){
     board[y][x+1].type = null;
     updates[board[y][x+1].id]= {x:x+1, y:y, type:null, removed:true};
     ++total;
     if (cols[x+1] == null ¦¦ y > cols[x+1]){
        cols[x+1] = y;
     }
     total += removeHelper(x+1, y, type);
  }
  if (board[y][x-1].type == type){
     board[y][x-1].type = null;
     updates[board[y][x-1].id]= {x:x-1, y:y, type:null, removed:true};
     ++total;
     if (cols[x-1] == null ¦¦ y > cols[x-1]){
        cols[x-1] = y;
     }
     total += removeHelper(x-1, y, type);
  }
  return total;
}
// general use variables for loops
var i, j, z, total = 0;

// shortcut to board
var board = this.board;

// track the lowest "hole" in each column
var cols = new Object;

// cells to update
var updates = new Object();

// how many items to skip when adjusting to "gravity"
var skip;
```

continues

```
// type of cell we are looking for
var type = board[y][x].type;

// mark the current cell, for now
board[y][x].type = null;

// mark as the lowest "hole" for the column, for now
cols[x] = y;

// mark all matching neighbors and get total
total = removeHelper(x, y, type);

// if it there's one or more neighbors, get busy
if (total > 0){

    // toss the clicked cell into updates
    updates[board[y][x].id] = {x:x, y:y, type:null, removed:true};

    // keep track of how many cells there are left
    this.totalLeft -= total + 1;

    // adjust each column for "gravity"
    for (j in cols){
       skip = 1;
       i = cols[j];
       for (z = i-1; z>-1; --z){
          if (board[z][j].type == null){
             ++skip
          }else{
             updates[board[z+skip][j].id].type =  board[z][j].type;
             board[z+skip][j].type = board[z][j].type;
             updates[board[z][j].id] = {x:j, y:z, type:null};
             board[z][j].type = null;
          }
       }
    }

    // broadcast that update event
    this.broadcastMessage("onKSUpdate", updates, this.totalLeft);

    // check for win, and if so broadcast it
    if (this.totalLeft == 0){
       this.broadcastMessage("onKSWin");
    }
}else{
    // whoops! no neighbors, reset the clicked cell
    board[y][x].type = type;
}
}
```

*The model's **remove** method.*

Just a quick note on the removeHelper method; yes, it is inside of the remove method, and yes, this is a perfectly legitimate thing to do, and in fact it makes a lot of sense in this case. When you define a method inside another in this manner, the inner method has access to all the outer method's variables but is not actually exposed to the outside world. Only the outer method can call it. In this case, where removeHelper is just a special "helper" method for remove and in doing its job removeHelper needs access to some of remove's variables, using a "inner" method like this not only makes sense, but is a good idea. This is because recursion is a memory-intensive type of operation to begin with and by using an inner method in this manner, you are preventing yourself from having to copy variables multiple times (which would be the case if it wasn't an inner method).

To keep the view as uncluttered as possible, this code will just live in its own .as file. Now that the model has been created, it's time to move on to the presenter.

Building the Presenter

As stated earlier, the presenter is a very simple class because the game doesn't call for any more. Here's its code:

```
_global.KeyStonePresenter = function(model, view){
    this.model = model;
    this.view = view;
}

KeyStonePresenter.prototype.remove = function(x, y){
    if (this.view.enabled){
        this.model.remove(x, y);
    }
}
```

The presenter's code. Yes, that's it!

All the remove method does is act as a filter; only if the view has its enabled variable set to true will the presenter pass the removal request on to the model.

Like the model, this code goes in its own .as file, KeyStonePresenter.as.

Building the View

The final part of the construction process is building the view. First, think a little about the actual assets used by the movie. For the actual game you are going to have four separate colors of cells. You could create four separate movieclips and when you update the stage just remove the old ones and replace it with the new colors; however, this would be very inefficient.

A better way to handle the cells would be to create a movieclip with five frames, one for each colored cell and another to represent a destroyed cell. This way all you have to do is place the cells once and then just use gotoAndStop to jump between the cell's possible states. This movieclip also has its linkage set to "cell" so that it can be dynamically attached (see Figure 5.3).

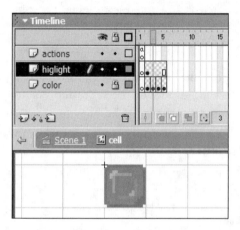

Figure 5.3 The cells movieclip has five frames, a blank one and then one for each color.

The only other user interface in the game is the reset button. This is a push button component with its handler set to "onReset".

The other "active" element on the stage is a textfield, total_txt, which represents the total number of cells left for the user to remove. In addition, this field also displays "You Won!" if the user manages to remove all the cells.

The first bit of code in the movie handles the inclusion of all the .as files and setting up a few constants you can later tweak to modify how the game works:

```
#include "EventBroadcaster.as"
#include "KeyStoneModel.as"
#include "KeyStonePresenter.as"

// constants
NUM_X = 15;
NUM_Y = 24;
NUM_TOTAL = NUM_X * NUM_Y;
CELL_WIDTH = 15;
CELL_HEIGHT = 15;
```

```
FADE_STEP = 3.5;
FADE_NUM = 10;

// properties
enabled = true;
```

The first part of the view code.

The NUM_X and NUM_Y variables represent the size of the grid. The CELL_WIDTH and CELL_HEIGHT variables represent the actual pixel size of each cell. The FADE_STEP variable represents how much to divide a removed cell's alpha each frame. The larger this number, the slower it will fade out removed squares. This number must be larger than 1. FADE_NUM is how many frames should be taken up waiting for the removed cells to fade out until the new state of the board is shown. Finally, enabled specifies whether the user can currently remove cells.

Next comes the two methods that listen for events coming from the model (and one that handles the fading of the cells):

```
// handle fading of the cells
fadeCells = function(){
    var temp;

    if (this.countDown == 0){
        for (var i in this.updates){
            temp = cells[this.updates[i].y][this.updates[i].x];
            temp._alpha = 100;
            if(this.updates[i].type != null){
                temp.gotoAndStop(this.updates[i].type+2);
            }else{
                temp.gotoAndStop(1);
            }
        }
        this.onEnterFrame = undefined;
        this.enabled = true;
    }else{
        for (var i in this.updates){
            if(this.updates[i].removed){
                temp._alpha /= FADE_STEP;
            }
        }
        --this.countDown;
    }
}
// handle if the user wins
onKSWin = function(){
    this.total_txt.text = "You Won!";
}
```

continues

```
// handle updates from the model
onKSUpdate = function(updates, totalLeft){
    this.total_txt.text = totalLeft;
    if (totalLeft == NUM_TOTAL){
        for (var i in updates){
            if(updates[i].type != null){
                cells[updates[i].y][updates[i].x].gotoAndStop(updates[i].type+2);
            }else{
                cells[updates[i].y][updates[i].x].gotoAndStop(1);
            }
        }
    }else{
        this.updates = updates;
        this.countdown = FADE_NUM;
        this.enabled = false;
        this.onEnterFrame = fadeCells;

    }
}
```

The view's methods to handle events from the model.

You can see that the onKSUpdate method first checks to see if the number of cells passed to it happens to be all the cells. If that's the case, then the method just goes ahead and draws all the cells. (This is the case in which the model has just been reset.)

If that is not the case, then the movie sets up an onEnterFrame loop to first fade out the cells that were removed, and then after the number of frames specified by FADE_NUM, the cell movieclips that were affected will all be updated.

Finally comes the last bit of code that handles the reset button and initializing the movie:

```
// function to be inserted into each cell
cellPress = function(){
    this._parent._parent.presenter.remove(this.x, this.y); }

// handle reset requests from the push button component
onReset = function(){
    this.model.reset();
}

// initialize the game
init = function(){
    var temp;
    var num = 0;

    this.grid_mc = this.createEmptyMovieClip("grid_mc", 1);
```

```
    this.grid_mc._x = 150;
    this.grid_mc._y = 15;

    this.cells = new Array()


    for (var i=0; i<NUM_Y; ++i){
       cells[i] = new Array();
       for (var j=0; j<NUM_X; ++j){
          temp = grid_mc.attachMovie("cell", "cell"+num, num++);
          temp._x = j * CELL_WIDTH;
          temp._y = i * CELL_HEIGHT;
          temp.x = j;
          temp.y = i;
          temp.onPress = this.cellPress;
          temp.useHandCursor = false;
          this.cells[i][j] = temp;
       }
    }

    this.model = new KeyStoneModel(NUM_X, NUM_Y, 4);
    this.model.addListener(this);
    this.presenter = new KeyStonePresenter(model, this);
    this.model.reset();
}

init();
```

The final code for the game.

To keep things as clear as possible, the actual instance of the KeyStoneModel used in the movie is named model, and the instance of KeyStonePresenter is, you guessed it, presenter.

First of all, in this last bit of code is the function that will be attached to each one of the cell movieclips. This code, as you can see, has to reference up two movieclips before it can reach the presenter object located here in the main Timeline. This is because all the cells are placed inside a movieclip that's dynamically created. This is so you can move the entire grid of cells around easily if you need to later.

Then comes the function, onReset, which captures the event coming from the reset push button component. As you can see, it just references the reset method of the model. This call could go through the presenter first, but in this case it's just easier to reference the model directly.

Finally, there's the init method. This is the code that does all the initialization of the movie. It's encapsulated into its own function for the sake of organization and so if needed you can reinitialize the whole game later.

This code first creates a movieclip, grid_mc, where the cell movieclips will live. It also positions grid_mc to the correct spot on the stage.

Then, there's the loop that actually creates the cell movieclips and places them in the correct position and assigns their onPress event, the cellPress method that was defined earlier.

Next there's the lines that create the instance of KeyStoneModel. The view (the main Timeline) is then assigned as a listener to model. Then, the presenter is created, and finally the model's reset method is called to start the game.

The last line of code in the game, init(); just calls the init method so that the game initializes as soon as it is loaded.

Be sure you walk through all this code a number of times. Reading explanations is a good first step, but to get the most out of this chapter you should go in and play with the code on your own. Try to add more features, perhaps a timer or maybe a way to make the grid squeeze together if there is an empty column. There are some examples of such modifications on this book's web site (http://www.wheelmaker.org).

Project Postmortem

Anytime you create any project, whether or not it's in Flash, you should conduct a postmortem analysis to find out where you encountered the most problems, and what you learned over the course of building the project. Even if you have done something similar before, you'll find that you learn something new each time you do it. By examining how a project progressed you can be sure that you can later capitalize on the knowledge you gained and avoid the pitfalls you fell into.

A good example of this is the postmortem I conducted when I finished designing and building KeyStone, but before I actually wrote this chapter. I have written two other games similar to KeyStone, but during the postmortem I realized that in KeyStone I came up with some new ways to handle making the cells drop. The way that the code only handles columns that have been modified and only works up from the lowest cell that was modified turned out to be quite a success. When I compared this code to my earlier attempts at similar games, KeyStone proved to be almost 10 times faster! I now know that though it results in more code, tracking the modified sections of the grid and only modifying those gives a huge speed improvement over just scanning through the whole grid. By conducting a postmortem, I learned even more about the code I created than I originally thought.

Conclusion

You've now seen the creation of an OOP project from start to finish. If you have written object-oriented code before, the structure and overall flow of this code may seem a bit foreign; however, the one thing to keep in mind at all times is that OOP is not about sticking to strict rules. Instead it's about following some core guidelines to make your job as a programmer easier.

Another lesson to remember is that ActionScript is neither Java nor C++. Although as an ActionScript programmer you can learn a lot from these languages, if you had tried to emulate how Java works in making this game, you would have been bogged down very quickly. By playing with ActionScript and Flash's strengths you watched KeyStone rise from an idea, to a plan, and finally to reality quite quickly.

Object-oriented programming is all about working smarter instead of harder. If you stick to the basic rules of abstraction, encapsulation, and inheritance while utilizing ActionScript's unique strengths, you can create incredible applications in Flash remarkably quickly.

II

Components

6

Using UI Components

By Samuel Wan

From Building Blocks to Real Machines

The first time I saw *Star Wars*, I wanted to learn everything there was to know about building robots. I think it was the idea of interacting with a machine that fascinated me, rather than the nitty-gritty details of electronics and mechanics. Every month, I would max out my library card by checking out all the robotics books. Most of them described how to build the electronic components of robots from scratch. I was probably six years old, and eventually realized that I didn't have the math or physics background to learn basic electronics. Discouraged, I went back to building imaginary robots with Lego blocks and eventually lost interest in robots altogether.

Years later, I read an article about the Lego Mindstorms robot kit and eagerly bought the kit from a local hobby store. The Lego Mindstorms system allows kids to build simple robots by combining a "logic" brick and a couple of motors with regular Lego pieces. By snapping together a few Lego pieces, you can build a programmable robot within minutes. Even better was the fact that I'd found a group of hackers who had ported the Java Virtual Machine to Lego Mindstorms. Other Java programmers had even written some reusable libraries for advanced Lego programming.

Armed with a Lego Mindstorms kit and a Java compiler, I suddenly had the tools to build a very sophisticated robot. The simple design of reusable Lego machines with object-oriented code was all I needed to see a childhood dream come true. In the same way, many user interface designers find themselves faced with the laborious task of building UI components from scratch, even though they're just interested the interface as whole. Flash components work like the Lego Mindstorms system in the sense that components allow you to build what you want to build without spending too much time on low-level details. In this chapter, we'll explore how the different components can snap together to create a complete interface.

Introduction

Components will change the way you approach interface design in Flash. In previous versions of Flash, even the most common interface elements, such as scrollbars and pull-down menus, required a lot of redundant work. You either had to rebuild common UI elements from scratch for each new project, or change the code beyond all recognition. With Flash MX, however, developers have access to standard user interface components engineered for ease of use, flexibility, and customizability.

Although other books and the Flash documentation will tell you all about the basics of using components, I'd like to give you a sense of what's possible with Flash components by introducing some more advanced strategies for combining components into useful interfaces. Along the way, you'll see how components function as individual pieces, and you'll see how they can work together as a cooperative system of parts.

We're starting the components section of this book with a chapter on how to *use* components instead of jumping straight into *building* components. After you get a sense of how components are used in the real world, you can design your own components in a way that meets the user's needs.

If Flash designers can drag and drop components easily to build complex interfaces, what does that mean for Flash programmers? Will they become less important? The answer is that components will give Flash programmers more freedom to do more valuable work. Components free up Flash programmers from reprogramming the same basic interface widgets, so that programmers can now focus on taking web applications to a new level of complexity and power.

In this chapter, we'll use an interactive form to demonstrate the power and flexibility of various components. Discussing every feature of every component would require more pages than are available in this book, and the official Macromedia documentation already does a pretty good job of it. Rather, we'll discuss strategies for programming with components and using ActionScript to "glue" them into a cohesive interface.

How and Where to Get Components

To begin, let's talk about where components come from. After installing Flash MX, press F11 to open the Components panel. By default, the Components panel contains the Flash UI Components Set, which provides most of the standard interface widgets found in applications and operating systems. This panel acts like the Forms toolbox in Dreamweaver, where you can drag interface widgets onto the stage and then customize them.

Downloading Macromedia Components

Beyond the standard UI Components, we'll discuss two other component sets in this chapter: Flash UI Components Set 2, and the Charting Components. You can download these and other components from the Macromedia Exchange at `http://www.macromedia.com/exchange/flash/` (see Figure 6.1).

Figure 6.1 The Macromedia Flash Exchange site.

To download and manage these components, you need to download the Macromedia Exchange Manager. You can find the download link at the bottom of the Macromedia Exchange homepage (`http://www.macromedia.com/exchange/`). After downloading, run the installer and follow the instructions.

At the time of writing, the main page of the Flash Exchange web site has direct links to the Flash UI Components Set 2 and Charting Components download pages. You might need to sign in to the exchange to get the links later. Download the .mxp file for both component sets, and save them somewhere permanent on your computer. Double-click each .mxp file, and the default installed Macromedia Extension Manager program should open up to install them individually, as shown in Figure 6.2. If the On/Off checkbox is checked, then the component set is already installed on your computer. Simply restart Flash MX and you'll find these component sets available in the authoring tool.

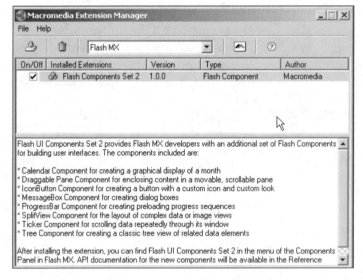

Figure 6.2   The Extension Manager.

Components In the Authoring Environment

The Components panel only shows one set of components at a time. To access the other component sets, click the down-arrow icon in the upper-right corner of the panel, and select from the pop-up list of component sets. Figure 6.3 shows the pop-up list of all three Macromedia component sets in the Components panel.

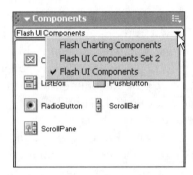

Figure 6.3 Accessing other component sets.

To start, you'll use one of the components as an example of how to access and customize the component. Be sure you change the Components panel back to the original Flash UI Component Set. With the Components panel open, drag the push-button component onto the stage. Keep the push button selected, and look at the Property Inspector as shown in Figure 6.4.

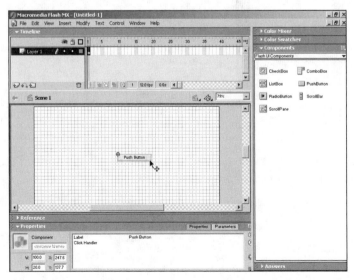

Figure 6.4 Property Inspector for Components.

The Component Property Inspector is similar to other property inspectors in that it allows you to set the instance name of a component to make it identifiable in ActionScript. The area on the right side of the Property Inspector contains component parameters, which are rows of customizable values that change the way a component appears or behaves.

Getting Information on Components

There are three good ways to look up information about components. The most comprehensive way is to use the Flash MX documentation or the Reference panel. The second way, with code hints in the Actions panel, is the most immediate way to pop up a list of a component's methods and properties. The third way is to use the online documentation for packaged components, such as the charting and Flash UI Set 2 component sets.

Code hints offer the quickest way to look up the methods and properties of a component. Each component has a specific suffix you can add to the end of the component's instance name. For example, typing **myButton_pb.** in the Actions panel pops up all the methods and properties of the Push Button component, and typing **myListBox_lb.** pops up information about the listbox component. Figure 6.5 shows the code hints popping up as soon as the user typed in the suffix _pb. as part of the instance name push_pb.

Figure 6.5 Component code hints.

For your convenience, I've compiled a list of all the special suffixes that trigger code hints for Macromedia components:

Flash UI Component Set 1

Suffix	Component Object
_ch	Check Box
_pb	Push Button
_rb	Radio Button
_lb	List Box
_sb	Scroll Bar
_cb	Combo Box
_sp	Scroll Pane
globalStyleFormat	Style Format

Flash UI Component Set 2

Suffix	Component Object
_mb	Message Box
_dp	Draggable Pane
_tick	Ticker
_tree	Tree
_tn	Tree Node
_ib	Icon Button
_pr	Progress Bar

Flash Charting Components

Suffix	Component Object
_bc	Bar Chart
_lc	Line Chart
_pc	Pie Chart

To get information on the component parameters of the Push Button component, you'll find plenty of valuable tutorials and descriptions in the Flash MX help files. Click on Component Help – UI 2 or Component Help – Charts in the Window pull-down menu to access documentation for Flash UI Component Set 2 and the Charting Components.

Changing Component Parameters

Changing a component's parameter can change its appearance. In the case of the push button, we'll use this button as the submit button for the interactive form, so change the value of the Label parameter to Submit as shown in Figure 6.6.

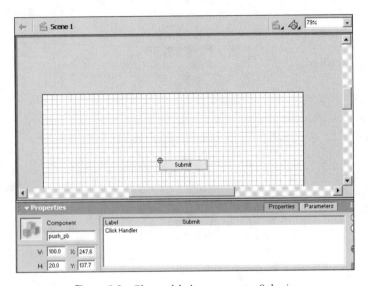

Figure 6.6   Change label parameter to Submit.

At author time (inside the Flash authoring tool), a component can give you a continuously updated author-time representation of how it will appear a run-time (in the Flash player). This feature is called Live Preview. What you see when you're using a component is the component's live preview swf movie playing on stage. The live preview display of a component on stage plays a small Flash movie that communicates with the Component Parameters in your Property Inspector to display the most current configuration. If you've placed too many components on stage, the large number of live previews running simultaneously can sometimes use up a lot of resources. To save on resources, you can deselect the Enable Live Preview option in the Control pull-down menu.

The other parameter, Click Handler, allows you to type the name of a function as a String value. This is known as a callback event handler, described in more detail in the earlier chapters on object-oriented programming in Part I, "OOP and ActionScript." Most components support callback handlers, and the name of the callback handler (a function in the parent Timeline) can be defined in a component's event handler parameter.

For example, if you type `submitForm` into the click handler parameter, any click on the push button will call a function named `submitForm` in the parent Timeline. In this case, clicking on the push button calls a function in the main Timeline, which is the Push Button component's parent Timeline. Many component event handlers receive a reference to the event source (the component) as the first argument of the event handler. For example, the `submitForm` event handler would accept the event source component like so:

```
function submitForm(component)
{   trace(component);
}
```

*Simple event handler for the **push_pb** push button.*

You can also set a component's event handler dynamically in ActionScript, as shown here:

1. Give the push-button an instance name of **push_pb**.

   The suffix _pb triggers code hints in the Actions panel, which is where we're going next.

2. Click on the keyframe in the main Timeline and open the Actions panel. Type in the following code to set the event handler for the push button:

   ```
   push_pb.setClickHandler("submitForm");
   ```

3. Now test the movie, and you'll notice that the `submitForm` executes every time you click on the push button.

   You'll also notice that the `submitForm` traces out the target path to its main parameter, `component`, which refers to the `push_pb` movieclip.

To get a list of all the code hint suffixes for every Macromedia component, go to the custom actions configuration folder for Flash MX, Flash MX\Configuration\ActionsPanel\CustomActions. Then, open any of the XML documents and look for code hint suffixes near the bottom of the XML files, inside the <codehints> node. All the component suffixes were also listed earlier in this chapter.

Macromedia's official components support many similar ActionScript methods for controlling the components. You can access information on these standard methods by opening the Reference panel. Click on the Flash UI Components node in the Reference panel menu (see Figure 6.7), and select any of the methods in the Methods folder to view complete documentation of a component's API method.

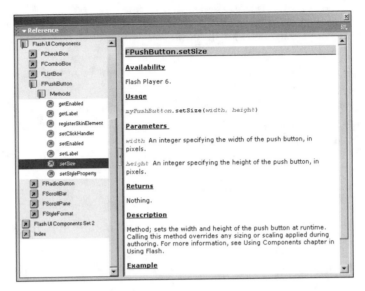

Figure 6.7   Reference panel for components.

At this point, we've established the fundamentals of using components. As you can see, components are easy to customize, and provide a handy set of methods for ActionScript programmers to use in their work as well. Components work well together to build complex interfaces, but interfaces aren't of much use unless they enable you to manipulate information. In the next section, we'll discuss one of the most popular components, the listbox, as an example of how to manage data with components.

Data-Aware Components: ListBox

Some components, described as *data-aware*, can handle multiple pieces of information through a standardized API written "behind the scenes." The flow of information among data-aware components is a reason why Flash MX components can perform complex tasks so easily. Macromedia established the standards for data-aware components in anticipation of Flash applications that needed to communicate and share information with other applications.

Predefining and Retrieving Data

Before we get into too much detail about data-awareness, we'll use the listbox as the perfect example of manipulating information with components. This section uses the file 02_GetDataFromListBox.fla from the downloadable files for this chapter.

1. Open the file 02_GetDataFromListBox.fla.

   You'll find the same submit button, with three input textfields and a listbox component. The three textfields have instance names of `author_txt`, `title_txt`, and `price_txt`, while the listbox component has an instance name of `list_lb`. The suffix `_lb` triggers code hints in the Actions panel for the listbox.

2. Select the listbox with your mouse, and look at the Property Inspector.

   Here, you can see that the listbox has two array parameters called `Labels` and `Data`. These two parameters specify the information stored in the listbox. The `Labels` parameter contains a list of string values to be displayed as a list of names in the listbox. The `Data` parameter contains a list of string or numeric values that aren't displayed, but are associated with the labels in the `Labels` parameter.

3. With your favorite books in mind, try adding author's names for the `Labels` parameter, and book titles for the `Data` parameter as shown in Figure 6.8.

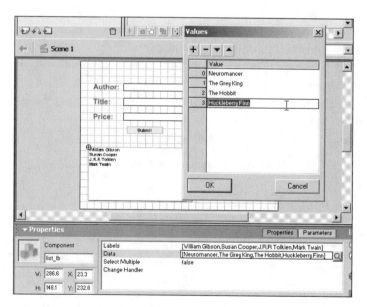

Figure 6.8 Listbox contents.

4. Test the movie now. As shown in Figure 6.9, you'll see that the information in the `Labels` parameter (author names) shows up, but not the information from the `Data` parameter (book titles).

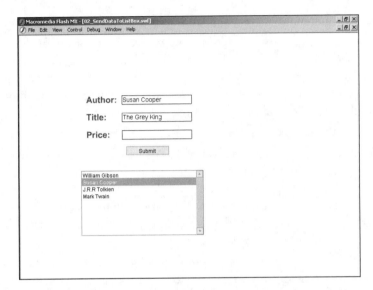

Figure 6.9   Selecting an item from the listbox populates the textfields.

To access the data, you'll have to write some code that makes use of the listbox's methods. Keep in mind that elements in the listbox Data parameter can contain strings, primitive data types such as numbers, Booleans, and even variable references to objects.

5. Open the Actions panel in the first keyframe, and you'll see the following code:

```
function getItem(component_lb)
{
    var item = component_lb.getSelectedItem();
    author_txt.text = item.label;
    title_txt.text = item.data;
}

list_lb.setChangeHandler("getItem");
```

Event handler for the list_lb listbox.

Again, we've written some ActionScript to dynamically set the listbox event handler. Any time a user selects an item in the listbox, it calls a function in the parent timeline with the function name getItem, and passes a reference to itself as the first argument of the function call.

The first line of this code, component_lb.getSelectedItem(), retrieves an object representing the currently selected item in the listbox. This retrieved object actually contains both the Label and Data values of the currently selected item in the listbox. In Figure 6.9, you see that the author "Susan Cooper" is selected in the listbox. Making the selection triggers the getItem() function, and the function creates a local variable item that receives an object from the listbox.

```
var item = component_lb.getSelectedItem();
```

The item object returned by the listbox.getSelectedItem() method is a simple object containing two properties: label and data. These two properties correspond to the label of the selected item, which would be the author's name, and the data of the item, which would be the book's title. After retrieving those two pieces of information into the item object, the getItem() function populates the author_txt and title_txt textfields with the item.label and item.data properties.

Dynamically Setting Data

Sending information to a data-aware component should be as easy as retrieving information. Again, all the work is performed through the use of component APIs, such as the addItem() and addItemAt() methods. We will use the file 03_SendDataToListBox.fla to look at code for sending data to a component.

1. Open the Actions panel in the first keyframe, and you'll see the same function name used to define the event handler for the Submit push button:

```
function submitForm(component)
{
   list_lb.addItem(title_txt.text, author_txt.text);
}

push_pb.setClickHandler("SubmitForm");
```

The addItem() method takes two parameters, Label and Data, and pushes the new information into the existing data of the listbox component. Anytime you have a lot of components, however, it's a good idea to define all of your event handler functions together in one section of your code, and then set the component event handlers after the function definitions:

```
function getItem(component_lb)
{   var item = component_lb.getSelectedItem();
    author_txt.text = item.label;
    title_txt.text = item.data;
}

function submitForm(component_pb)
{   list_lb.addItem(title_txt.text, author_txt.text);
}

//Initialize
list_lb.setChangeHandler("getItem");
push_pb.setClickHandler("SubmitForm");
```

2. Test the movie by typing information into the textfields and pressing the Submit button.

Sending Data Objects to ListBox Data

Listbox components and other data-aware components such as combo-box and charting components accept two parallel arrays, Label and Data. By now you're probably wondering, "Hey, what if I have a lot more than two fields for my data? What about the third textfield in the form, price_txt?"

To answer this question, open the file 04_SendDataObjectsToListBox.fla.

1. Look at the ActionScript in the first keyframe. Modify the submitForm() function to accommodate the third textfield, price_txt:

```
function submitForm(component_pb)
{
    //Old code
    //list_lb.addItem(title_txt.text, author_txt.text);

    //New code
    var item = {author: author_txt.text,
                title: title_txt.text,
                price: price_txt.text}
    list_lb.addItem(author_txt.text, item);

} // submitForm
```

Again, you're using the `listbox.addItem(label, data)` method to send a label that will show up in the list, and a `Data` parameter to hold information corresponding to each list item. However, this time we're passing an associative array to the `Data` parameter, with a name:value pair for each textfield.

An *associative array* in ActionScript can be thought of as an array that uses string keys instead of numbers to represent the location of an element in an array. However, associative arrays do not have any array specific properties or methods such as `length`, `sort()`, `push()`, `pop()`, and so on. Associative arrays are actually objects in ActionScript, and you can create them as objects. For more information, refer to Chapter 15, "Data Structures: Sculpting Information To Suit Your Needs."

Here's an alternative approach for creating the item object:

```
var item = new Object();
item.author = author_txt.text;
item.title = title_txt.text;
item.price = price_txt.text;
list_lb.addItem(author_txt.text, item);
```

The first approach you used is commonly known in JavaScript as "creating an anonymous object," where the two curly braces `{}` denote the creation of a new `Object()`. The inner name:value pairs, separated by commas, represent the name of the object's property and the value of the property. For the sake of legibility, we recommend using the shorthand method of creating anonymous objects. We also recommend indenting the name:value pairs after each comma on a new line. Once you've added all the name:value pairs, you must close the last line with a `}` (curly) brace:

```
var item = {author: author_txt.text,
       title: title_txt.text,
       price: price_txt.text}
```

2. To retrieve the data, simply modify the `getItem()` method to treat the `item.data` property as an object, and grab values from the properties of the `item.data` object:

```
function getItem(component_lb)
{   var item = component_lb.getSelectedItem();

   var dataObject = item.data;
```

continues

```
        author_txt.text = dataObject.author;
        title_txt.text = dataObject.title;
        price_txt.text = dataObject.price;
    }
```

3. Try testing the movie; enter data into all three textfields and press the Submit button to send to the listbox, as shown in Figure 6.10.

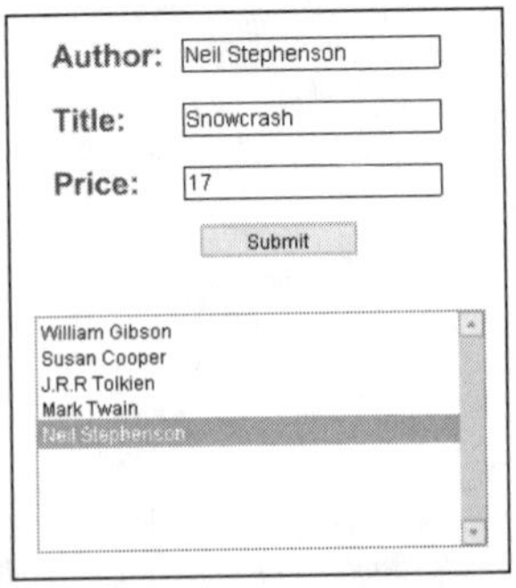

Figure 6.10 Send data objects to the listbox.

As you deal with more complex data, you'll run into the limitations of using component parameters to predefine data. Because we're treating the data value of each listbox item as an object with its own properties, the component parameter, Data cannot be used to contain objects.

Don't worry, there's an even better way to send data objects, such as the item variable in the example. In fact, you can send data to multiple components and synchronize them to the same data source as well!

Using *DataProviderClass* As a Common Data Source

To accommodate the manipulation of complex data with Flash components, Macromedia components support a standard data object known as the Data Provider. Any data-aware component from Macromedia will define the constructor for this data provider object in the _global scope, and the constructor has a name of DataProviderClass.

The DataProviderClass was originally designed to work behind the scenes, but the unexpected popularity of components generated a lot of interest from ActionScript programmers. Consequently, many advanced ActionScript programmers use the DataProviderClass, but this aspect of components is not documented in great depth in the help files.

Each of the Macromedia Component Sets contains a few data-aware components that support the `DataProviderClass` standard:

Flash UI Component Set
Listbox
ComboBox

Flash UI Component Set 2
Tree Menu

Charting Components
Bar Chart
Line Chart
Pie Chart

You can always tell whether a component supports the `DataProviderClass` by the following steps:

1. Create a new Flash movie.

2. Drag the component onto the stage.

3. Look for a symbol named DataProvider in the library folder Flash UI Components\Core Assets – Developer Only\FUIComponent Class Tree\DataProvider.

You can "bind" any of the data-aware components listed previously to a specific data provider object by using the `setDataProvider()` method. The `setDataProvider()` method is available in the API of any data-aware component. As long as you drag a data-aware component onto the stage, you can also call the `DataProviderClass()` constructor from any scope as well, because the data-aware component will define `DataProviderClass()` in the `_global` scope. Once a data-aware component appears in the Flash movie's library, you should be able to call the `DataProviderClass()` constructor even after the components are removed from the stage.

1. Open file 05_DataProviderClass.fla to see an example of the `DataProviderClass` technique.

   This file contains an extra listbox component named `list2_lb`.

2. Open the Actions panel for the first keyframe, and you'll see the following code:

   ```
   function getItem(component_lb)
   {   var dataObject = component_lb.getSelectedItem();
       author_txt.text = dataObject.author;
       title_txt.text = dataObject.title;
       price_txt.text = dataObject.price;
   }
   ```

continues

```
function submitForm(component_pb)
{
   var item = {label: author_txt.text,
               author: author_txt.text,
               title: title_txt.text,
               price: price_txt.text}
   dp.addItem(item);
} // submitForm

//Initialize
list_lb.setChangeHandler("getItem");
push_pb.setClickHandler("SubmitForm");

dp = new DataProviderClass();
list_lb.setDataProvider(dp);
list2_lb.setDataProvider(dp);
```

The differences between this code and previous examples may appear subtle, but are significant. In the initialization section of the code, you create a data provider by calling the `DataProviderClass()` constructor and passing a reference of the object to a variable named dp.

```
dp = new DataProviderClass();
```

Then, the listboxes register themselves with the data provider object by using the `setDataProviderClass()`:

```
list_lb.setDataProvider(dp);
list2_lb.setDataProvider(dp);
```

Now that both listboxes are registered with the dp data provider, they will update themselves to reflect any changes in the data provider's contents.

3. Write some code to make changes to the dp by modifying the `submitForm()` method:

```
function submitForm(component_pb)
{
   var item = {label: author_txt.text,
           author: author_txt.text,
           title: title_txt.text,
           price: price_txt.text}
   dp.addItem(item);
} // submitForm
```

As done previously, the values of all three textfields are gathered into an associative array object named `item`. The main difference here is that you're not adding the `item` object directly to any listbox component. Instead, you're adding the `item` object to the data provider, which has a variable name of `dp`.

```
dp.addItem(item);
```

As explained earlier, any components registered with a data provider reflect changes made in the data provider's content. Because you are adding an `item` object to the data provider, both listboxes (which registered with `dp`) reflect the newly added data.

It's important to note that you only sent one parameter to the `dp.addItem(data)` method, while previous examples called the `addItem(label, data)` method with the first parameter indicating the label shown in the listbox. Instances of the `DataProviderClass` and components that implement data provider methods can both accept two kinds of arguments for the `addItem()` method. Both kinds of objects recognize how many arguments have been passed. If one argument is passed, then the single argument is used as the data for an item. If two arguments are passed, then the first argument is used for label, while the second argument is used for data. With data providers, you can also define a property in your associative array with the name `label`, and a listbox or combobox will automatically recognize the label property.

To summarize these three methods of providing labels/data to a `dataprovider` and data-aware component, you could say that the `addItem()` method accepts three possible forms of arguments: one data argument, label and data arguments, or an associative array object with one of the properties having a name of `label`. In this case, you are going with the third form, that is, sending an object to the `addItem()` method.

4. Try testing the code now by entering values into the input fields and pressing the Submit button. (See Figure 6.11.)

   You'll see how information from all three textfields is now sent to both listboxes at once, through the common data provider object.

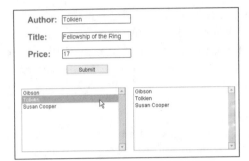

Figure 6.11   Both listboxes are registered with the common dp data provider.

There is no label argument supplied to the addItem() method call, only a single item object stored in the dp data provider object. The listbox can still retrieve information from the data provider to which it is registered.

5. Use the same method that you used before to retrieve data from the dataprovider, but the method now returns an object from which you can retrieve specific properties.

```
function getItem(component_lb)
{   var dataObject = component_lb.getSelectedItem();
    author_txt.text = dataObject.author;
    title_txt.text = dataObject.title;
    price_txt.text = dataObject.price;
}
```

The most notable difference between the modified getItem() method and previous versions is the direct retrieval of an object through the getSelectedItem() method. Previous versions of this example used the following code to retrieve the selected item.label and item.data:

```
function getItem(component_lb)
{   var item = component_lb.getSelectedItem();
    var label = item.label;
    var dataObject = item.data;
```

6. Because the listbox now returns a single object referenced by the item variable name, you can modify the code to treat the retrieved item as the container for author, price, and other data:

```
function getItem(component_lb)
{   var dataObject = component_lb.getSelectedItem();
```

The data object sent to the data provider comes back in the exact same form and structure.

7. You can retrieve values by their property names from the object, as you did previously:

```
author_txt.text = dataObject.author;
title_txt.text = dataObject.title;
price_txt.text = dataObject.price;
```

Using the data provider class in this section of the chapter reveals that data providers can handle data in a variety of formats. Specifically, the `addItem()` method accepts three forms of arguments: data, label and data, and associative array objects as arguments. The data can be retrieved from a data provider in its original structure through two methods: `getItemAt()` and `getSelectedItem()`. Most importantly, you have seen that sending and retrieving associative array objects into a data provider is a more efficient way to manage larger pieces of data through components. In the next section, you'll further explore this idea with the advanced use of data-aware components.

Advanced Use of Data-Aware Components

It's possible for multiple components to use a common data provider object as a way to visualize and manipulate the same set of data. Such flexibility lends quite conveniently to the design of complex interfaces. For example, if you typed in the author names, titles, and prices of several books, you might want to compare them visually on a graph, such as a bar chart. If you wanted to find more information about the least expensive book, you might want to click on an item in the bar chart and display more information about that book. Is all this possible? Of course! All you have to do is take advantage of the components' API and the Data Provider API.

Although little documentation exists on the `DataProviderClass` because it was originally intended for internal use by Macromedia components, it's a powerful aspect of Flash components. To that end, we have included documentation of the `DataProviderClass` API in the accompanying web site for this book.

> It's interesting to note that data-aware components can use externally defined data provider objects, but data-aware components will generate their own internal data provider if their setDataProvider() method is never called.

Binding Charts to Data Providers

Open the file 06_BarChartDemo.fla, and you'll see one more example of the power of data-aware components. This file is exactly the same as the previous example file, with only one new component and three new lines of code. Figure 6.12 shows the final result of the bar chart demo.

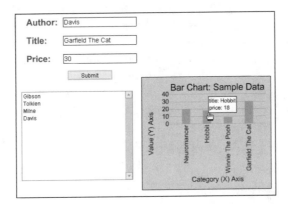

Figure 6.12   A bar chart hooked into the same data provider object.

First, we've dragged a bar chart component onto the stage (refer to the earlier part of this chapter for information on how to download and install other components). The bar chart component is given an instance name of barchart_bc, where the suffix _bc triggers code hints for the bar chart API in the Actions panel.

Open the Actions panel, and you'll see three new lines of ActionScript at the bottom of the code:

```
// Register dp with Bar Chart
barchart_bc.setDataProvider(dp);
barchart_bc.setLabelSource("title");
barchart_bc.setValueSource("price");
```

Again, you register the bar chart component with the `dp` data provider object. The next two lines specify which fields of the data provider to use for assigning values to the bar chart's x-axis and y-axis. Earlier, the `submitForm()` function was defined to create an associative array with three fields: `author`, `title`, and `price`. Then, it adds the associative array to the `dp` data provider:

```
var item = {label: author_txt.text,
       author: author_txt.text,
       title: title_txt.text,
       price: price_txt.text}
dp.addItem(item);
```

Because the data provider has the field's `title` and a numeric field `price`, you simply tell the bar chart to use `title` as the source of labels on the x-axis:

```
barchart_bc.setLabelSource("title");
```

Then, you tell the bar chart to use the field `price` as the source of numeric values on the y-axis:

```
barchart_bc.setValueSource("price");
```

You could just as well use another field, such as `author` to populate the labels on the x-axis, but the y-axis of a chart only accepts numeric values. (For more form validation techniques, refer to the `restrict` textfield property and `textfield` event handlers in Chapter 13, "Textfield Mangling.") The `textfield.restrict` property allows you to restrict text input to characters in a string, such as `price_txt.restrict = "0123456789."`. If you enter string values rather than numeric values for the price_txt input field, the chart will simply evaluate the string to a numeric value of 0.

```
barchart_bc.setLabelSource("author");
barchart_bc.setValueSource("price");
```

Editing and Deleting From Data-Aware Components

When dealing with complex data or multiple components, the task of editing and deleting from data-aware components is best performed on the data provider object. Open the file 07_EditingAndDeleting.fla for an example of these two tasks.

1. Test the movie 07_EditingAndDeleting.fla by typing in different values for the form.

2. Then, select an item from the listbox and click Edit to edit that item.

   As soon as you click the Edit button, the label in the Submit button will change to Overwrite Record.

3. Make changes in the data in the form, and then click Overwrite Record to store your changes as shown in Figure 6.13.

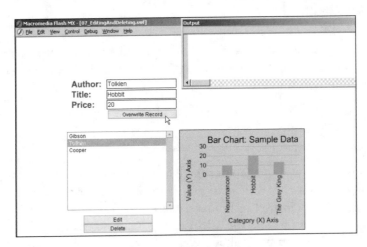

Figure 6.13 Editing and deleting.

Editing

Editing a record in a data provider involves two steps: determine which record to edit, and overwrite the record with new data (if this were a database-driven application, the action would be called an "update" rather than "overwrite"). The first step requires you to know which record is currently selected. For example, the listbox component (as well as other components) has a method called getSelectedIndex(), which allows you to retrieve the position of the currently selected item in the listbox. If you've selected the topmost item, then getSelectedIndex() will return a value of 0. If you've selected the next item, it will return 1. If you select the next item, it will return 2, and so on. You'll see an example of getSelectedIndex() later in the chapter, but first, open the Actions panel for the first keyframe.

Several changes have been made here to accommodate editing, deleting, as well as to improve the usability of the form. First of all, the input textfields will now clear as soon as you've submitted the data. This is accomplished by defining a `clearForm()` function, and calling it at the end of the `submitForm()` and `overwriteForm()` methods. By clearing the form after every submission, the form behaves more consistently with HTML forms. (Don't worry, the `overwriteForm()`method is explained in a minute.)

```
function clearForm()
{   author_txt.text = title_txt.text = price_txt.text = "";
}
```

Also, we've deleted the event-handler registration for the listbox, because we've got a new Edit button to choose an item from the listbox. Select the Edit button underneath the listbox with your mouse, and you'll see that its Click Handler refers to a function named `editRecord`. After you press the Edit button, it should trigger the `editRecord()` function. Then, the function should populate the form with data from the selected item, and change the label of the submit button to display `Overwrite Record`.

```
function editRecord()
{   storedIndex = list_lb.getSelectedIndex();
    getItem(list_lb);
    push_pb.setLabel("Overwrite Record");
    push_pb.setClickHandler("overwriteRecord");
    Selection.setFocus(author_txt);
}
```

The `editRecord()` function performs several tasks. First, it retrieves the position of the currently selected item from the listbox, and stores the index position in a variable named `storedIndex`:

```
storedIndex = list_lb.getSelectedIndex();
```

Then, we'll call a function defined in earlier examples, `getItem(list_lb)`, which will populate the textfields with data from the currently selected item:

```
getItem(list_lb);
```

Now that the form's textfields are populated, the next time you click the Submit button should be when you overwrite the record's data with changed values from the textfields. So, we'll call the push button's `setLabel()` method to change the label displayed on its front panel to read `"Overwrite Record"`:

```
push_pb.setLabel("Overwrite Record");
```

Next time you click the Submit button (which is now the Overwrite Record button), you want to overwrite the selected record instead of adding a new record. So, you'll change the push button's event handler to call another function instead. The new event-handler function is defined as `overwriteRecord()`:

```
push_pb.setClickHandler("overwriteRecord");
```

Finally, once you've clicked the Edit button, the code should help you by setting the focus to the first input textfield in the form. (More powerful textfield selection techniques are described in Chapter 13, "Textfield Mangling.")

```
Selection.setFocus(author_txt);
```

Okay, so after you've clicked the Edit button, all these things happen. The next time you click the form button, it will trigger a function called `overwriteRecord()`. This function should grab the values of all the textfields, combine them into an associative array, and then send that information to the data provider. However, you don't want to simply add data as you did in previous examples. Here, you want to delete the currently selected item from the data provider object (variable name `dp`), and replace it with a new item in the data provider object:

```
function overwriteRecord()
{
    var item = {label: author_txt.text,
            author: author_txt.text,
            title: title_txt.text,
            price: price_txt.text}
    dp.removeItemAt(storedIndex);
    dp.addItemAt(storedIndex, item);
    push_pb.setLabel("Submit");
    push_pb.setClickHandler("submitForm");
    clearForm();
}
```

The first chunk of code, defining the `item` object, is identical to previous examples. Earlier on, we retrieved the index of the selected item in the listbox, and stored it in a variable named `storedIndex`. Now, it's time to use that number to delete a specific record from the data provider:

```
dp.removeItemAt(storedIndex);
```

In its place, we'll simply add a new record item to the same location in the data provider, at the index number of the `storedIndex` variable:

```
dp.addItemAt(storedIndex, item);
```

The deed is done! Out with the old item, in with the new item, exactly in the same spot! Now that the job's finished, you can reset the `push_pb` button to show a label of Submit, and reset its click event-handler to the `submitForm()` function instead.

```
push_pb.setLabel("Submit");
push_pb.setClickHandler("submitForm");
```

Of course, the form should also clear itself after you've finished editing the data, so call the `clearForm()` method as the last statement in this function.

Deleting

Deleting an item from the data provider really only requires two lines. You already know that the `getSelectedIndex()` method retrieves the position of the currently selected item in the listbox component. So, we simply retrieve the index number, and remove an item from the data provider, which corresponds to the index number:

```
function deleteRecord()
{   var index = list_lb.getSelectedIndex();
    dp.removeItemAt(index);
}
```

The delete button below the listbox has a click handler set to `deleteRecord`. Whenever the user selects an item in the listbox and presses the delete button, the `deleteRecord()` executes to remove the selected item from the data provider. It's important to realize why this task is so convenient with data providers. The selection index corresponds to both records in the data provider and in the listbox because of the following line of code at the bottom of the Actions panel:

```
list_lb.setDataProvider(dp);
```

Because the listbox uses the data provider as its source of data, its selection index will correspond exactly to the order of items in the data provider.

Well, that's it for data-awareness. Let's move on to something more fashionable, like style-awareness...

Skinning

"There's more than one way to skin a cat." That's probably the most common joke we heard while developing the Macromedia components! However, the phrase aptly describes the number of ways you can modify the appearance of components. The ability to modify a component's appearance is commonly known as "skinning" the component.

ActionScript jokes won't enhance your programming skills, but they'll seriously boost your geek status!

Skinning is a relatively straightforward process that's thoroughly explained in the Flash documentation, so I'll only briefly describe the process here. First, you can modify the basic appearance of a component by changing its graphics symbols in the library. Secondly, you can use the FStyleFormat object in ActionScript to define sets of styles for individual components, groups of components, or all components. FStyleFormat can also be used to programmatically skin your manually changed skin graphics, giving you the best of both worlds should you need to combine both features.

Library Skins

Open the file named 08_LibrarySkinning.fla. In the library, look for the folder named Flash UI Components. This folder should contain another folder named Component Skins. Open the folder named FscrollbarSkins. This folder contains all the graphics for the scrollbar component, which comes prepackaged with the listbox component to help you scroll through the listbox items.

Double-click on the fsb_DownArrow symbol to edit the graphics for the Down button in a scrollbar. Here's what you'll see if you open the Actions panel for the first keyframe in the README layer:

```
var component = _parent._parent;
//::: don't delete the above

//::: SKIN ELEMENT REGISTRATION
/*    To add styleFormat properties to your skins :
  1) Break up your skin into individual movie clips (skinElements)
  2) add a registerSkinElement line of code for each skinElement

component.registerSkinElement(skinElement, propertyName)
// makes the skinElement Listen to the propertyName specified (eg: "background")
                                                      n*/
component.registerSkinElement(arrow_mc, "arrow");
component.registerSkinElement(face_mc, "face");
```

```
component.registerSkinElement(shadow_mc, "shadow");
component.registerSkinElement(darkshadow_mc, "darkshadow");
component.registerSkinElement(highlight_mc, "highlight");
component.registerSkinElement(highlight3D_mc, "highlight3D");
```

Follow these instructions if you're going to make direct changes to the component skin that should also be available for programmatic skinning with the FStyleFormat object. If you simply want to change the graphics and have no intention of using ActionScript to manipulate skinning, then you don't have to worry about this part at all.

You can replace the movieclips in this fsb_DownArrow movieclip, but be sure you give them the proper instance names that correspond to the instance names in the registerSkinElement() function calls. Doing so will allow your component skins to be accessible via the FStyleFormat skinning system in ActionScript.

Also, be sure you don't delete the first two lines of code:

```
var component = _parent._parent;
//::: don't delete the above
```

If you want to completely change the appearance of a component's skins, be sure that you work thoroughly to change every skin movieclip for every "state" of the components' interface elements. In the file 08_LibrarySkinning.fla, I've changed the scrollbar skin symbols, fsb_downArrow_disabled so that the black down arrow now looks like an upside-down crescent moon (see Figure 6.14). It's not a major change, but it'll give you an idea of how Library skinning works.

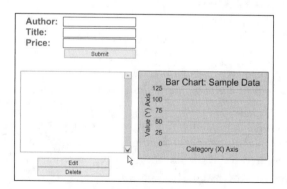

Figure 6.14   Changing the scrollbar skin symbols.

FStyleFormat Object

As mentioned earlier, there's a way to change the appearance of components through pure ActionScript code. After you drag a Macromedia component onto the stage, a class named `FStyleFormat` is automatically defined in the `_global` scope, so you can create new style format objects anywhere in the Flash movie, much like the `TextFormat()` object for formatting textfields. (For more information on the `TextFormat()` object, refer to Chapter 13.)

You can find documentation for the `FStyleFormat` in the Flash MX Help Files. You can also access quick information about its methods and properties in the Reference panel, under the folder "Flash UI Components\ FStyleFormat." The reference panel lists all the properties you can use to customize the appearance of a component.

FStyleFormat

The `FStyleFormat` works by enabling you to create a new instance of the `FStyleFormat` class, define style properties of the object, and then apply that style to a component. New style format objects can be applied to components at any later point in time. For example, check out the file 09_FStyleFormat.fla. Open the Actions panel for the first keyframe, and scroll down to the bottom of the code:

```
//Create a style format object
//Register several components as listeners
//Apply style changes to all listening components
mystyle = new FStyleFormat();
mystyle.face = 0x99BBFF;
mystyle.background = 0x55FF55;
mystyle.addListener(list_lb);
mystyle.addListener(edit_pb);
mystyle.addListener(delete_pb);
mystyle.applyChanges();
```

Here, a new `FStyleFormat` object called `mystyle` is created. The object's properties, `face` and `background`, are given new hexadecimal values to denote RGB color values, similar to the `#FFFFFF` values in HTML tags. Then, three components are added as listeners to the `mystyle` format object. When you call the format object's `applyChanges()` method, the background and face style properties are applied to all the components registered as listeners. As a result, the button faces and the listbox background change color. For example, Figure 6.15 shows the Listbox, Edit button, and Delete buttons with modified colors.

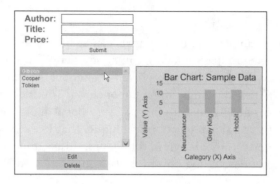

Figure 6.15 Applying the `FStyleFormat` to Listbox, Edit, and Delete buttons.

A simpler but less powerful approach involves calling a component's `setFormat()` method to directly set the value of a style property. In this example, you set the face of the push_pb button to a red color:

```
//Directly set the "face" style property
//of the push_pb component
push_pb.setStyleProperty("face", 0xFF0000);
```

Not all components support all properties, so you'll have to look up their support in the Reference panel, or in the online documentation for the other component sets. For example, all the components in Flash UI Components Set have complete support of Format Styles, but the Flash UI Components Set 2 have limited support, while the charting components rely completely on Library skinning instead.

globalStyleFormat

The `globalStyleFormat` object exists globally in the `_global` scope. It's basically an instance of the `FStyleFormat` class to which all components on the stage are registered by default. Making any changes to the `globalStyleFormat` from any timeline in the Flash movie affects the appearance of all components that support the `FStyleFormat` object.

For example, the following code will tell all components to use a "_serif" font instead of the default "_sans" font:

```
//Globally define style properties for all components
globalStyleFormat.textFont = "_serif";
globalStyleFormat.applyChanges();
```

Conclusion

As seen in these examples, Flash developers can adapt components easily and quickly to their own projects. Individually, components can do some neat stuff, but together, they can combine into powerful interfaces that perform useful tasks. The possibilities for combining components are limitless, and we don't have enough pages in this book to discuss every detail about every component. However, the data manipulation techniques that I've explained in this chapter are not commonly known in the Flash industry, and they'll help you establish an edge in developing powerful Flash applications for the future.

7

Building Your First Component

By Samuel Wan

Reinventing the Wheel—For the Last Time

I remember during the first week of Integral Calculus in high school, having to approximate the area underneath a curve on a graph. As you might know, you can calculate the area of a rectangle by multiplying its height by its width (Area = w × h). To calculate the area under a curve, we had to slice the curve roughly into a series of vertical rectangles. Then, we had to calculate the area of each rectangle, and add them up into a total sum, known as the Riemann Sum. The more thin rectangles we used, the more accurately we could "guess" the true area under the curve.

As you can imagine, this was a lot of work! Sir Isaac Newton invented Integral Calculus so that we wouldn't have to calculate a zillion rectangles by hand. However, our teacher said we had to learn the *hard way* before we learned the *calculus way*.

Well, I was the kind of student who cared more about finding the *quickest way* to finish my homework. I didn't know Integral Calculus, but I did know how to program my graphing calculator. Rather than doing the homework, I spent a few hours writing a program that would calculate Riemann Sums for me. This program allowed me to define two parameters. The first parameter asked for the equation that defined the curve. The second parameter asked me how many rectangles or "slices" I wanted to divide the curve into. Then, the calculator would crunch numbers, and report the area of each rectangle as well as the total sum of areas.

In the end, it probably took longer to write the program than to do the homework by hand, but now I could do any Riemann Sums homework in the blink of an eye. I woke up the next day, punched in the formulas five minutes before class, and wrote down the results on a piece of paper. When the teacher suspiciously asked me to show my work, I showed her the calculator with code on the screen. She sighed and said, "Well, as long as you understand how it works…"

Components: Reusable Solutions

Reusable solutions can eliminate a lot of repetitive work and give you more time for other tasks. However, a reusable solution should have enough flexibility to adapt to variations of a problem. If I had programmed my calculator to solve a single equation, then I would have had to customize the program for each homework assignment. Instead, the program accepted user-defined parameters, so that it could apply the same logic toward solving problems that were similar in nature, but different in detail.

Flash MX Components are reusable solutions in the problem space of building user interfaces. They also support user-defined parameters so that you can adapt the behavior and appearance of a component for different projects. In this chapter, we'll walk through the construction of a simple component. The goal is to help you understand how to build a component from scratch, so that you can build your own reusable components in the future.

Components can be very simple or very complex. As a rule, the more user-friendly a component, the more complex code it contains. The official Flash UI Components provided by Macromedia were carefully built to be very user-friendly, adaptable to many different situations, with the fastest performance and lowest file size. A lot of ingenuity and effort went into the design of these components, and one of the components engineers, Nigel Pegg, describes the process of building such powerful components in Chapter 8, "The Hidden Architecture of Components."

The best way to learn about building components is to dive right into the process. However, the amount of design, engineering, and testing that goes into an "official" Macromedia component can be pretty overwhelming, so we'll start off with something more straightforward: a slideshow component. Figures 7.1 and 7.2 show the slideshow component at runtime and at authoring time.

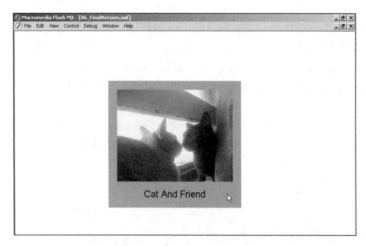

Figure 7.1 Slideshow component playing at runtime.

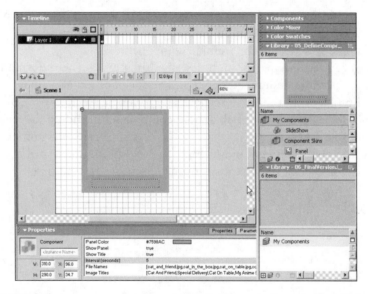

Figure 7.2 Slideshow component dragged from the library to the stage at authoring time.

Steps for Constructing a SlideShow Component

Building a component involves several steps. Nigel's Chapter 8 describes some of the more subtle steps for advanced components, but in this chapter, we'll stick to the basics:

1. Define the specifications for your component.
2. Build a visual model and keep the library organized.
3. Write the ActionScript to drive your model.
4. Make the model customizable with parameters.

Step 1: Write the Component Specification

The first step is to define the goals and the design of your component. In short, write a brief specification outlining what it should do, what it should look like, and how it can be customized. It doesn't have to be formal or complex, but the specification should help you organize your ideas. Figure 7.3 is an example specification of a simple component.

As you can see, the specification describes the purpose, behavior, and appearance of the slideshow component. The specification also addresses any potential problems in the issues section. The parameter section defines each parameter for customizing the slideshow component, including the parameter name, the data type, and a brief description. Revision dates and authors are listed at the top. Comments and revisions are shown in more detail at the bottom of the specification, in case anyone else wants to read them.

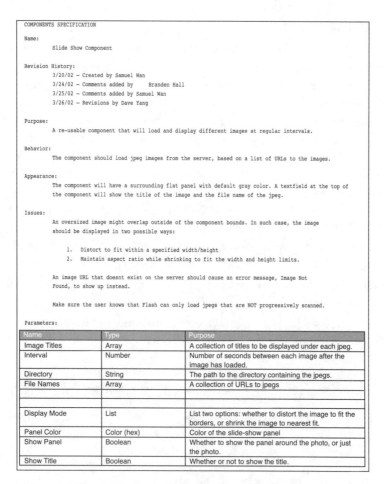

```
COMPONENTS SPECIFICATION

Name:
        Slide Show Component

Revision History:
        3/20/02 — Created by Samuel Wan
        3/24/02 — Comments added by     Branden Hall
        3/25/02 — Comments added by Samuel Wan
        3/26/02 — Revisions by Dave Yang

Purpose:
        A re-usable component that will load and display different images at regular intervals.

Behavior:
        The component should load jpeg images from the server, based on a list of URLs to the images.

Appearance:
        The component will have a surrounding flat panel with default gray color. A textfield at the top of
        the component will show the title of the image and the file name of the jpeg.

Issues:
        An oversized image might overlap outside of the component bounds. In such case, the image
        should be displayed in two possible ways:

        1.   Distort to fit within a specified width/height
        2.   Maintain aspect ratio while shrinking to fit the width and height limits.

        An image URL that doesnt exist on the server should cause an error message, Image Not
        Found, to show up instead.

        Make sure the user knows that Flash can only load jpegs that are NOT progressively scanned.

Parameters:
```

Name	Type	Purpose
Image Titles	Array	A collection of titles to be displayed under each jpeg.
Interval	Number	Number of seconds between each image after the image has loaded.
Directory	String	The path to the directory containing the jpegs.
File Names	Array	A collection of URLs to jpegs
Display Mode	List	List two options: whether to distort the image to fit the borders, or shrink the image to nearest fit.
Panel Color	Color (hex)	Color of the slide-show panel
Show Panel	Boolean	Whether to show the panel around the photo, or just the photo.
Show Title	Boolean	Whether or not to show the title.

Figure 7.3 A complete component specification.

Step 2: Build a Visual Model

Now that you have defined the component on paper, it's time to build a visual model in Flash. I've gone ahead and built one for you as file 01_SlideShow_VisualModel.fla in case you want to skip ahead. You can find it in the downloadable files for this chapter. We'll also walk step by step through the construction process with comments.

Create Graphics

The first thing you need to do is to create the graphics for your model:

1. Draw a rectangle on the screen with no border stroke, and fill it with gray. Draw a smaller rectangle inside with another color, such as blue, and convert the inner blue shape into a movieclip symbol named Container. Select the outer gray rectangle and convert it into a movieclip symbol named Panel (see Figure 7.4). When you're creating symbols, be sure the registration point is in the upper-left corner, so that the upper-left corner will always correspond to a movieclip's internal coordinates (x=0, y=0), and always represent the movieclip's external _x and _y coordinates. As you'll find out over time, setting the registration point simply makes life easier for ActionScript programmers.

   You now have two movieclips on the stage, one rectangle named Panel and another inner rectangle named Container.

2. Select both movieclips and press F8 to convert them into a single movieclip symbol named SlideShow.

   This creates a SlideShow movieclip containing a gray movieclip named Panel and a blue movieclip named Container.

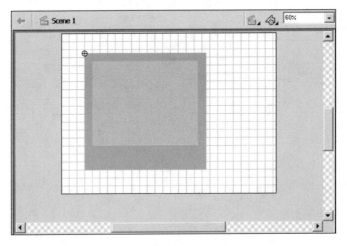

Figure 7.4 SlideShow movieclip.

3. A textfield label is needed to show the title of each image, but before you add the textfield label, first be sure all your assets are organized into proper layers. Go into the SlideShow movieclip and create the following layers:

   - Script:
   - Container
   - Label
   - Panel

4. Put the Panel movieclip in the Panel layer, and give it an instance name of panel_mc. Put the Container movieclip inside the Container layer, and give it an instance name of container_mc.

5. Then create a dynamic textfield in the Label layer, just below the Container movieclip. Set the textfield to use _sans font at 22pt, and give it an instance name of label_txt (see Figure 7.5).

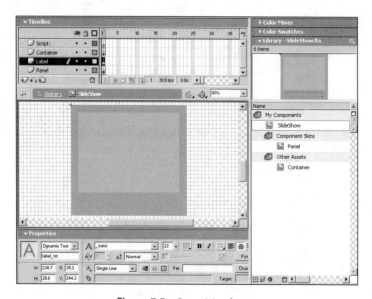

Figure 7.5 Organizing layers.

The _mc and _txt suffixes enable the Action Panel to show code hints when you add ActionScript code later on. If you're not familiar with code hints, refer to Chapter 1, "Starting Off on the Right Foot."

Organize the Library

As you create new symbols in the library, you should organize them into folders according to their purposes. For example, all the assets for Macromedia Flash UI Components exist inside the FUI Components folder in the library. Of course, the FUI Components folder will only appear once you drag a Macromedia component into your movie. If you're defining your own group of components, you should create a folder for your own components as well. In this example, we'll create a library called My Components.

1. First, create a folder in the library and name it My Components. Then, move the SlideShow symbol into the My Components folder.

2. Inside the My Components folder, create a new folder called Component Skins.

   This inner folder contains all the graphics that define the appearance of a component. Any user who is reusing the SlideShow component can customize its appearance by going directly to the Skins folder and making changes to the graphics.

3. Move the component movieclip, SlideShow, inside the My Components folder, and move the Panel symbol into the Component Skins folder.

4. Create another folder inside the My Components folder, and name it Other Assets. This folder contains any symbols that you don't want other people to change. Put the Container symbol inside the Other Assets folder.

   The purpose of organizing your component assets into library folders is to maintain consistency and to prepare for the construction of other components. In the future, you can build other components and put them in the same folder structure. People who re-use your components will also be able to recognize the purposes of each folder. As you drag new components onto the stage, their assets will re-appear in the proper folders.

5. At this point, you'll notice that the SlideShow symbol appears at the bottom of the library, even though it is the main symbol that represents the Slide Show component.

6. To give the symbol a more prominent position in the library, add an empty space in front of the symbol's name. In other words, rename the symbol as "SlideShow." Now the symbol should rise to the top of the Library panel. Figure 7.6 shows how the library should look at this point.

Figure 7.6 Organizing the library.

Step 3: Write the ActionScript

As we write ActionScript for this component, keep in mind the example of the programmable calculator, where a single program was written to solve many math questions. In order for a solution to be reusable, the user should be able to define parameters, which will adapt the solution to different situations. An approach to designing components should follow the same strategy of making solutions adaptable and reusable. The SlideShow component should have some built-in flexibility, so that the user-defined parameters can customize its appearance and behavior.

Export Symbol for ActionScript

The first step in writing ActionScript for a component is to define an ActionScript class and register it with a specific movieclip. If you're not familiar with classes and object-oriented programming, be sure you've read the first part of this book on OOP. The class defines the data of a component, and tasks performed on the data. In other words, the class defines behaviors for a component, so when you register the ActionScript class with a symbol, the symbol inherits the behaviors of the class to form a full-fledged component.

To register a class with a movieclip symbol, you need to make the symbol accessible to ActionScript.

1. Windows users, locate the SlideShow symbol in your Library panel, right-click on the library symbol and select the Linkage option. Mac users, Command-click on the library symbol and select the Linkage option. In the pop-up menu for the SlideShow symbol shown in Figure 7.7, you can see the Linkage option as the ninth item from the top.

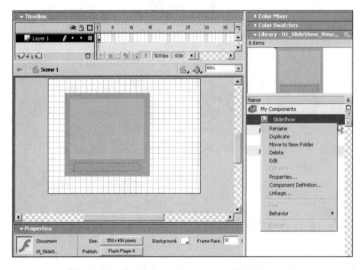

Figure 7.7 Linkage option in the Library panel.

2. In the Linkage Properties window that pops up, check the Export for Actionscript check box, and enter the name **FSlideShowSymbol** into the Identifier textfield.

Macromedia components all follow the same standard naming convention. Linkage identifiers for component symbols starts with "F", then add the name of the component, followed by "Symbol", as the linkage identifier for component symbols. The "F" prefix denotes this symbol as a Macromedia linkage ID, and the "F" prefix also helps to avoid naming collisions. The suffix "Symbol" helps clarify the different references in your code, between Symbol linkage IDs and Class definitions. Now, the SlideShow symbol has an export linkage ID of FSlideShowSymbol.

The pop-up window Linkage Properties in Figure 7.8 specifies a linkage ID of FSlideShowSymbol for the Library's SlideShow symbol.

This is a good naming convention because it will make your ActionScript code easier to read, which is why we've adopted the practice here.

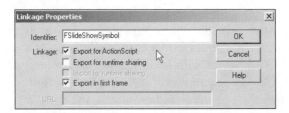

Figure 7.8 Export for ActionScript and assign a linkage identifier.

Define and Register an ActionScript Class

Now define a class in ActionScript to describe how the component should behave. If you want to skip ahead, this step has a corresponding file 02_DefineAndRegisterClass.fla; otherwise, continue with the previous example, 01_SlideShow_VisualModel.fla.

1. Open the SlideShow symbol, and open the Actions panel for the first keyframe in the Script: layer. Add the following code to the Actions panel:

```
#initclip

function SlideShowClass()
{
}
SlideShowClass.prototype = new MovieClip();
Object.registerClass("FSlideShowSymbol", SlideShowClass);

#endinitclip
```

The first and last lines of code, #initclip and #endinitclip, are known as pragma directives in the programming world. A *pragma* is a comment that informs the compiler to do something special before compiling the code into software. For various reasons, a component's class must be defined before anything else in the Flash movie, so the #initclip pragma tells the Flash player to interpret all code between the #initclip and #endinitclip pragmas before playing the movie.

The next three lines of code define an empty constructor, which we'll fill in later.

```
function SlideShowClass()
{
}
```

The constructor defines the class named `SlideShowClass`, which defines the behaviors for the SlideShow component. However, the SlideShow component is still considered an extended version of a movieclip because its `SlideShowClass` inherits from `FUIComponent`, which inherits the `MovieClip` class. To prevent the `SlideShowClass` from overwriting all the movieclip's methods and properties, the next line of code basically tells the `SlideShowClass` to inherit from the `MovieClip` class.

```
SlideShowClass.prototype = new MovieClip();
```

2. Now that `SlideShowClass` has been defined as an extension of the `MovieClip` class, you need to register the class with the `SlideShow` symbol in the library.

```
Object.registerClass("FSlideShowSymbol", SlideShowClass);
```

When you define more methods for the `SlideShowClass`, the `Object.registerClass()` command should move to the bottom of the code, mainly as a matter of programming style. The `Object.registerClass()` method informs the Flash player that any instance of the SlideShow symbol created on stage should inherit all the behaviors of the class `SlideShowClass`. You can drag an instance of the movieclip from the library to the stage, or use the `attachMovie()` method to attach the symbol dynamically to the stage. Either way, every new instance of the SlideShow symbol on stage executes the `SlideShowClass` constructor as an instance of that class.

3. How do you prove that the constructor is called as soon as an instance of the component exists on stage? Simply add a `trace` statement to the constructor, and drag a copy of the component onto the stage:

```
#initclip

function SlideShowClass()
{
```

```
    trace("SlideShowClass constructor was called");
}
SlideShowClass.prototype = new MovieClip();
Object.registerClass("FSlideShowSymbol", SlideShowClass);

#endinitclip
```

Class constructor for the slide show component is registered to the symbol,
***FSlideShowSymbol**, and called when the Flash player renders the symbol on stage.*

4. Test the movie, and you'll see the following trace statement in the
   Output panel:

   ```
   "SlideShowClass constructor was called"
   ```

   At no time did you ever call the constructor directly, so this proves
   that the `Object.registerClass()` method successfully registered the
   `SlideShowClass` in the ActionScript code with the `FSlideShowSymbol`
   in the library.

Create Model Data and Define Basic Functionality

Because you haven't defined user parameters yet, you can use some fake data
to simulate parameters. The goal is to build something that works, and then
add the parameters afterward. The simulated parameters data should be
declared and defined in an initialization method.

All methods of the class, including the initialization method, should be
defined *after* the class prototype inherits from movieclip. Otherwise, the
movieclip's prototype will completely wipe out any predefined class methods.
The prototype-overwriting issue wouldn't be a problem with some of the
inheritance systems proposed in Branden's Chapter 4, "Practical OOP:
Welcome to the Real World." However, Macromedia components use the
standard method of inheriting from the prototype of a newly instantiated
object, and because we're focusing on standard practices, it's important to
define a class method only after its inheritance has been defined.

The corresponding source file for this section is 03_BasicFunctionality.fla.

1. In the constructor, call an init function, and define the init function after the prototype inheritance:

```
#initclip

//Constructor
function SlideShowClass()
{   this.init();
}
SlideShowClass.prototype = new MovieClip();

//Initialize the component
SlideShowClass.prototype.init = function()
{
    //Array of filenames for the jpeg images
    this.fileNames_param = ["cat_on_table.jpg",
                        "cat_in_the_box.jpg",
                        "house.jpg"];

    //Array of titles for each jpeg image
    this.imageTitles_param = ["Sitting On Table.jpg",
                        "Special Delivery",
                        "House In Ann Arbor"];

    //Path to directory
    this.directoryPath_param = "images/"

    //Number of seconds between slides
    this.interval_param = 5;

    //Remember original container width and height
    this.origWidth = this.container_mc._width;
    this.origHeight = this.container_mc._height;

    //Current pointer to a position in the arrays
    this.imagePointer = 0;
}

Object.registerClass("FSlideShowSymbol", SlideShowClass);

#endinitclip
```

*The **init()** function initializes the component class.*

Notice all references to methods and variables have the prefix "this." Flash interprets the class definition before anything else exists on stage, so the class definition appears to occur in the base level of the movie, such as _level0 or _level2. The prefix "this" allows the code to refer to itself, because no scope exists at compile time.

In the `init` function, you define an array to hold the filenames of the jpegs. You also define a corresponding array with descriptive titles for each image. The `directoryPath_param` variable defines the path to the images folder, and the `interval_param` variable defines the number of seconds between each slide. The `origWidth` and `origHeight` variables capture the original dimensions of the container, so that you can resize oversized images later. The last variable, `imagePointer`, acts as a counter to refer to the same element in both the `fileNames_param` and `imagetTitles_param` arrays.

All these variables end with the "_param" suffix to indicate that you'll replace them with component parameters later. Again, using hard-coded variables instead of defining parameters makes the process easier by giving you easier access to the code at the programming stage.

2. The next function serves to load a new image into the `container_mc` movieclip. All the jpeg files are stored inside the images directory, so the following code will work if your Flash movie exists in the parent directory that contains the images directory:

```
//Load the next image into the container movieclip
SlideShowClass.prototype.loadNextImage = function()
{
   this.container_mc.loadMovie(this.directoryPath_param +
            this.fileNames_param[this.imagePointer]          );

   this.label_txt.text = this.imageTitles_param[this.imagePointer];

   this.imagePointer ++;
   if(this.imagePointer >= this.fileNames_param.length)
      this.imagePointer = 0;
}
```

Load the next image into the container movieclip.

The `imagePointer` variable increments every time the `loadNextImage()` method is called. If its value ever exceeds the length of the filenames, `imagePointer` reverts to 0 again. At each increment, the `container_mc` movieclip loads an external image based on the directory path and the filename:

```
this.container_mc.loadMovie(this.directoryPath_param +
            this.fileNames_param[this.imagePointer]          );
```

Load an external image based on directory path and file name.

Then, the `label_txt` textfield displays the title of the image from the `imageTitles_param` array:

```
this.label_txt.text = this.imageTitles_param[this.imagePointer];
```

3. Now that the `loadNextImage` function has been defined, the component should load the first image during initialization. So, add the function call to the last line of the `init()` method:

```
//Current pointer to a position in the arrays
this.imagePointer = 0;

//Load the first image
this.loadNextImage();
} // init
```

Initialize the component by loading the next image (first image) into the container movieclip.

4. Test the code (or run the file 03_BasicFunctionality.fla) and see for yourself! The component now loads a single image.

Load and Resize Multiple Images

You might have noticed that the image doesn't fit perfectly inside the square area of the container, and that the component only loads a single image. You'll fix those two issues in this section of the chapter.

▩ You can load the file 04_MultipleImages.fla to view the complete product for this section.

Once the `loadMovie()` command has been issued to load a jpeg, you need to check whether the jpeg is completely loaded, and then wait for a predetermined interval before loading the next image. The only way to check for jpeg loading completion is to compare the values returned by `getBytesLoaded()` and `getBytesTotal()`.

1. Add two lines of code to the `loadNextImage()` method.

```
//Wait for image to load before counting down to next image
clearInterval(this.loadNextID);
this.loadCompleteID = setInterval(this, "waitForLoadedImage", 100);
```

*Stop the **loadNext()** method from executing by time intervals, and begin executing the **waitForLoadedImage()** method by time intervals.*

The first line, which calls the `clearInterval()` function, stops the `loadNext()` method from executing at regular intervals. (I'll explain more about `clearInterval` and `setInterval` later.) The other line of code registers the `waitForLoadedImage` method to execute at every 100 millisecond interval.

2. The `waitForLoadedImage()` method should execute every 100 milliseconds and compare the value returned by `getBytesLoaded()` against the value returned by `getBytesTotal()`:

```
SlideShowClass.prototype.waitForLoadedImage = function()
{
   if(this.container_mc.getBytesLoaded() ==
   ➥this.container_mc.getBytesTotal())
   {   clearInterval(this.loadCompleteID);
      this.loadNextID = setInterval(this, "loadNextImage",
      ➥this.interval_param * 1000);
   }
}
```

A method to check whether the image has completely loaded.

ActionScript programmers should beware that `getBytesTotal()` won't always return the correct value due to delays in loading. If the loading hasn't even begun (because of a slow server, connection latency, and so on), then `getBytesTotal()` can sometimes return a value of zero. In such a case, `getBytesTotal()` would actually equal `getBytesLoaded()`, although the loading hasn't even begun. You can prevent this accidental detection by being sure that `getBytesLoaded()` is at least greater than 4 bytes.

```
if(this.container_mc.getBytesLoaded() > 4 &&
➥this.container_mc.getBytesLoaded() == this.container_mc.getBytesTotal())
```

A more robust way to check for loaded images (the same technique works with loaded sounds and movieclips).

If `getBytesLoaded` equals `getBytesTotal` and is greater than 4, then the previous method executing at an interval, which is the `waitForLoadedImages`, is cleared from the interval stack. Then, the `loadNextImage()` method is set to execute after a number of milliseconds defined by the `interval_param` variable. The resulting code is a component that checks to see if an image has completely loaded, and then starts counting a predefined interval of time (5 seconds) before starting to load the next image. Try testing the code now.

3. Okay, so some of the images are too big for the screen! The image won't render until it's completely loaded, so you can't calculate the best size for oversized images until getBytesLoaded() = getBytesTotal(). Insert the resizing code inside the if condition of the waitForLoadedImage() method.

```
//Wait for image to load completely before resizing and
//counting down to the next load.
SlideShowClass.prototype.waitForLoadedImage = function()
{   if(this.container_mc.getBytesLoaded() > 4 &&
➥this.container_mc.getBytesLoaded() == this.container_mc.getBytesTotal())
    {   clearInterval(this.loadCompleteID);
        this.loadNextID = setInterval(this, "loadNextImage",
        ➥this.interval_param * 1000);

        //Reset to original scale
        this.container_mc._xscale = this.container_mc._yscale = 100;

        // Test for over-sized image
        if(this.container_mc._width > this.origWidth ||
           this.container_mc._width > this.origHeight)
        {
           var wRatio = this.origWidth / this.container_mc._width;
           var hRatio = this.origHeight / this.container_mc._height;

           //Test if it's too wide or too tall
           if(wRatio < hRatio)
           {
              //too wide, shrink to fit width
              this.container_mc._width *= wRatio;
              this.container_mc._height *= wRatio;
           } else
           {
              //too wide, shrink to fit height
              this.container_mc._width *= hRatio;
              this.container_mc._height *= hRatio;
           } // if-else
        } // if oversized
    } // if loaded
} // waitForLoadedImage
```

*Final version of the **waitForLoadedImage()** method.*

Now that the slide show works, it's time to make it customizable by defining parameters.

Step 4: Define Component Parameters

The specifications written during Step 1 described several parameters for customizing the behavior and appearance of the SlideShow component:

Name	Type	Purpose
Panel Color	Color (hex)	Color of the Slide Show panel.
Show Panel	Boolean	Whether to show the panel around the photo, or just the photo.
Show Title	Boolean	Whether to show the title.
Interval	Number	Number of seconds between each image after the image has loaded.
File Names	Array	A collection of URLs to jpegs.
Image Titles	Array	A collection of titles to be displayed under each jpeg.
Directory	String	The path to the directory containing the jpegs.
Display Mode	List	List two options: Whether to distort the image to fit the borders, or shrink the image to nearest fit.

Each parameter should support its own data type to fulfill its purpose. It only takes a few steps to add a parameter to a component. Locate the SlideShow symbol in your Library panel, and right-click/Command-click on the symbol to select the option labeled Component Definition (see Figure 7.9).

Figure 7.9 Component Definition option.

The Component Definition Panel

Once you're in the Component Definition panel, you can click on the + or − icons to add or remove a component parameter. Each component parameter is represented as a row, and the row is divided into separate columns to define different aspects of the parameter. Here's a description of each column and its purpose:

Component Parameter	Purpose
Name	The name that the user sees in the Property Inspector. Does not have any affect on the ActionScript code for the component.
Variable	The variable name used in ActionScript to access the parameter. Each parameter represents a variable defined within the scope of the component class.
Value	The default value of a parameter.
Type	The data type for the parameter.

Component Parameter Data Types

Component parameters support a variety of data types, some of which can be extremely user-friendly and powerful. Here's a review of each data type, how it's used, and what it's good for:

Data Type	Definition	Purpose
Default	Generic data type, a single basically a string.	Used to store simple information in parameter.
Array	Allows the user to add/list of data remove/reposition elements in an array parameter. Array elements can hold strings and numbers.	Great way to let the user control items, such as a list of email addresses, grocery items, photo file names, and so on.
Object	Creates an associative array of name/value pairs. For example, an object parameter could contain city names for the object name and city population for the object value. The name of the object can contain numbers, spaces, and special characters.	Users can store name/value pairs in a convenient parameter. To retrieve values from an object parameter "population," you could write `this.population["Paris"]`, or `this.population["New Orleans"]`.

Data Type	Definition	Purpose
List	Supplies a list of possible string or numeric values. User can choose one (and *only* one) item from the list. The parameter creates a variable with the value of the selected item. To choose a list item as the default selected value, check the box on the left side of the item.	Allow the user to select one of several predefined options for a parameter, without letting the user define his/her own parameter value. For example, useful for choosing display modes, or a limited set of sizes.
String	Explicitly casts the value of the parameter variable as a string.	User can enter any kind of value for the parameter, but it will be interpreted as a string regardless of the value.
Number	Only accepts numerical values. If you try to enter any illegal characters, such as alphabet characters or punctuation marks, the parameter variable will have an undefined value.	Good way to enforce numbers-only parameters, and prevents the component from mistakenly interpreting a character as a numeric value.
Boolean	Only allows the user to select between true or false input.	Good way to restrict user input to true or false Boolean.
Font Name	Allows the user to select from all available fonts on the computer.	Restricts user's input to names of available fonts only. Prevents the user from mistyping the name of a font. However, keep in mind that choosing a font for a component parameter will not automatically embed a font. For more information on embedding fonts, refer to Chapter 13, "Textfield Mangling."
Color	Allows user to select color from a color interface identical to the toolbar's Color panel. Users can select from a general palette, type in their own HTML numbers (for example #RRGGBB), or control a finer selection from an advanced custom color panel.	Very user-friendly interface for presenting color selection options. You can enter the color in the traditional HTML format of #RRGGBB, where R, G, and B are numeric characters, and the pairs of RR, GG, and BB represent intensity values for red, green, and blue, respectively. Although color parameters accept values in the #RRGGBB format, the values are actually converted to a regular numeric value at runtime. Therefore, if you want to change the value of a color parameter at runtime via ActionScript, you have to supply the value as a decimal or hexadecimal number.

Keep in mind that the Property Inspector can only display six component parameters at a time before requiring the user to scroll down further. If you can, try to limit the number of parameters so that the user doesn't get confused with too many options. If you absolutely need to provide more than five parameters, be sure the most important parameters are displayed at the top of the parameters list so that users won't miss them by accident.

Define Component Parameters for the Slide Show

Now we'll add the parameters from the specs into the Component Definition panel. If you want to jump ahead to the final product, open the file 05_DefineComponentParameters.fla. Otherwise, continue with the previous source file from 04_MultipleImages.fla.

When you create parameters, try to keep the parameter names short, but descriptive enough to convey the purpose of the parameter. For the parameter variable names, it's a good habit to use a _param suffix, to indicate the origins of these variables in your ActionScript code.

You can define the default values of each parameter by double-clicking on the Value column of a parameter. However, be sure you've selected the most appropriate data type first! Figure 7.10 shows the most appropriate data types for the SlideShow component parameters, based on the descriptions in the component specification from Step 1.

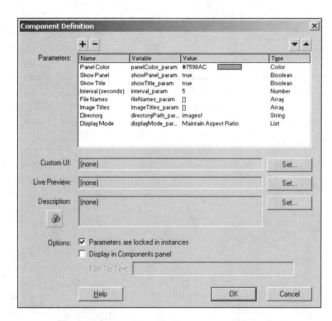

Figure 7.10   Component parameter definitions.

Initialize ActionScript Based On Parameter Values

Now that the component has a defined set of parameters with default values, you can change the `init()` method of the `SlideShow` class to initialize the component based on the parameter values. Depending on your preference, commenting in a list of the parameter variables, which you need to adapt into the component code, can save you the extra step of referring to the Component Definition panel:

```
/* COMPONENT PARAMETERS
panelColor_param     - Color
showPanel_param      - Boolean
showTitle_param      - Boolean
interval_param       - Number
fileNames_param      - Array
imageTitles_param    - Array
directoryPath_param  - String
displayMode_param    - List
*/
```

Commented list of component parameters for quick reference.

You'll need to rewrite much of the `init()` method to accommodate these parameters. Let's start with the `panelColor_param` and the `showPanel_param`.

1. If `showPanel_param` is false, then make the panel movieclip invisible:

```
//Initialize the component
SlideShowClass.prototype.init = function()
{
    this.panel_mc._visible = this.showPanel_param;
```

Initialize the panel_mc movieclip to be invisible.

2. Set the panel color with the value of the `panelColor_param` parameter variable:

```
var panel_color = new Color(this.panel_mc);
panel_color.setRGB(this.panelColor_param);
```

*Initialize the panel movieclip color to the **panelColor_param** parameter.*

3. The `showTitle_param` determines whether to show the `label_txt` textfield:

```
this.label_txt._visible = this.showTitle_param;
```

*Initialize the visibility of the **label_txt** textfield.*

4. In previous versions of the `init` function, you manually defined the arrays for `fileNames_param` and `imageTitles_param`. Now that the component parameters have two array parameters with those variable names, you can delete those manual array definitions entirely. You also manually defined the value of the `interval_param`, to specify the number of seconds between slides.

```
//Number of seconds between slides
this.interval_param = 5;
```

Remove this code because the variable is already defined as a component parameter.

However, the value for `interval_param` is now provided as a component parameter, either as a default value, or changed by the user at authoring-time. Because `interval_param` is now a component parameter, you can simply remove the manual definition from the `init()` method and use whatever value exists in the component parameter.

5. The only remaining variable definition to be replaced by component parameter values is the variable `directoryPath_param`. So, remove the following definition to prevent the component parameter from being overwritten as well:

```
//Path to directory
this.directoryPath_param = "images/"
```

Remove this code because the variable is already defined as a component parameter.

So, the final version of the `init()` method should look like this:

```
//Initialize the component
SlideShowClass.prototype.init = function()
{
    this.panel_mc._visible = this.showPanel_param;
    var panel_color = new Color(this.panel_mc);
    panel_color.setRGB(this.panelColor_param);
    this.label_txt._visible = this.showTitle_param;

    //Remember original container width and height
    this.origWidth = this.container_mc._width;
    this.origHeight = this.container_mc._height;
```

```
//Current pointer to a position in the arrays
this.imagePointer = 0;

//Load the first image
this.loadNextImage();
} // init
```

*Final version of the **init()** method, to accommodate newly defined component parameters.*

What about the two remaining parameters that you still have to adapt to this component, `directoryPath_param` and `displayMode_param`? Well, the `directoryPath_param` doesn't have to be initialized because it's defined as a component parameter, so the `loadNextImage()` method still relies on the same variable name, and no changes are required:

```
this.container_mc.loadMovie(this.directoryPath_param +
                this.fileNames_param[this.imagePointer]               );
```

In the `displayMode_param` component definition, the parameter is a list with two possible string values: `"Exact Fit"` or `"Maintain Aspect Ratio"`. These values are used to direct the manipulation of an oversized image. Either it will distort to fit exactly into the container's dimensions, or it will shrink to a size that will fit into the container without losing its aspect ratio, preventing distortion.

To accommodate this final parameter, you have to make a simple modification in the `waitForLoadedImage()` method. After testing for oversized image in that method, the code should decide whether the `displayMode_param` variable contains the string `"Maintain Aspect Ratio"`. If so, then it should follow through with the original shrinking ratio algorithm. If the `displayMode_param` variable contains a value of "Exact Fit", then the code should resize the `container_mc` movieclip to fit the exact original dimensions stored in `origWidth` and `origHeight`:

```
// Test for over-sized image
if(this.container_mc._width > this.origWidth ||
   this.container_mc._width > this.origHeight)
{
    // Test for displayMode_param
    if(this.displayMode_param == "Maintain Aspect Ratio")
    {
    var wRatio = this.origWidth / this.container_mc._width;
    var hRatio = this.origHeight / this.container_mc._height;
```

continues

```
//Test if it's too wide or too tall
if(wRatio < hRatio)
{
  //too wide, shrink to fit width
  this.container_mc._width *= wRatio;
  this.container_mc._height *= wRatio;
} else
{
  //too wide, shrink to fit height
  this.container_mc._width *= hRatio;
  this.container_mc._height *= hRatio;
} // if-else wider or taller
} else
{
// Exact Fit
this.container_mc._width = this.origWidth;
this.container_mc._height = this.origHeight;
} // if-else Maintain Aspect Ratio or Exact Fit
} // if oversized
```

Code for resizing image. Either maintains or doesn't maintain aspect ratio depending on the **displayMode_param** *parameter.*

Try it for yourself! Drag multiple instances of the component onto the stage, and try playing around with the parameter settings. You can even put a folder full of jpegs in the same location as the Flash movie to display other images. Simply change the directory path parameter, and enter both their filenames and image titles into the component parameters. Try changing the shape of the graphics in your Library Component Skins folder for even deeper appearance changes. Voilá, a reusable component for all your slide show needs!

Conclusion

In this chapter, you've seen how the power of component parameters enables you to adapt the behavior and appearance of a component. Parameters are simply a user-friendly interface to define variables at author time. They save the user a lot of work in customizing components to different scenarios without having to modify or even look at the internal ActionScript code.

As you've seen from the sequence of steps in this chapter, a successful component begins with careful thought and planning. Writing specifications will help you define a planned approach in building the component, especially if many people are involved in using the final component. After you've established what you want to build, creating the graphics will provide a frame of reference before you start programming. Organizing your assets with library folders, layer labels, and movieclip instance names will establish a basic architecture to support your code. Once you've finished with the planning and graphics, it's time to build a working model without using any parameters. Building a working model before defining parameters will help you adjust and debug the code before you start separating the initialized variables into component parameters. All these basic strategies can save you a lot of time and effort in future components projects.

Next Steps...

Compared to the official Macromedia components, you may have noticed some room for improvement in this simple slide show component. For example, changes to the parameters should immediately be reflected in the appearance of the component on stage (a feature known as Live Preview). Also, you can add public methods to a component so that other people can use ActionScript to manipulate a component without having to look at its internal code.

These are all design questions that we'll start to answer in the next two chapters. Chapter 8, "The Hidden Architecture of Components," describes a Macromedia engineer's strategy in building components. Chapter 9, "Building an Advanced Component," applies some advanced techniques to extend this slide show component and make it even more powerful and user-friendly. The final chapter on components, Chapter 10, "Component Live Previews," explores ActionScript programming techniques for building live previews.

8

The Hidden Architecture
of Components

By Nigel Pegg

Introducing Nigel Pegg,
Component Engineer, Macromedia

By the time I'd finished my fifth or sixth Flash site, I was sure of one thing: I was bloody sick of fiddling with scrollbars. A designer friend and I had been working on a wacky little site for a few months, and I'd promised to build a library of widgets that we used to construct it. It seemed pretty simple to build these pieces at first, divorced from the realities of using them together.

The problem was partly bad structural design on my part, and partly our fickle natures. We'd gone back and forth a few times about the way we wanted scrolling to perform (both with plain text and with graphic content under masks) and look. I'd rebuilt the scrollbar nearly from scratch about three times and tensions were starting to get a little high. My friend would make design changes on-the-fly that I was finding hard to keep up with. Pieces of widget were scattered over various .fla libraries and everything was generally a mess. I vowed that I would never make a scrollbar again if I could help it.

It turns out I couldn't really help it. Landing a job soon afterward at Macromedia, I found my job was going to be developing what are now known as the prebuilt Flash MX UI components. My first assignment: the scrollbar.

My experiences building a site over months with a designer became indispensable for the challenge. My first focus was on separating the graphics from the code, so that design changes would be easy to make. I got a chance to correct the structural mistakes I'd made the first time, by using library folders and layers to tame the vast bulk of the components. Really, this was a chance to make a framework that would be flexible enough to accommodate the fickle interests of people like my friend and I. After a year and a half of full-time development, this framework is mature enough to be released into the wild.

Introduction

"Component" is a term as loaded as is it vague. It has any number of implications: flexible, structured, reusable, and interchangeable. Building blocks used to build higher platforms for bigger-problem solving. All sorts of happy thoughts.

It's a really positive word, but it's a tricky one to tack any hard definition to in Flash MX. Especially as components get released into the wild, we're going to see them used in any number of different ways, ranging from a company's in-house stash of customizable buttons, an open-source community archive of code, or a company selling advanced UI widgets or server components. The only truly common thread to all components is that to qualify, they have to save Flash authors' time in the end.

This chapter focuses on the more advanced nuances of creating commercial-grade components in Flash MX. Primarily, we're going to examine ways to use Flash MX to hold together the important elements of components. Where does the code (especially the public methods) live? How can Flash be used to build a class framework for components? How can we ensure that graphic symbols are included? Where does the organization of the library fit into the construction of a component? This chapter will be a guide to solving the structural problems of holding together the elements that make a component. There's more hidden structure to these animals than you might expect.

The Philosophy and Goals of Robust Components

Components solid enough to be used by a variety of users and in a range of situations are a balancing act of different goals. Building a component is an iterative design process that follows a set of defined steps. Imagine building the component with the first goal in mind. Once you've finished, move on to the second goal and make a pass through your design to optimize the component for this goal, then move on to the next. The very last goal, and indeed the bottom line, is to make a final pass through the design to try to reach compromises in accommodating as many of the other goals as possible, keeping in mind the relative importance of each. These design considerations are detailed in the following sections, in order of importance.

Goal 1: Components Should Be Easy to Build With

The key to easy-to-build-with components is to write them keeping your audience in mind. Beginning audiences will be more likely to use Component parameters and on-stage sizing of components, whereas advanced developers are more likely to use ActionScript to do most of their work. A robust component gives something to both camps.

One of the most important ways a component author can make a component easy to work with is to package it in a way that emphasizes the parts of it the user is more likely to want to explore. Expose the features your users need and hide the structure they don't. The library is one of the cornerstones of this strategy, as we'll see later in the section "The Library Is the Component Home."

A good example of packaging components to reveal what is most important can be found in the basic Macromedia set. Figure 8.1 shows the library added to the .fla when I bring in a scrollbar.

We can see that only the scrollbar is at the topmost level, most exposed to the user. The skins are the next most important detail of the component, and are shown one level down. This is an important way to guide the user to the preferred ways of manipulating the component. All other assets (other graphics, component hierarchy code) aren't really useful for the initial user, and so are hidden away. Abstracting details like this makes it easier for the user to get on with building with the component as a "black box," rather than spending too much time digging through it.

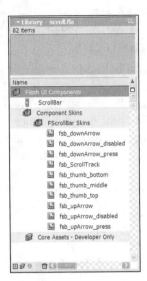

Figure 8.1 The scrollbar's assets.

A few other considerations make components easier to work with. Tailor the way the component is interacted with so that it fits into patterns the user is accustomed to. If the component is resizable, take advantage of the Scaling tool to make the resizing happen. Keep everything as WYSIWYG as possible, to make the component easier to layout and design with. Take advantage of the live preview feature (covered in Chapter 10 of this book, "Component Live Previews") to give as much feedback as possible on stage. Make the authoring experience as natural as possible.

Goal 2: Be as Bandwidth–Sensitive as Possible

As the component developer, your ultimate responsibility extends all the way to the user of the web application. If part of the user's experience of the app is a long load time because of component bloat, you're partly to blame. Try to keep in mind that if you can create something the 56K users can stand, users on higher-speeds won't even notice it loading at all.

The key strategy for this goal is simple: share. If your components share the same code or assets, then the cost of downloading more than one is smaller than the sum of its parts. For example, Macromedia's built-in scrollbar component is reused in many of the other components as well (such as the `listBox` or `scrollPane`), which means that your user is already downloading the scrollbar to scroll text—he/she is getting it for free when it's used in the `scrollPane`.

Goal 3: Don't Waste the CPU's Time

It's important to try to make your code as efficient as possible. It's all about the speed of the user's interaction; the way it *feels*. If it's slow or awkward for simple tasks, it's not a successful component.

The best way to get efficient is to be careful with algorithms and data structures. Keeping the number of executed commands down to a minimum is the key. Not only will your CPU not have to work as hard, but often as not, less code reduces bandwidth as well. Become familiar with the number of executions your code is cycling through on a given task. Find a computing science textbook covering basic algorithms and data structures (Sedgewick's *Algorithms* is the reference I use most), and read up on ways to store information in data structures that take the least amount of cycles to store and retrieve. Flash's `Object` type makes for a convenient hash table, so feel free to abuse it as much as possible. A good example comes from the `listBox`.

The multiple–select `listBox` needs to remember every selection made in it. It's important to be able to get two important pieces of information about the current selection:

- What items are selected.
- Whether a specific item is selected.

It might not seem like a big deal at first, but both of these details are demanded over and over and over again as a `listBox` is scrolled up and down. A common first attempt at storing the selections would be to use an array:

```
selected[0] = 2;
selected[1] = 4;
selected[2] = 6;
selected[3] = 9;
```

A basic array for holding selection.

This array is flat. All it tells us is that the first selected item is #2, the second selected item is #4, and so on. Take a second to ponder accessing and storing the two details we need the most with this kind of data structure. Sure, we can figure out what items are selected by looping over the array and returning the values. But the problem in this case is that if I needed to know if item #13 is selected, I end up looping over the entire array just to confirm that it isn't there. As the number of selections increases, it gets harder and harder to find out if any given item is selected. And this information is needed for different items dozens of times for each time the `listBox` is scrolled. This data structure cripples scroll performance, once the amount of selections gets high enough.

Fortunately, the Object type gives us a really simple way to store the same information. Taking the same information, we can structure it this way:

```
selected["2"] = true;
selected["4"] = true;
selected["6"] = true;
selected["9"] = true;
```

An Object holding selection information.

This structure makes it possible for me to look up whether an item is selected or not with only one array access. One line of code is enough to find out (here "i" is any item's index).

```
if (selected[i.toString()])
```

By using an Object (or associative array) with the items' index itself as the property name, we've taken a problem that took N comparisons and shortened it down to one. This is the kind of use of data structures that can have a visible impact on the performance of a component (as it did in this case).

Goal 4: Don't Let Components Use Too Much Memory

From experience, I can say memory is the easiest place to let a component get out of control. It doesn't seem like it would be such a big deal, until you realize that if you want your component to play with lots of others, it has to use memory in proportion with how much functionality/aesthetic value it has to offer.

Managing memory is about keeping data structures and the number of movieclips used to a minimum. Exploring ways to lessen the memory consequences of your component is an overarching theme in this chapter.

Goal 5: Aim for Reusability and Flexibility

It can be hard to picture the different situations your work can be put into. But for a component author, dreaming up usages and scenarios is a large part of the process. Often, having one feature missing will be the difference between someone using your component or building something from scratch. Your component will be as popular as the number of situations it can fit into. If you can cover most reasonable cases, ask yourself what the unreasonable users would want. A good place to find reasonable cases is to look at components made for developers of other languages. If your users are likely to be at the JavaScript level, see how extensive the JavaScript equivalents of your component are. If you expect a component to be comfortable to a Java–level programmer, then looking at Java's APIs is advisable.

Other than providing extensive methods for various functionalities, a large part of reusability involves the separation of graphics from code. If you make components that can have their graphics slipped in or changed by a designer, then you've made something that can be reused far more than something with a static look.

The key here is to make sure that all code resides in a centralized place. Keep code off the graphics themselves—no more onClipEvent actions! The central code will just attach graphic symbols to be used for display; as long as the user can modify these graphics, he can be blissfully unaware of the deeper things going on in your component, and still be able to change the look completely. Lastly, be sure that any code you use to attach these symbols can handle variable sizes of graphics. For example, when the scrollbar attaches the up and down arrow buttons into itself, it measures them before laying them out. This way, a user can have arrows of any reasonable size within the scrollbar, and it will adapt accordingly.

Goal 6: Provide a Framework to Extend Functionality

After authors have been working with your component long enough, it won't be too hard to envision them coming across more complex situations that your work just can't handle with simple methods. When this time comes, you can either expect them to try to make their own or provide some way of adding new layers of functionality to your component. The advantages of this approach are obvious; it wouldn't be too shabby if your work becomes the base work that founds a variety of far-reaching applications.

The most obvious approach to this problem is through object-oriented programming. Through the course of this book you're likely to come across a wealth of techniques for writing code that is clean and built for extension. As we'll see in "The Library Is the Component Home" later in this chapter, the library can be a useful medium for representing class and inheritance structures.

Goal 7: Keep All the Goals Above in Balance

Now that we've covered the main points, it's back to the over-arching theme we started with; it's of vital importance that each goal respect the importance of the rest. If a component is amazingly rich in features but is a 30K download, it might not be as useful as a more lightweight component. Likewise, a component that uses vast data structures to ease CPU use can hog so much memory that only one can be on the screen at once. For example, in a 3D-rendered component, it might be tempting to create a lookup table for each trig function at every angle, as well as the results of every calculation done on your set of points to be used later. This would vastly reduce the amount of calculations the CPU has to worry about, but could end up so large in memory that the computer is forced to swap pages of RAM back and forth from your hard drive, which would cancel out your performance gains.

There really isn't any quick solution to this goal. It's a matter of careful consideration and common sense. Above all, it's going to be dependent on the intentions behind the component. Deciding where to make compromises is never easy, but it becomes an important part of defining the other design choices you'll make.

Do I Really Need to Think This Hard About My Basic In-House Components?

Well, umm, no. For those of you making components that don't need to be as robust, the balancing act isn't as difficult. But it pays to be forward-looking; even if a component looks like a one-off for a project now, if it has a flexible design, it might be able to grow into the next project's needs. Keeping your eyes open for more open structure possibilities is never a bad thing, even if you don't get around to filling in all the details the first (or twentieth) time.

Flash MX's New Features Make Components Possible

Although component authors are certainly going to be a driving force of components from now on, their foundation is based on a series of authoring and runtime features in Flash MX that make them possible. It's not even conceivable to do most of this authoring in Flash 5; it doesn't have the backbone needed to keep the various pieces together. The most obvious is the Components panel—and we should be thankful for it—but it's really only the method of transportation for components. The stuff that truly holds together components is subtler than you might think. Let's thank these new features and give them their due.

The Library Is the Component Home

One of the main drawbacks of the library in Flash 5 was that it didn't hold its folder structure as library items were dragged from .fla to .fla. You could spend an hour structuring your library, but it was forever trapped in one .fla. (See Figure 8.2.) Flash MX solves this problem by reproducing the folder structure of the library item dragged over in the new library.

Figure 8.2   Flash UI Components' library structure.

This unbelievably useful feature means that the portable library structure can now be used to convey guidance as to the way a component is used. Symbols that should be touched can be brought to the top levels of the folder hierarchy, and things better left unseen by all but the developer can be buried somewhere further back. All symbols nested inside a component are guaranteed to be copied into the new library; this is a feature we'll learn to exploit effectively as the section progresses.

The second way in which the library makes component development easier is the way it handles collisions of symbols. If a symbol is brought on stage and the library finds that the same symbol with a different last-modified time is already in the library, it gives you the option to update (and hence all instances on stage or nested inside other library symbols) to the new symbol. This means that updating an older .fla to newer components is (hopefully) only a matter of dragging them to the stage of the old .fla. The library automatically finds all symbols that changed and updates them, which is an invaluable help in development.

The Event Model Lets You Centralize Code

One of the keys to building a successful component is to keep its structure centralized to make access to code as simple as possible. In Flash 5, this could be a difficult task, because of the way event handling worked. In general, a symbol had to have "clip events" attached to its instances to do things like catch mouse clicks or key presses. In the Flash 5 authoring tool, this meant clicking on symbol instances to check whether or not they had code attached to them. Especially when dealing with other people's project files, it could be easy to miss a large chunk of functionality by overlooking events attached to a symbol instance on stage. It also made for code with a decentralized and scattered feel.

Flash MX solves these problems with its great new event model. It's fair to say there is almost no need for "clip events" as we knew them in Flash 5 anymore. The beauty of the new event model is that it treats events as though they were member functions of the movieclips they are attached to. And since member functions of a movieclip can be added and removed at any time in your code, we're given a huge amount of flexibility in how an event can be caught and handled.

For example, I have a movieclip, `circleButton`. I want this movieclip to react to mouse events by tracing its name. So I define a function (on the timeline that hosts the movie), like this:

```
this.reactToEvent = function()
{
    trace("something happened to " + this._name);
}
```

An inline function to be used for event handling.

With this function defined, I am free to add it to my movieclip as the response to any of the events it handles (see Chapter 3, "Event Wrangling: When To Do What," for more details of the event model). So, with `circleButton`, I can try a few things:

```
circleButton.onPress = this.reactToEvent;
circleButton.onMouseMove = this.reactToEvent;
```

*Assigning event callbacks to **circleButton**.*

What makes this so powerful is that inside a component, you generally define a library of functions. This entire library can be put on one frame in a Methods layer of the component, and when it comes time to add events to a symbol inside the component, the preceding technique can be used to dynamically assign a function to the event desired. In the end, it means your component has only one place that needs code in it; the first frame in the

Methods layer. This could be an #include to an .as file, or the code itself in the Actions panel. Either way, one-stop shopping for code makes your component easier to use, maintain, and extend.

Why Are *#initclip* and *Object.registerClass* So Important?

Probably the most crucial feature for components with methods is the combination of #initclip and Object.registerClass. They might seem a little daunting at first, but after you've used them more than once they become second nature.

The biggest problem with defining reusable movieclips with custom methods in Flash 5 was that they weren't usable to the outside world until one frame after they were put on stage. Put simply, the code written inside a movieclip isn't done initializing until the frame the clip is in is already done. This was a problem, because developers just aren't used to the idea that a component on stage needs warm-up time to be usable.

Flash MX solves this problem with #initclip/#endinitclip. By putting these compile-time pragma in your method layer, around all the methods that belong to the component, it ensures that code within the pragmas gets initialized before the movieclip that contains it does. Thus, when you put your component on stage, the code within the component is ready to use it by the time the component hits the stage. No more waiting for code to run means your component behaves much more naturally for developers used to UIs like those of Java or C++.

> Although #initclip works in most cases, there is one significant time where it does not function. If the component is nested inside another component in authoring time, the methods of the inner component will not be available by the time the host component is constructed. The host component should use attachMovie to nest all inner components, such as when a scrollPane hosts scrollbars by using attachMovie to initialize them from its own methods.

Object.registerClass is another godsend for component developers. Thanks to #initclip, we know that the methods we write inside a component are going to be ready on time. But what if we need some code to run *every* time a component is initialized—to set up some variables, or manage the initial UI state? This is a common task in object-oriented programming, covered by the *constructor* of the instance being initialized. Object.registerClass does this by linking a constructor to a movieclip symbol, so that the constructor runs every time the symbol gets instantiated. It's the bond between a constructor and a symbol that really makes a component what it is: a movieclip with a class that controls it from the inside.

What About Clip Parameters?

Although they are important, clip parameters (now named "component parameters") are very easily produced by-products of the component methods you have written. We'll see in Chapter 10, "Component Live Previews," how this feature of Flash 5, which is still very much the same, can be combined with the new Live Preview feature for some exciting possibilities; once your component has had its methods defined, the clip parameters can be used to trigger these methods in the Live Preview, reflecting the effect of the method at authoring time. For instance, your clip parameter for color could trigger a `setColor` method in the component, which takes the parameter value and colors the component—right on stage as the author watches. For now, it's time to dig deeper into techniques for structuring components with respect to our commercial-strength goals.

Component Structure: Library Management

A properly organized library, if it's really good, is almost unnoticeable. This is probably why it's not exactly the most glamorous part of building a component, but it's definitely one of the most important aspects.

Library management is the study of how symbols are broken up and organized in the library based on their utility to the end user (who is, after all, the one who gets the library dumped in their .fla). In this section we'll talk about the division of symbols in a component, what each kind is useful for and to whom, and how to organize them in a library.

Making a Skinnable Component: The Division of Symbols

It's important to lay down some terminology at this point. Once we know how to name the different elements of a component, it will be a little clearer what the relationships are between them (see Figure 8.3).

Let's start from the topmost level.

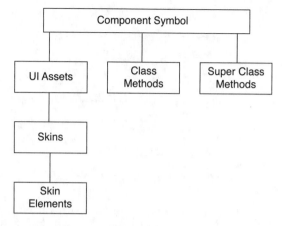

Figure 8.3 The division of symbols.

The Component Symbol

At the top of the ladder is the Component symbol. To the most basic end users this is all your component is; there's more than a fair chance they won't even notice the assets this "host" adds to their library—if you've done your homework. Therefore, the component needs to have all the other symbols it will use nested within it. As well, the component should have a Method layer inside itself—this is where the code that runs the overall component will be found. The rest of the layer structure of the component symbol will be covered in the section "Component Structure: Layers and Asset Management."

UI Asset Symbols

The layer below the Component symbol is the UI (User Interface) Assets within it. This concept is a little tricky, but generally, a UI asset is a symbol in the library that represents the states a piece of UI can be in. As shown in Figure 8.4, a basic button component might have these states: ButtonUp, ButtonOver, ButtonDown, and ButtonDisabled.

Figure 8.4 The button states UI asset.

The UI Asset symbol for this button—excitingly named `Button States` in the library—contains all these states as labeled keyframes in its timeline. We're going to be manipulating the symbol with our Class Methods; sizing it, moving it from state to state, and so on, so this means we need some way of getting a hold of it. In the library, we call up the Linkage dialog of the symbol, and choose Export for ActionScript, along with Export In First Frame. I'm giving it the Linkage name `ButtonStatesAsset`. Now, when the class constructor of the button component is called, we can use `attachMovie` to bring `ButtonStatesAsset`, and initialize it to the size and state we want.

So we're off to a good start; but what exactly does this have to do with skinning? It's time to move down a level in our hierarchy and find out.

Skin Symbols

Each state of a UI Asset is a skin symbol. The entire concept of skinning is to have symbols in the library that a designer can modify in order to change the look of the component. It's important that each skin is only one state (wherever possible). This keeps the designer in a two-dimensional picture; having to know anything more is just too much work. For example, Figure 8.5 shows the skin symbols in the library.

Here you can see that the only thing a designer is going to have to edit in each skin symbol is the graphics. The skin symbols are nothing other than vessels to be filled with artwork—no logic needed. This is because the UI Asset symbol (which contains all the skin symbols), along with the Class Methods, already does the work of defining the logic between symbol states. Isolating skin symbols down to simple graphics means a designer with no idea how the component works has a fair shot at being able to redesign its look anyhow. This is why it's important to structure the library so that it exposes its skin symbols more than any other assets.

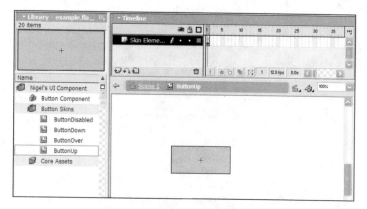

Figure 8.5 The Button Component's skins.

Skin Element Symbols

Skin elements are simply the movieclips that make up each skin symbol. Dividing a skin symbol into sub-movies isn't really necessary. The only reason to do so is to allow the skin to comply with `FStyleFormats`. For each skin element you make, you can define a color style property that will be used to color it, using `registerSkinElement` (see "FUIComponentClass," later in this chapter, for details on how to use `FUIComponentClass` to enable FStyleFormats). Most users probably won't want to do this; the preferred way to skin a component is to delete the old skin elements and draw a new skin in their place. Dividing up the skin symbol into skin elements should usually be treated as an afterthought—it's much easier to do your drawing in the skin symbol first, then break it up. Building skin element movieclips first and then trying to assemble skin symbols using them is a frustrating process at best.

For now, let's focus on the importance of the library in organizing all these levels of complexity.

Organizing the Library for Maximum Usability

The common nerdy urge is to want to organize a library structurally. Because the component has a hierarchical structure in the way symbols are nested, it's tempting to make a library in exactly the same structure (see Figure 8.6).

Figure 8.6 A structural library.

So, each level explicitly shows the symbols it contains through use of folder hierarchies. This appeals to a sense of tidiness and helps us understand the overall relationships between symbols. The only problem being, the user really doesn't care much about the overall relationships of the symbols, she cares about what she can do with those symbols, or whether she should touch them at all. Generally, there's a sliding scale of things the user might care about, listed here from most important to least. We'll take a prebuilt MX checkbox as a running example of what we're talking about:

- **The Component symbol itself**—In the case of the checkbox, this is the entire checkbox component—the symbol dragged off the Component panel. It's highly exposed, for obvious reasons.

- **Skin symbols**—For checkboxes, this would be a symbol for the individual states of the checkbox: the unchecked state, the checked state, and the disabled states. These symbols should be somewhat exposed so that the user can change the look of the component.

- **Class Method symbols**—In the checkbox world, the only Class Method used is FUIComponentClass, the SuperClass of all prebuilt Flash UI Components. It needs to be included as part of the checkbox so that it may inherit its methods. It's possible a user might want access to these, but they're certainly not as important as a skin symbol.

- **UI Asset symbols**—For checkboxes, a UI Asset symbol is the symbol that holds all the separate skin symbols. It's going to be a movieclip with one frame per skin symbol inside it, and will be attached by the component methods. It's pretty unlikely a user would want to mess with this, so it's kept pretty well hidden.

- **Skin Element symbols**—The Skin Element symbols of a checkbox are all the individually colored pieces of the skin symbol—the sides of the box, the checkmark graphic, and the background of the box. We don't really want the user to modify these symbols at all from the library (to skin the component they should be drawing their own skins, not editing the current skin element symbols, except "in place" from the skin symbol itself), so they're kept as deep down as possible.

In order to manage the users' fickle interests in your component, the best way to organize the library is *functionally* rather than *structurally*. Put simply again: Expose the symbols users are more likely to want to use, and hide the ones they aren't. Compare the list above to the order in which the library shown in Figure 8.7 is built.

This keeps a lot more confusion out of using your components, because the user is less apt to stray into territories he shouldn't. Happily for us, it also makes development of your component more straightforward; you'll find you have easier access to pieces you need to develop on a regular basis, and the stuff you don't is hidden from you.

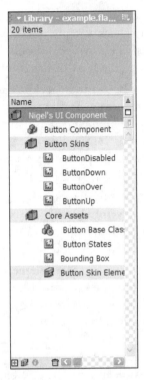

Figure 8.7   A functional library.

A Word on Class Hierarchies in the Library

I don't want to stray too far at this point of the discussion, but it's probably a good time to mention (in passing) that the library is also a good place to represent class hierarchies. If you drag one of Macromedia's built-in `ListBox` components to the stage, you can see a bit of this theory in action. Open the library and travel down through the first folder to `Core Assets / FUIComponent Class Tree / FUIComponent SubClasses / FSelectableList SubClasses` (see Figure 8.8).

This looks pretty daunting for right now, but what it does to help usability is show the structure of the `SuperClass` hierarchy of the components. I know I just finished arguing against structural organizations, but in this case, a user is more likely to use/study the classes at the top, which means it's both structurally and functionally organized, so everyone wins.

Figure 8.8 A library class hierarchy.

Component Structure: Layers and Asset Management

One of the subtler mysteries of component architecture is the way assets are packaged inside the component. As mentioned before, a component must nest every symbol it's going to need inside itself at some level, so that these assets are dragged from .fla to .fla with the component. It turns out that the choices you make in structuring your components' insides to include these assets can have a fairly large impact on bandwidth, memory consumption, and CPU use.

Using Layers to Structure Your Component

The basic unit of organization in a component symbol are the layers in the component's main Timeline. Layers are useful in separating code from UI, as well as helping to control memory and bandwidth consumption. Figure 8.9 reviews the layers a typical component might need.

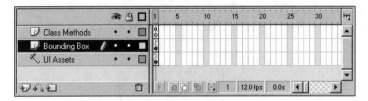

Figure 8.9   A typical component layer structure.

Class Method Layer

This layer is code-only. As we covered earlier, this layer contains the constructor and method code for the component, all surrounded in `#initclip` pragmas and with an `Object.registerClass` to link the constructor code to the symbol that contains it.

A useful feature of Flash MX deserves attention here. If the layer selected has code in it, it is automatically displayed in the Actions panel. What is more, the last selected layer of each symbol is saved in the .fla upon saving. This means if you make sure that during development, you leave your code layers as the last selected, as soon as someone edits the component by double-clicking the symbol in the library, the component code is displayed in the Actions panel. This makes it possible to use the library as a code browser, because as soon as a symbol is double clicked, you can have the Actions panel ready to start editing code (see Figure 8.10).

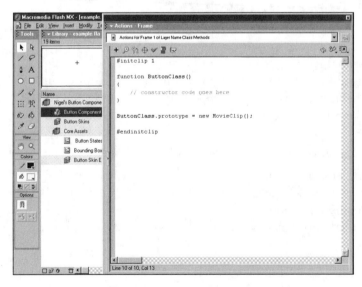

Figure 8.10   Using the library as a code browser.

When you're already done putting in your other assets, using Flash MX in this kind of code-centric way can vastly speed up development time.

UI Asset Layers

We've already seen one of the asset types we're going to need in the component: UI Assets. Most UI assets get used over and over again in a component; destroyed, brought back, and assembled in different ways. This makes `attachMovie` the best way to instantiate these assets in many cases. We made sure the UI asset symbols were exported in the first frame (in the Linkage dialog), which means they'll download before the main .swf starts, ready by the time your component wants to `attachMovie` them into existence. This is fine, but we also have to be sure that these symbols are able to hop from .fla to .fla. Which means any time you have a UI asset, you need layers to hold them inside your component.

Holding UI assets as instances in (normal) layers has an unforeseen consequence: Anything in those layers will instantiate inside your component before the component is done initializing. This presents a problem: We only really wanted the assets there so they would be nested in the component and hop from .fla to .fla, not so they would initialize and become instances in the movie (potentially including executing constructors). In fact, if you let your UI Assets initialize, you are eating away at valuable memory and CPU resources, while your component is initializing—a very time-sensitive part of a component's execution cycle, especially as it gets more complex.

Fortunately, there is an answer to this problem that is familiar to most animators: guide layers. Guide layers are layers that are seen at authoring time but not exported in the .swf. They also have the happy side effect of dragging symbols nested in them from one .fla to another, which means they can be used to transport the symbols but not initialize them—exactly what we needed. Look back on Figure 8.9 for a moment to review the layer structure we've seen so far.

One UI asset layer we haven't explained in the figure is the Bounding Box. It's useful to have your component draw itself based on size given to it through scaling, and the Bounding Box gives your users an even area to stretch on stage. Its size on stage will determine the Component's Live Preview size (See Chapter 10, "Component Live Previews," for details). It actually gets initialized on stage (usually to be used inside the component as a hit area), so its layer won't be guided out.

> The last type of layer a component might have is a SuperClass asset layer. If you're building a component that inherits methods from a SuperClass symbol, this is where you would put it. This would be the start of an involved discussion, so we'll skip it for now and talk more about SuperClasses and inheritance in Part III, "High-Level ActionScript," coming up shortly. We have one topic left to cover in Part II. Maddeningly enough, it shows that sometimes, guide layers don't work.

Compromising Goals: Dead Air Versus Memory

There's a flaw in the cleverness of using guide layers to transport UI assets. The problem is, it depends on the Export in First Frame feature of the Linkage dialog in the library. As mentioned earlier, Export in First Frame means that the symbol downloads *before* the rest of the .swf plays. This is important because there's no way to play anything while the assets load. A load progress display is out of the question—unless you load a component .swf into a host .swf using loadMovie. This technique is worth exploring, but beyond the scope of this section.

This is definitely a problem worth considering. How much "dead air" are you willing to let a user watch—5K, 10K? Depending on users, using loadMovie is inconvenient and unlikely in some cases. In the end, we have to follow "Goal 7: Keep All the Goals Above in Balance." Let's talk a bit about Export in First Frame.

You choose to Export a Symbol for ActionScript and another checkbox, Export in First Frame. So, if you uncheck this second checkbox, when is the symbol exported so you can use attachMovie? The answer is: after it's been initialized somewhere on stage. So to export a symbol without dead air, we have to abandon the guide layer idea and let the symbol initialize on a normal layer in the component.

It's not a fun compromise to make, but the key here is *balance*. If a UI asset is light in memory consumption but heavy in bandwidth, then let it instantiate on a normal layer in the component. If it's heavy in memory but light in bandwidth, it's best to use a guide layer and let it export before the first frame. Most cases will be somewhere in between, but because low amounts of dead air is probably slightly more important, it might make sense to err on the side of leaving more assets on normal layers, and try to keep dead air down to less than 10K for any .swf.

Component Structure: Class Management

This last segment deals with practical methods of class management, using code completely inside .fla files (without .as files). Using class hierarchies is a good way of making more shared, extensible code. If five components all need to do a set of identical tasks, then it's a good idea to put these methods in one symbol, so they only need to be downloaded (and defined) once. The first topic at hand is making a base class.

Packaging a Base Class

In this discussion we'll focus more on symbols than code; OOP being the subject of the book, there are plenty of examples of how to make good object-oriented code. But here's the basic template of a component's base class code:

```
#initclip 0

function ButtonBaseClass()
{
    // constructor code goes here
}

ButtonBaseClass.prototype = new MovieClip();

// method code goes here

#endinitclip
```

A basic component definition.

There are three interesting things to note about this code. First of all, there's a 0 after the #initclip line. This is a parameter that controls the order in which the code is compiled, zero being the first. In order for a base class to be defined before its subclasses, it needs a lower number than those subclasses. Our ButtonClass component would need an #initclip number of one or higher.

Second, notice that the base class is prototyped to be a subclass of the MovieClip class. This way, components that inherit from the base class also inherit all the MovieClip methods you'll want to use with the component.

Third, notice that the code has no `Object.registerClass` line. It doesn't need one. Because this code-only component never needs to be instantiated on stage, we don't need to worry about registering it to a symbol. As mentioned previously, all we have to do is place the Super Class symbol in a Super Class asset layer in the component, and it's ready to be used for prototyping your component (see Figure 8.11).

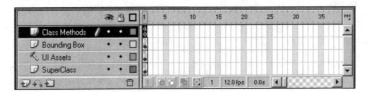

Figure 8.11   A component with a SuperClass layer.

To make our `ButtonClass` inherit the methods of the `ButtonBaseClass`, all we need is the following line in the ButtonClass Class Methods layer:

```
ButtonClass.prototype = new ButtonBaseClass();
```

This line gives `ButtonClass` access to all the base class's methods. If multiple components use this symbol as prototype, they all get these methods, which only need to be downloaded once.

FUIComponentClass

Macromedia's built-in components ship with a common base class, which can be used with our custom components; `FUIComponentClass`, found in `/ FUIComponent Class Tree / FUIComponent SubClasses / FSelectableList SubClasses`. (Refer to Figure 8.8.) This class is fairly expansive and covers a broad spectrum of functionality; in this section we'll only cover an area pertaining to skin elements.

> For further information on using `FUIComponentClass`, I recommend checking the Macromedia Exchange (`http://www.macromedia.com/desdev/mx/flash/`) regularly for articles and documentation updates.

In Chapter 6, "Using UI Components," we saw how to customize a Macromedia component using style formats. We can make use of this feature of `FUIComponentClass` in our own components, so that they can also use style formats.

If, instead of using `ButtonBaseClass`, I put `FUIComponent` in the SuperClass asset layer of `ButtonComponent`, I inherit the `FStyleFormat` methods I need to power my own component. The secret to using `FStyleFormat` is to do a little digging in your skin assets, and register the skin elements therein to some style property of the component.

Let's say the `ButtonUp` symbol is made up of two skin elements: one named `border_mc`, and the other named `face_mc`. `FUIComponent` gives you the capability to give each of these elements its own style property for color, through the wonders of this method:

```
FUIComponentClass.registerSkinElement(element_ref, propertyName)
```

This method allows you to assign a style format property to color a certain element reference. In the skin for `ButtonUp`, we'd be likely to see two lines of code like this:

```
this._parent._parent.registerSkinElement(border_mc, "border");
this._parent._parent.registerSkinElement(face_mc, "face");
```

By registering the skin elements to the component (`this._parent._parent`, from the skin we're in) to style property names, a user can customize the colors of these two elements by using style format code like so:

```
globalStyleFormat.border = 0xff0000; // red border
globalStyleFormat.face = 0x0000ff; // blue face
```

To see `registerSkinElement` in action, check the skin symbols of the built-in MX components. What we're seeing from this example is that object-oriented code, when packaged effectively, can be used to give common functionality to a broad range of components, and save bandwidth at the same time.

Should I Use *FUIComponent* as My Base Class?

The answer to this question depends on two factors. First, does your component need features like keyboard navigation, focus management, and style formats to be successful? And second, is it worth the time of familiarizing yourself with the Class methods of `FUIComponent` to see how they can be used? For many components, it won't be necessary at all to spend time studying `FUIComponent`; it's only when one gets to the point of needing a lot of features mentioned previously that the power of this base class outweighs the cost of learning to use it. For more resources on learning to use `FUIComponent`, watch Macromedia's developer exchange (`http://www.macromedia.com/desdev/mx/flash/`) for updates.

Final Thoughts on Class Hierarchies

The best reason to use class hierarchies (base classes, subclasses, and so on) is to keep your code clean and forward-looking enough so that it's easy to extend. Choosing whether to go with this a strategy depends on how far you intend to go with a component; for a component that's almost definitely a one-off with little potential to be reused other than in an identical situation, it's not really worth the effort to add the extra structure. But if your component aims to solve a class of problems shared by a lot of other components, then it's probably time to start thinking of your code in terms of a class structure. Again, it's a balancing act; your initial time versus the time you're likely to save later by being able to easily reuse your code.

Conclusion

Although it's in a book about object-oriented ActionScript, this chapter focused more on how to package your component structure itself to be object-oriented, and to complement the OOP patterns of this book with the subtle strategies needed to package your code and graphics in a way that is easy to use, flexible, extensible, and optimized for memory and bandwidth consumption. We've seen that these are problems and goals to be respected; so many facets go into building a component that it often becomes a balancing act between different interests.

The biggest point I can stress is this: Structure your component to be as usable as possible for your intended audience and purpose. It sounds like a self-evident truth, but properly selecting and emphasizing certain goals (out of the seven outlined in the beginning of this section, among others) to fit the people you imagine using your product is really the subtlest process of all in creating a component. Once you've got an outline of what overall standards you're trying to stick to, making the detailed design choices you'll need will be a process with much more purpose and understanding. Keeping an eye on the big picture while hiding the details isn't always easy. Once you put yourself in the shoes of your users, however, you'll discover that the big picture is the only part of your component that they want to see.

9

Building an Advanced Component

By Samuel Wan

Picking Up Where We Left Off

In Chapter 7, "Building Your First Component," you built a SlideShow
component that demonstrated the basic features of components. The chapter
started with the draft of a component specification document to help you
plan ahead. Then, we covered some important concepts such as class definition,
movieclip inheritance, and class registration with component library symbols.
Toward the end of the chapter, we defined some component parameters so
that the user could customize the behavior and appearance of the component.

This chapter builds on top of concepts from the previous chapters, so be sure you've read all the previous
components chapters first.

In Chapter 8, "The Hidden Architecture of Components," Nigel outlined
some of the main goals and potential pitfalls to watch out for in developing
Flash components.

Because the simple SlideShow component had several disadvantages,
we'll use this chapter to address those issues, starting with a recap.

Recap: The SlideShow Component

If you want to view the final version of the Advanced SlideShow component, open the file named FinalVersion_AdvancedSlideShow.fla. This final version shows two components, both of which have parameter values for displaying two images, as well as several new features. Rather than rebuild a new component from scratch, you'll build an Advanced SlideShow component by extending the original class, SlideShowClass, into a new class, AdvancedSlideShowClass. Throughout this chapter, we'll cover the improvements made to the original SlideShow component:

- In the simple slideshow, the user had no control over the slide show playback. An advanced slide show should support buttons for skipping back and forward to other photos. To extend this behavior without completely over-hauling the code, the first thing we'll study is how class inheritance works with components. We'll want to keep the original code for displaying different images, but also add some functionality to force the slide show to the next image.

- Rescaling the component to extreme width/height ratios would distort the component. So, we'll add some anti-distortion code. The solution calls for all the inner movieclips to be attached dynamically, so that they can be repositioned as the component is resized. The init method is the first method called when constructing an instance of the class, so the init method should be responsible for attaching inner movieclips.

- Publishing the Flash movie is the only way to see the results of changing component parameter values. Here, we'll build a simple live preview to reflect the component parameters in real-time, inside the Flash authoring tool. Chapter 10, "Component Live Previews," offers a more detailed look at the live preview feature.

- The SlideShow component lacked any ActionScript commands. In this example, you'll add a simple API command to set the size of the component. The setSize() method is commonly found in other Macromedia components, accepting width and height parameters. Developers should be able to resize the component in ActionScript via the setSize() method.

Component Inheritance: Extending a Component Class

Instead of completely rewriting the `SlideShowClass` ActionScript from scratch, we're going to apply an inheritance technique to create a new class named `AdvancedSlideShowClass`.

To extend the `SlideShowClass`, you'll need to get a copy of the source code to work with. The source files for this chapter include a file named 00_SimpleSlideShow.fla, which contains the final version of the slide show component from Chapter 7. You can open this file and follow the steps that follow, or jump ahead and see the result in the file 01_AdvancedSlideShowClass.fla. Like Chapter 7, all the examples in this chapter will use jpeg images stored in a local folder named images.

Now that we've got the file opened in the Flash MX authoring tool, it's time to get busy:

1. Select the SlideShow symbol and duplicate it in the folder My Components.

    You can duplicate a symbol by right-clicking (or Command-clicking for Mac users) on the library symbol and choosing the Duplicate command.

2. Rename the new symbol "AdvancedSlideShow" with a space in the first character. While you're in the Convert To Symbol dialog box, be sure that you click the Advanced button to gain access to the linkage options as well. Give this movieclip an external linkage ID of `FAdvancedSlideShowSymbol` with no space in the front (see Figure 9.1).

    You're duplicating the symbol because you want to reuse most of the component parameters, and it would be a hassle to re-create those parameters by hand.

3. You don't need any of the code in the duplicated symbol, so delete all the ActionScript code. Double-click the AdvancedSlideShow symbol to edit its contents. Then, open the Actions Panel for the first keyframe of the Script: layer. Select all the ActionScript code and delete it. Delete all the other layers as well.

    Now, you've got a movieclip with defined parameters and a single blank layer named Script:. (see Figure 9.2).

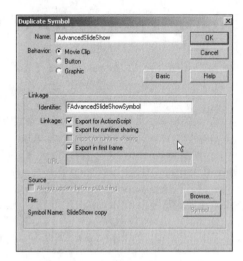

Figure 9.1   Duplicate the SlideShow symbol to create the AdvancedSlideShow symbol.

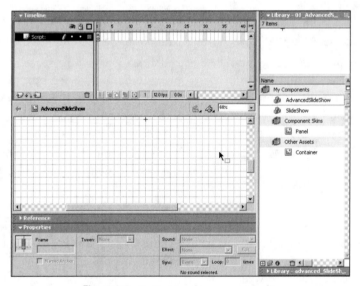

Figure 9.2   Setting up the new movieclip.

4. Add the following ActionScript code into the Actions panel for the first keyframe in the Script: layer.

```
#initclip 2

// Constructor
function AdvancedSlideShowClass()
{   this.init();
}
AdvancedSlideShowClass.prototype = new SlideShowClass();

Object.registerClass("FAdvancedSlideShowSymbol", AdvancedSlideShowClass);

#endinitclip
```

Laying down the foundations for the Advanced SlideShow component.

This code lays down the foundation for the new Advanced SlideShow component, while inheriting most of the features of the simpler SlideShow component. As you can see, the code looks very similar to the first few steps from Chapter 7. The code defines a new class named `AdvancedSlideShowClass` after the `SlideShowClass` is already defined in the other component. Then, the new class inherits all of the methods and properties of the `SlideShowClass` class. Then, it registers the class with the symbol's linkage ID, `"FAdvancedSlideShowSymbol"`.

The first line of code, `#initclip 2`, serves the same purpose as the `#initclip` pragma from Chapter 7. However, this initclip has a priority of 2, so that all the code executes after any initclip with a lower number and higher priority. Don't let the numbering system confuse you…the lower the number, the higher the priority. An initclip number 0 would have the highest priority, and thus execute before initclip 1 and initclip 2. The SlideShow component, which co-exists in the Library panel, actually has an initclip without any specified priority, so it defaults to a priority of 0. Therefore, the `SlideShowClass` is defined in the SlideShow symbol before the `AdvancedSlideShowClass` is defined in the `AdvancedSlideShow` symbol.

The initclip priority plays an important role because it allows the `AdvancedSlideShowClass` class to inherit from `SlideShowClass` only after the `SlideShowClass` has been defined. The inheritance occurs on line 7:

```
AdvancedSlideShowClass.prototype = new SlideShowClass();
```

In Chapter 7, the `SlideShowClass` inherited from the `MovieClip` class. Here, `AdvancedSlideShowClass` inherits from `SlideShowClass` instead of `MovieClip`, thus inheriting from `MovieClip` indirectly.

The inheritance chain looks like this:

```
MovieClip -> SlideShowClass -> AdvancedSlideShowClass
```

Thus, `AdvancedSlideShowClass` doesn't have to inherit directly from `MovieClip`, yet it still retains all the powers of a movieclip symbol. It inherits methods and properties from the `MovieClip` class such as `gotoAndStop()`, `play()`, `_width`, and `_height`. It also inherits methods and properties from the `SlideShowClass`, such as `init()` and `loadNextImage()`. This means that you can call any method on the `AdvancedSlideShowClass` and have it resolve to a method in the super class, `SlideShowClass`. If the `SlideShowClass` doesn't support that method, then the method call will resolve to the next class in the hierarchy, which would be the `MovieClip` class. Method calls will resolve all the way up the inheritance chain if child classes don't have a definition of the method. Therefore, the call to `this.init()` on line 5 will actually call the `SlideShowClass.init` method unless you overwrite it with your own definition of `init()` for this class:

```
// Constructor
function AdvancedSlideShowClass()
{   this.init();
}
```

By default, `AdvancedSlideShowClass` inherits a method called `init` from the `SlideShowClass`, so it should already have an `init` method defined. The process of redefining an inherited method is called *overwriting*.

Okay, so let's review how component class definition works. The order of movieclip export, class definition, class inheritance, and symbol registration executes in the following sequence:

1. Class Definition: `MovieClip` class is natively defined by the Flash player.

2. Export Symbols: `FAdvancedSlideShowSymbol` and `FSlideShowSymbol` are loaded into the Flash player before any movieclip begins playing.

3. Class Definition: The class `"SlideShowClass"` is defined and inherits from the `MovieClip` class.

4. Symbol Registration: `SlideShowClass` is registered with the `"FSlideShowSymbol"` movieclip.

5. Class Definition: The class `"AdvancedSlideShowClass"` is defined and inherits from the `SlideShowClass`.

6. Symbol Registration: `AdvancedSlideShowClass` is registered with the `"FAdvancedSlideShowSymbol"` movieclip.

7. Initialization: All the components on stage initialize themselves by calling the class to which they're registered.

Now that the `AdvancedSlideShowClass` inherits from `SlideShowClass`, you need to overwrite some of its methods, beginning with the `init()` method.

Overwriting the *init()* Method

For this section, you can continue with the file 01_AdvancedSlide-ShowClass.fla, or skip ahead to 02_OverwriteInitMethod.fla for the final result. Double-click on the AdvancedSlideShow to edit its contents now.

We need to over-write the `init()` method in order to add the anti-distortion features and change the layout of the component.

1. Overwrite `init()` simply by defining the function for the `AdvancedSlideShowClass.prototype.init` variable:

```
#initclip 2

// Constructor
function AdvancedSlideShowClass()
{   this.init();
}
AdvancedSlideShowClass.prototype = new SlideShowClass();

AdvancedSlideShowClass.prototype.init = function()
{
}

Object.registerClass("FAdvancedSlideShowSymbol", AdvancedSlideShowClass);

#endinitclip
```

*Define **init()** method for the **AdvancedSlideShowClass**.*

The `init()` method initializes the `AdvancedSlideShow` component with an anti-distortion algorithm. When a user rescales a movieclip to stretch it horizontally or vertically, the contents of the movieclip tend to appear distorted. This is a particularly bad problem when you're building a component with user interface elements such as labels and buttons.

The AdvancedSlideShow component features two buttons and a title label, so you need to make sure the component will not distort those buttons and labels at runtime if the user has resized the component at author-time. However, the layout of the component's interface should use all the available space of the component area.

Anti-Distortion

Anti-distortion is an important aspect of Flash components, because it allows you to resize a component without distorting its internal contents. For example, a web browser's scrollbar must always fit the height of the browser, but the up/down buttons of the scrollbar should always remain the same size. It would look pretty weird if the scrollbar's up/down buttons grew taller or shorter, depending on the browser's window size. In other words, a user interface element should resize to fit the available space, but its internal contents should only change position, not size.

The anti-distortion technique requires relatively simple steps in Flash MX:

1. When the component is resized, record initial width and height.

2. Un-resize the component by setting _xscale and _yscale back to 100.

3. The component has an internal rectangular movieclip called boundingBox_mc, which should be resized internally to the recorded width and height.

4. The component attaches movieclips internally, such as buttons and labels.

5. Then, the internally attached movieclips are repositioned to the component's new width and height.

6. At this point, the component still has _xscale and _yscale at 100. However, its width and height fit the initial width and height due to the internally resized boundingBox_mc movieclip. The component's internal elements are repositioned to expand or shrink according to the available width and height.

So how do these steps translate into ActionScript? First, record the initial _width and _height values of the component into componentWidth and componentHeight variables. Secondly, rescale the component movieclip so that _xscale and _yscale are normally scaled at 100 percent. Finally, resize an internal rectangular movieclip to the originally recorded values of componentWidth and componentHeight. This internal movieclip contains a simple rectangular shape. The result of anti-distortion is a movieclip with zero distortion (_xscale and _yscale = 100), but whose _width and _height remain the same as its original dimensions before the anti-distortion occurred.

For an example, check out 90_anti_distortion_example.fla. When you run this example, pay attention to the black boxes in the lower half of the example that are distorted according to the dimensions of the movieclip. On the other hand, the black boxes in the upper half of the example don't distort, even though the main square distorts (see Figure 9.3).

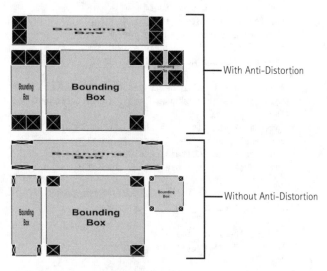

Figure 9.3   Anti-distortion example.

Before you apply any anti-distortion technique, you need to be able to attach movies. Without any attached movieclips, there would be nothing to anti-distort! The SlideShow component needs to dynamically attach movieclips to serve as buttons, a bounding box, an image container, and a title label. Once these movieclips are attached into the SlideShow component, they are internal movieclips.

For now, anti-distortion is a concern, so the only movieclip you'll need for anti-distortion is the boundingBox_mc movieclip. To build the boundingBox_mc movieclip, create a simple gray rectangle in a new layer named "Bounding." Then, convert the shape into a movieclip symbol named "BoundingBox," with an export linkage ID of SSC_BoundingBox. The prefix "SSC" indicates that the bounding box belongs to the SlideShowComponent family of assets. Give it an instance name of boundingBox_mc, and in your Library panel, put the BoundingBox symbol inside the Component Skins folder.

Here's what the final `init()` method should look like, including the anti-distortion code:

```
// Initialize the component
AdvancedSlideShowClass.prototype.init = function()
{
    //Record original dimensions and then
    //perform anti-distortion.
    this.componentWidth = this._width;
    this.componentHeight = this._height;
    this._xscale = this._yscale = 100;
    this.boundingBox_mc._visible = false;

    //Set size with originally recorded dimensions
    this.setSize(this.componentWidth, this.componentHeight);

    this.panel_mc._visible = this.showPanel_param;
    var panel_color = new Color(this.panel_mc);
    panel_color.setRGB(this.panelColor_param);
    this.label_txt._visible = this.showTitle_param;

    // Current pointer to a position in the arrays
    this.imagePointer = 0;

    // Load the first image
    this.loadNextImage();
} //  init
```

Final version of the ***init()*** *method.*

In the code shown here, the original dimensions are stored in variables named `componentWidth` and `componentHeight`. Then, `_xscale` and `_yscale` are reset to 100 percent to perform anti-distortion.

The next step is to set the internal `boundingBox_mc` movieclip's dimensions to the recorded `componentWidth` and `componentHeight` variables. This step should be part of a `setSize()` method so that users can resize the component via ActionScript. Before the `setSize()` method is called, however, set the `boundingBox_mc` movieclip's `_visible` property to false, so that the rectangular graphic doesn't show up anymore. The movieclip's width and height are still determined by all elements that exist in the frame of the movieclip, even if they're not visible at the time. So the next step in the `init()` method is to call a new method, `setSize()`, which sets the size of the component to its original dimensions.

The rest of the code found in the `init()` method is identical to code found in the `SimpleSlideShow` component:

```
this.panel_mc._visible = this.showPanel_param;
var panel_color = new Color(this.panel_mc);
panel_color.setRGB(this.panelColor_param);
this.label_txt._visible = this.showTitle_param;

// Current pointer to a position in the arrays
this.imagePointer = 0;

// Load the first image
this.loadNextImage();
}
```

The rest of the `init()` *method comes from Chapter 7.*

For more explanation about the remaining code in the `init()` method, refer to Chapter 7, "Building Your First Component," which details the `SimpleSlideShow` component.

Before we move on to the `setSize()` method, take a look at the last line of code in the `init()` method—it's the same `loadNextImage()` method called from the previous example! Because `AdvancedSlideShowClass` inherits from `SlideShowClass`, any method not defined by the current class resolves to a method in the parent. We're basically going to reuse previously defined methods for much of the SlideShow component's functionality—that's the power of OOP in ActionScript.

Automatic Layout with the *setSize()* Method

The `setSize()` method allows the component to automatically arrange its internal contents (such as buttons and other widgets) according to the component's new size. Macromedia engineers typically design the `setSize()` method to allow the user to dynamically change a component's size at runtime. Usually, the component will also call `setSize()` internally after it has finished anti-distortion, during initialization. This is pretty important when you consider what happens if a user has resized the component at authoring time: With anti-distortion, the internal buttons and widgets are no longer distorted, but they're no longer in the right position if the user has changed the component's width or height.

Last Step of Anti-Distortion

So once the init() function begins to execute, it captures the original dimensions into componentWidth and componentHeight, then sends those two values as arguments for the setSize() method:

```
// Initialize the component
AdvancedSlideShowClass.prototype.init = function()
{
    //Record original dimensions and then
    //perform anti-distortion.
    this.componentWidth = this._width;
    this.componentHeight = this._height;
    this._xscale = this._yscale = 100;
    this.boundingBox_mc._visible = false;

    //Set size with originally recorded dimensions
    this.setSize(this.componentWidth, this.componentHeight);
```

Last step of the anti-distortion code.

Now define setSize() to receive the two arguments as variables w and h:

```
AdvancedSlideShowClass.prototype.setSize = function(w, h)
{
    this.componentWidth = w;
    this.componentHeight = h;

    this.boundingBox_mc._width = w;
    this.boundingBox_mc._height = h;
```

*Using **setSize()** to set the width and height of the internal boundingBox_mc movieclip.*

The arguments are reassigned to componentWidth and componentHeight in case setSize() was called at runtime by the user's ActionScript. In such a case, anti-distortion isn't required, but you'll need to capture the intended dimensions again. Other methods may also need the values of componentWidth and componentHeight, so it's important to keep those two variables updated whenever setSize() is called. The next two lines of code set the boundingBox_mc movieclip to the intended dimensions of the component, so that the component now has the correct width and height. This last step completes the anti-distortion process.

From now on, anyone who uses the AdvancedSlideShow component should use setSize() to set the width and height of the component. Users should avoid setting the values of _width and _height at all costs, because doing so will totally negate the advantage of anti-distortion!

Adding New UI Elements

Now the component's at the right size, and at a natural scale of 100%, but it's still missing some internal elements, such as the label and buttons. Rather than walk you through the simple steps of creating those buttons, I've gone ahead and built them in the file 03_SetSize_AddUIElements.fla. Open that file and open the Actions panel for the first keyframe in the AdvancedSlideShow movieclip. Jump ahead to 04_WorkingVersion.fla if you want to see the final result.

Now you're going to add some code to the setSize() method to dynamically attach the interface elements:

```
AdvancedSlideShowClass.prototype.setSize = function(w, h)
{
    this.componentWidth = w;
    this.componentHeight = h;

    this.boundingBox_mc._width = w;
    this.boundingBox_mc._height = h;

    var depth = 0;
    this.attachMovie("SSC_BoundingBox", "Panel_mc", depth++);
    this.createEmptyMovieClip("outerContainer", depth++);

    // Create shortcut to accommodate earlier functions
    this.container_mc = this.outerContainer.createEmptyMovieClip("innerContainer",
    ➥depth++);

    this.attachMovie("SSC_BoundingBox", "containerMask", depth++);
    this.attachMovie("SSC_SlideButton", "leftButton_mc", depth++);
    this.attachMovie("SSC_SlideButton", "rightButton_mc", depth++);
    this.attachMovie("SSC_TitleBar", "titleBar_mc", depth++);
```

Attach movieclips into the component.

The previous SlideShow component had all its interface elements (movieclips) stored inside the component's keyframes. In this version, we're dynamically attaching the interface elements so that their presence doesn't interfere with the anti-distortion process during initialization. If the interface elements, such as buttons and labels, were in the frame by default, their presence could affect the initial dimension of the component. Only the boundingBox_mc movieclip is required for anti-distortion when initializing a component, so we don't attach movieclips until anti-distortion has completed. As the final detail, all the elements have external linkage ID's with a prefix of "SSC" to indicate that they belong to the SlideShow component.

Note also the slightly unusual technique of incrementing a local variable, "depth," at the same time as passing it as the depth parameter for attachMovie() and createEmptyMovieClip():

```
var depth = 0;
this.attachMovie("SSC_BoundingBox", "Panel_mc", depth++);
this.createEmptyMovieClip("outerContainer", depth++);

// Create shortcut to accommodate earlier functions
this.container_mc = this.outerContainer.createEmptyMovieClip("innerContainer",
➥depth++);

this.attachMovie("SSC_BoundingBox", "containerMask", depth++);
```

Efficient techniques for attaching multiple movies with returned references and incremented depths.

By incrementing the depth variable at the same time as passing it to the attachMovie() or createEmptyMovie() method, you can rearrange the sequence without having to rearrange hard-coded depth values.

You're also creating two empty movieclips instead of using a predrawn container_mc movieclip. The outer movieclip, outerContainer, holds the inner movieclip, innerContainer. The reason we're doing this is because we'll need to mask the image as it loads, to prevent the flickering found in the original Slide Show component. However, a movieclip loading an image cannot be masked, unless you put the container movieclip inside an outer movieclip and mask the outer movieclip (we'll set the mask later).

Since the inherited method, loadNextImage(), loads a jpeg into a movieclip referenced with the container_mc variable, we assign a shortcut to the innerContainer movieclip to accommodate the loadNextImage() method.

```
// Create shortcut to accommodate earlier functions
this.container_mc = this.outerContainer.createEmptyMovieClip("innerContainer",
➥depth++);
```

Did you know, attachMovie() and createEmptyMovieClip() both can return a reference to the newly created movieclip? The following line of code is now legal in Flash MX: var clipReference = createEmptyMovieClip("foo", 1);.

At this point, you could drag an instance of the Advanced SlideShow component onto the stage and test the movie (see Figure 9.4). The only problem is that all the dynamically attached elements are still positioned at (0, 0), in the upper-left corner of the screen.

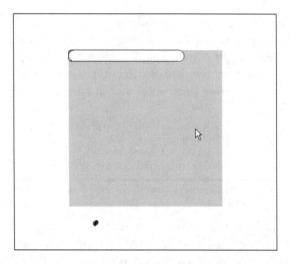

Figure 9.4   Attaching component elements without layout code.

Adding some layout code positions the component elements according to the available dimensions of the component:

```
// Bottom border of the image, minus the height of the button
this.bottomBorder = h - this.leftButton_mc._height;

// Set the dimensions of the Panel_mc
this.panel_mc._width = w;
this.panel_mc._height = this.bottomBorder;

// Set the mask for the container. The mask prevents flickering.
this.containerMask._width = w;
this.containerMask._height = this.bottomBorder;
this.outerContainer.setMask(this.containerMask);

// Set the dimensions for photos based on original dimensions
this.origWidth = w - this.margin_param * 2;
this.origHeight = this.bottomBorder - this.margin_param * 2;

// Position the title bar and buttons
this.leftButton_mc._x = 0;
this.leftButton_mc._y = this.bottomBorder;
this.leftButton_mc.blackArrow_mc._rotation = 180;
this.rightButton_mc._x = w - this.rightButton_mc._width;
this.rightButton_mc._y = this.bottomBorder;
this.titleBar_mc._x = this.leftButton_mc._width;
this.titleBar_mc._y = this.bottomBorder;
this.titleBar_mc._width = this.rightButton_mc._x - this.titleBar_mc._x;
```

Code used to layout the attached movieclips inside the component,
using all the available width and height.

This code is fairly straightforward, mostly simple arithmetic. For example, the left button belongs in the lower-left corner of the screen, and the right button belongs in the lower-right corner. The titlebar_mc movieclip, which provides a background for the label textfield, should stretch between the left and right buttons. The only interesting parts of the layout code are resizing and setting a mask for the container movieclip:

```
// Set the mask for the container. The mask prevents flickering.
this.containerMask._width = w;
this.containerMask._height = this.bottomBorder;
this.outerContainer.setMask(this.containerMask);
```

Set the containerMask movieclip as the mask for the outerContainer movieclip.

Here, the rectangular containerMask movieclip becomes a mask for the outerContainer movieclip. The outerContainer movieclip holds an innerContainer movieclip, which is used to contain the externally loaded jpeg.

As a result, the layout code will position the component elements, such as the buttons, labels, and masking rectangle, without distorting them to fit the component dimensions. You can try resizing the component by stretching it up or down, and when you test the movie, the buttons will look the same, but their position will reflect the amount of space available in the component.

The layout code also can accommodate user-defined margins around the edge of the photo. The variable used in the algorithm is called "margin_param", so simply add a parameter to the AdvancedSlideShow component with the variable name "margin_param" and a numeric data type (see Figure 9.5).

Figure 9.5 Attaching movieclips inside the component with layout code.

Finally, we add the textfield label as the last step:

```
// Position the textfield over title bar
this.createTextField("label_txt", depth++,
        this.titleBar_mc._x, this.titleBar_mc._y,
                         this.titleBar_mc._width,
                         this.titleBar_mc._height);

this.label_txt.type = "dynamic";
var tempFormat = new TextFormat();
tempFormat.align = "center";
this.label_txt.setNewTextFormat(tempFormat);
```

Create and format the label's textfield.

Because the `label_txt` textfield receives a new string value for each new image loaded, the textfield acquires the `tempFormat` object through `setNewTextFormat()` instead of the regular `setTextFormat()` method. As a result, any new values sent to the textfield will receive the same text-formatting styles defined in the `tempFormat` object, and you won't have to reapply the text format every time the title changes.

The last few lines of the `setSize()` method simply define button event handlers for the left and right buttons, so that they interrupt the loading process and jump ahead/behind to the next image.

```
this.leftButton_mc.onRelease = function()
{        this.clearInterval(this.loadcompleteID);
    this._parent.imagePointer -= 2;
    if(this._parent.imagePointer < 0)
        this._parent.imagePointer = 0;
    this._parent.loadNextImage();
}
this.rightButton_mc.onRelease = function()
{
    this.clearInterval(this.loadcompleteID);
    this._parent.loadNextImage();
}
```

*Define **onRelease** event handlers for left and right buttons.*

Extending a Super Class Method to Center Loaded Images

You can add images to the component parameters on stage and test the movie now to observe the final effects of the `setSize()` method. Any resizing of the component results in an undistorted layout of the buttons, title, and photo area to adapt to the component's new space. The buttons also let you skip back and forth.

We'll make one more modification to the Advanced SlideShow component to illustrate an OOP concept before moving on. As you may have noticed, loading images that are smaller than the slideshow area show up in the upper-left corner of the screen. The following code centers the image as soon as it has finished loading:

```
AdvancedSlideShowClass.prototype.waitForLoadedImage = function()
{
    super.waitForLoadedImage();

    // Center the photo if it's too small
    if(this.container_mc.getBytesLoaded() > 4 && this.container_mc.getBytesLoaded()
    ➡== this.container_mc.getBytesTotal())
    {
        if(this.container_mc._width < this.componentWidth)
            this.container_mc._x = (this.componentWidth - this.container_mc._width) /
            ➡2;
        else
            this.container_mc._x = 0;
        if(this.container_mc._height < this.bottomBorder)
            this.container_mc._y =(this.bottomBorder - this.container_mc._height) /
            ➡2;
        else
            this.container_mc._y = 0;
    }
} // waitForLoadedImage
```

Wait for image to load, and then align the image.

But wait, didn't you already define the `waitForLoadedImage()` method in the `SlideShowClass`, which this class inherits? By overwriting the method, aren't you preventing the method from performing its main duty, which is to wait for the image to finish loading? If you were completely overwriting the method, then you would lose all the functionality of the method defined for `SlideShowClass.waitForLoadedImage()`. However, the first line of the newly overwritten method actually calls a method of the same name in the super class (the class which `AdvancedSlideShowClass` inherited from):

```
super.waitForLoadedImage();
```

By calling `super.waitForLoadedImage()` first, the `AdvancedSlideShowClass` class actually calls a method from its super class, `SlideShowClass.waitForLoadedImage()`, before executing the code in the new version of the method. This technique allows you to call a previously defined method from a class you've inherited, and still extend the old method by overwriting it in your new class.

You may have noticed an additional condition in the `if` statement:

```
if(this.container_mc.getBytesLoaded() > 4 && this.container_mc.getBytesLoaded()
➥== this.container_mc.getBytesTotal())
```

This conditional statement also makes sure that `getBytesLoaded()` returns a value greater than 4. Sometimes, externally loaded movieclips or images will experience a delay in initialization, so that `getBytesLoaded()` and `getBytesTotal()` both have a value of 0. In such a case, it's important to make sure `getBytesLoaded()` returns more than 4 bytes, to avoid mistaking a delayed loading as a completed loading. For more information, refer to a description of this problem in Chapter 7.

Using Guide Layers for Super Class and Library Packaging

Many of the symbols don't exist as instances in the component's Timeline. Consequently, they won't accompany the component if you drag it to a new Flash movie stage. This can be a problem if you want to re-use the symbol in many different projects.

The solution for "binding" library symbols that are brought onto the stage dynamically is to put the symbols in guide layers. The ActionScript and regular contents of the symbol won't execute at runtime, but the symbol is now part of the component, so it will accompany the component into other library panels if you drag the component into other Flash projects. A more detailed explanation for this technique can be found in Chapter 8.

To implement this solution for the Advanced SlideShow component, create two guide layers, one named SuperClass and one named Assets. The class from which the `AdvancedSlideShowClass` inherits is defined inside the SlideShow component, so put an instance of the `SlideShow` component in the SuperClass guide layer. Put all the other dynamically attached movieclip symbols into the Assets layer. Make the two guide layers invisible in the Timeline so that they don't interfere with your work. Now, try dragging your component into other Flash projects, and you'll see those symbols reappear in identical folder structures in the Library panel (see Figure 9.6).

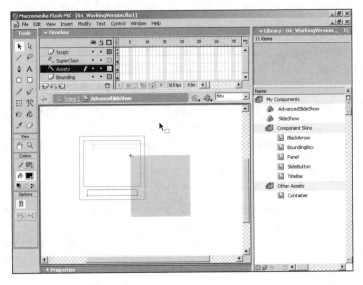

Figure 9.6   Guide layers.

Live Preview

Chapter 10 discusses live preview at length, but just for the sake of
completeness, we'll follow through with the creation of a live preview
for this component. Actually, live preview works easily if you've designed
the component well. The process consists of making a new Flash movie
with the component in the main stage and writing two event handlers
important for previews: onUpdate and Stage.onResize. The Stage.onResize
event handler is available to all Flash movies, but the onUpdate event handler
is unique to live preview movies.

1. First, create a new Flash movie.

2. Drag an instance of the Advanced SlideShow component onto the stage
   with the component's origin (upper-left corner) at the upper-left corner
   of the stage (0, 0).

3. Give the component an instance name of "preview_mc," and then save
   the Flash movie with any name you want.

   For this example, I've saved the live preview Flash movie in the source
   code directory as AdvancedSlideShow_LivePreview.fla.

4. In the first keyframe of the main Timeline, add the following ActionScript:

```
Stage.align = "TL";
Stage.scaleMode = "noScale";
listen = new Object();
Stage.addListener(listen);

listen.onResize = function ()
{   preview_mc.setSize(Stage.width, Stage.height);
}

function onLoad () {
    preview_mc.setSize(Stage.width, Stage.height);
    this.onUpdate();
}

function onUpdate()
{
    preview_mc.panel_mc._visible = xch.showPanel_param;
    var panel_color = new Color(preview_mc.panel_mc);
    panel_color.setRGB(xch.panelColor_param);
    preview_mc.label_txt._visible = xch.showTitle_param;
}
```

Live preview code in the first keyframe of the live preview movie.

The purpose of the stage settings is explained in Chapter 10. Those first two lines of code tell the Flash plug-in not to distort the Flash movie to fit available screen space, and to align the stage to the top-left corner of the available space. What's interesting here is the onResize method of the listen object, which executes when the stage area is resized. By creating an object called "listen" and calling Stage.addListener(listen), we've created an object that acts as a listener for the stage's onResize event. Because this movie will exist in the Flash authoring environment as a live preview, any resizing by the user triggers the onResize event of the live preview's stage. Once the onResize event triggers, the onResize event handler in the listener object sets the component's width and height according to the width and height of the stage:

```
listen.onResize = function ()
{   preview_mc.setSize(Stage.width, Stage.height);
}
```

*Use the **listen** object to handle the stage's **onResize** event.*

When the user makes any changes to the component parameters, the live preview should also reflect those changes in the appearance of the component. Any component parameter changes will trigger the onUpdate event-handler in the live preview movie. The onUpdate event-handler should grab any relevant properties of the xch object, which is an "exchange" object whose properties reflect the values of the component parameters in the authoring environment.

The SlideShow component only has a few properties that affect appearance (not including the margin property, which requires a loaded image to display). So, grab those properties from the xch object and assign the values to corresponding properties in the preview_mc movieclip:

```
function onUpdate()
{
    preview_mc.panel_mc._visible = xch.showPanel_param;
    var panel_color = new Color(preview_mc.panel_mc);
    panel_color.setRGB(xch.panelColor_param);
    preview_mc.label_txt._visible = xch.showTitle_param;
}
```

Event-handler to capture event when the component parameters have been updated.

5. Now, save the Flash movie and publish it to the same directory as your AdvancedSlideShow component's source file.

Now we're going to assign the newly created AdvancedSlideShow_LivePreview.swf as the live preview movie for the AdvancedSlideShow component.

6. Open up the file 05_CreateLivePreview.fla, which contains the same component we've built up to this point.

7. Right-click (or Command-click) on the AdvancedSlideShow symbol in the library. Select the option Component Definition. Near the middle of the pop-up dialogue panel, click the Set button next to the Live Preview textfield.

8. Choose either the option Live Preview in External .swf file, or Live Preview with .swf File embedded in .fla file (see Figure 9.7).

9. Browse to the live preview .swf you just created, and open it.

That's all you need to do to register an .swf as a live preview movie! The main difference between Live Preview External and Live Preview Embedded is the location of the Live Preview's .swf file. As you've probably guessed, an external live preview loads the external .swf into a mini-projector onto the stage, to represent the component's live preview. Flash MX records a relative path to the external swf. On the other hand, an embedded live preview stores the .swf file inside the .fla file. If the live preview .swf has changed, you can update the component's live preview by clicking the "update" button in the Live Preview dialog box.

Choosing between either options is a matter of convenience. If you want to keep your .fla file size small, and if you're working on a team where another person is still developing the live preview file, then you should choose the external option. Once the component is completed and ready for use, it's a good idea to choose the embedded option so that the user doesn't have to keep track of external .swfs when dragging the component into different projects.

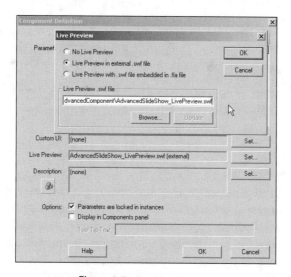

Figure 9.7 Set Live Preview.

Just a brief warning—the live preview movie that plays on stage in the Flash editor does not have error handling for infinite loops. So if you have an infinite-loop bug in your live preview code, it's possible to freeze the Flash editor unwittingly.

Now, try making changes to your component's panel color, show panel, and show title parameters. Your changes to the component parameters should be reflected in the live preview. Try resizing the component, and you'll notice that the buttons remain the same size, although they change position to use up all the available space in the component's live preview (see Figure 9.8).

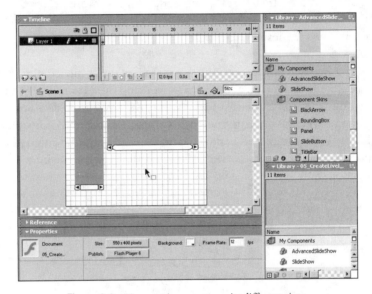

Figure 9.8 Live preview on stage, in different sizes.

Conclusion

Building a simple component is easy, but building a user-friendly component with many parameters, API, and live previews involves a lot of intricate steps. The process is straightforward, but it involves a lot of smaller details. Keeping your assets organized in the library and planning ahead with a specification document will help you avoid many mistakes that would cost a lot of time to fix. Hopefully, this chapter gives you an idea of the engineering process behind very advanced components such as the official Flash MX UI components. It's tempting to go overboard and design something overly powerful, but before you decide to build a component, be sure that you've defined your needs, so that you can build a component that's reusable and flexible within a feasible time frame and reasonable file size.

10

Component Live Previews

By Nigel Pegg

The Beginnings of Live Preview

Note: This personal anecdote was written by Branden Hall.

I first met Nigel when Flash MX was still just a twinkle in the eyes of Macromedia's Flash team. He and I chatted over email quite a bit about scrollbars. We discussed everything, from all the ways users expect to be able to interact with them to how to make them "skinnable." A few weeks after our initial conversations, I was told about how he was working on making the "live preview" for the scrollbar. At the time I sort of nodded and blew off the idea. I mean, a scrollbar is a scrollbar, why would you need a preview of a scrollbar?

Fast forward to today—each and every time I demo components to users groups or students, the very first thing I show is how you can just drag a scrollbar and drop it onto a textfield and like magic it snaps to the textfield and resizes itself properly. When it comes to making components easy to use for all levels of Flash users, live preview is key.

Introduction

Live preview is perhaps one of the most mysterious and misunderstood features of Flash MX components. Looking at it from the component users' perspective, it really seems as though you are no longer using movieclips anymore—you've crossed some line into full-fledged objects, complete with their own behaviors, that you're manipulating on stage at author time. From a component developer's perspective, it seems as though some incredibly complicated voodoo is going on, and it's often the case that developers I've talked to treat live preview with a kind of superstitious awe or distrust.

The strange thing is, live previews are very much a postscript to component creation, and involve very little magic at all. In fact, we'll see in the course of this chapter that the best live previews are almost ridiculously easy to make, once you've structured a component in the right way.

This chapter is meant as a basic primer and a set of guidelines for making live preview .swfs.

What Is Live Preview and Why Does It Matter?

The idea behind using Flash MX components is that you are authoring with something reusable and modular. You don't need to look inside; all you need is to understand the parameters and methods the component developer has given you. Live preview allows the component to render itself as you author—showing important details about the way it is configured, so that it lends the feeling that you are using a real, "live" object, as opposed to a movieclip that you might be tempted to dig into.

A live preview is really an .swf file that fills the space of the bounding box of your component—only during authoring time. It's as though your movieclip on the authoring stage has become the stage of a little Flash projector, which is running the .swf file you hooked up to it. You can do almost anything in a live preview that you can do in a .swf; note that this doesn't necessarily mean you *should*.

The biggest impact of live preview is psychological (see Figure 10.1). With the new face, your component has life beyond any other asset on the stage. It makes the component tangible in a way that a "movie clip" never could be. But there are several practical reasons for live preview that help lend your component more usability, which are covered in the following sections.

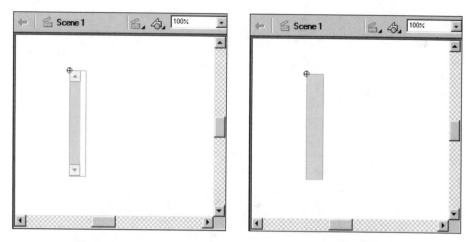

Figure 10.1 A scrollbar, with (left) and without (right) live preview.

WYSIWYG Sizing

One of the most important authoring-time aspects of any component is its sizing and layout on stage. Flash gives us a true "What-You-See-Is-What-You-Get" (WYSIWYG) environment in which to lay out content. This is one of its greatest strengths as an authoring tool. Placing an asset on the stage and scaling it to dimensions that fit your layout give Flash an intuitive interface for design. It's worth making sure your component responds by laying its internals out in a meaningful way to scaling, so that your users really are getting what they see.

The live preview feature of the authoring tool can be turned on and off by selecting Control, Enable Live Preview.

Live preview is extremely useful in this case by offering immediate feedback to the way the component reacts to scaling. Notice that in Figure 10.2, the live preview of the listBox (on the left side) shows that it is not as tall as the dimensions of the scaling. Because listBoxes must have an integer number of rows, a listBox snaps down to the nearest whole number size it can hold, and this behavior is clearly shown in the live preview.

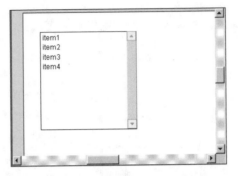

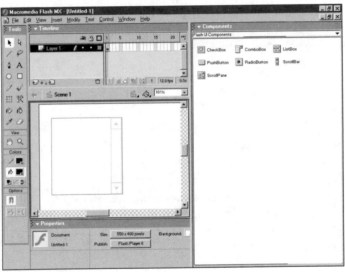

Figure 10.2 A scaled listBox, with (top) and without (bottom) live preview.

The listBox without live preview is a lot less informative and a little misleading to a designer looking to use it for strict layout demands. Its sleeker look notwithstanding, the live preview makes the listBox *more* usable.

Other Affairs of State

There are other obvious advantages to using live preview—you can display the items added in the component parameters panel, which helps give a picture as to how the component reacts to certain settings. It's not of the most vital importance, because any frame actions used to manipulate the component aren't expressible in the live preview, but it helps to set expectations for the way in which the component will behave as you put it into different states.

For example, in Figure 10.2, the listBox shows labels added to it. Component parameters could be used to set *any* parameter available to *any* method in the component. They could set the colors of the component, the text to be displayed, or trigger methods that affect the layout of the component (does the scrollPane have scrollbars by default or not?).

Limitations and Caveats

We've seen so far how much a live preview can add to a component's perception and functionality; these are all good things. But of course, the natural tendency is to go too far and try to push live preview further than intended. We know what a live preview is good for, so what sorts of things should be avoided? What *can't* a live preview do?

Live Previews Slow Down Authoring

It's really important to remember that live previews get rendered during authoring time, when a user is most likely to be spending his/her time *authoring*, not gazing in admiration at your beautiful live preview. Try to avoid live previews .swfs that do too much work or take a long time to instantiate— any time the author using your component switches to a view that shows your live preview, that .swf needs to instantiate, and can considerably slow down the editing process. Don't build live previews that are constantly doing something while they sit on the stage; no polling, no ticking away time, no seeking out network connections. Most importantly, if your component is likely to be used in multiple instances on one stage, mixed in with other components, have respect for the fact that *every* one of those needs to execute a live preview. Don't go overboard in what the live preview is doing, especially during instantiation, or authors will be likely to turn off live previews.

An additional reason to avoid intensive-when-idle live previews is that the live preview players in the authoring tool are throttled down to 1 fps. The only time the live preview is sure to be updating is as the user makes changes to it (via scaling or component parameters). So doing a little animation to entertain your users is probably out.

Mouse Interaction Doesn't Work

It's also tempting to take your live preview and hook it up so that you can configure its associated component using mouse interactions during authoring time. This is definitely an exciting possibility, but one that hasn't really had its day as of yet. Mouse events are blocked by the fact that clicking on the live preview triggers selection in the authoring environment, and doesn't register mouse events in the live preview itself. In a sense this is a blessing, in that it allows us to focus on what's most important—the component design itself—rather than have the ante upped by making components that can be directly manipulated during authoring time.

Live Previews Are Islands

Another exciting temptation is to build live previews that interact with other live previews or components. Unfortunately, this is not really practical. A live preview, contrary to some superstition, is unable to determine what other components are in the same authoring environment, so they can't really "hook up" in any pragmatic way (I probably shouldn't mention that there are *technical* ways to do it, but there are). All this is meaning to say is that while there is some very exciting potential with advanced live preview techniques, it's really best left to simplicity. My own personal bias is to treat live preview as a purely optional feature—with many components, it's quite likely that she/he will *turn off* live preview to make for a quicker authoring experience. Don't pin any required functionality on them.

Building a Basic Live Preview: The Essentials

It's time to cover the basic steps involved in building a live preview. The first thing to keep in mind is: This is really pretty easy. The component we're going to make over the course of this chapter is a simplified example case, more for the sake of getting used to live preview than for any vast display of functionality. Simply put, we're going to construct a label component (basically a container for text) with rounded edges, called RoundLabel. Here's a first look at the component itself (see Figure 10.3).

Looking at what we have so far, it's obvious we have a ways to go. All the component itself seems to be is *a white rectangle*. And, strangely enough, that's pretty much all the component really is. But add some parameters and a bunch of code on the inside and eventually you'll have a completed component. For now, we're going to focus on making a basic live preview for this rectangle.

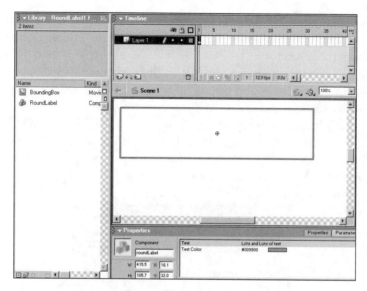

Figure 10.3 A component, its library, and parameters.

Step 1: A Component Starts With a Bounding Box

The first step in building the component is to draw a rectangle on the stage. Nothing too exciting about this. Select the rectangle and choose Insert, Convert to Symbol, which will bring up the Convert to Symbol dialog box (see Figure 10.4).

Figure 10.4 The Convert to Symbol dialog box.

As shown, name it BoundingBox. That's about it. Click OK and select the instance you now have on stage. Enter boundingBox_mc as instance name in the Property Inspector.

Lastly, you need to wrap this instance in the component itself; select boundingBox_mc once again and Insert, Convert to Symbol. Name the symbol RoundLabel.

Go to the advanced settings of the dialog (see the highlighted button in Figure 10.4) and be sure that the symbol has been exported for ActionScript, under the name "RoundLabelSymbol" (see Figure 10.5). Click OK, and you now have all the assets you need for this example.

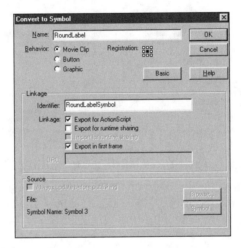

Figure 10.5   The Convert to Symbol dialog box for RoundLabel.

Step 2: Adding Component Parameters

All that's left before you actually make a live preview is to define the component parameters. Right-(Option-) click on the component symbol in the library and choose "Component Definition."

You start with two basic text parameters: Text, which is the content of the label, and Text Color, which is the color of the text (see Figure 10.6). Note that the two parameters have display names as well as variable names, labelText and textColor. The display names are only for the users, but remember these variable names, because you will use them shortly.

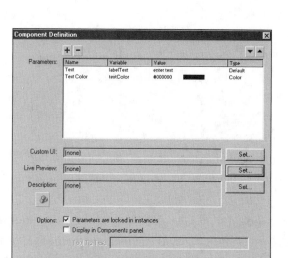

Figure 10.6   The first parameters for RoundLabel.

Also note that there's an empty space for setting a live preview .swf. Sounds like something you should get around to making; which means it's time to move on up to the next step. Click OK and save this .fla as RoundLabel1.fla.

Next, you're going to make the .fla that will be the source of the .swf to be projected inside your component.

Step 3: Creating the Live Preview .fla

Next up is actually making the .fla source for the live preview. This will be the lion's share of the work involved in this example; I know I promised that live preview was an afterthought, but for the purposes of examining how it works, we'll dive right in and do it before the rest of the component ("smoke and mirrors" comes to mind). Here are the steps:

1. Press Ctrl(Command)+N to start a new .fla, and then Ctrl(Command)+S to Save As "RoundLabel1LP.fla."

2. From the library of RoundLabel1l.fla, drag the BoundingBox symbol onto the stage of RoundLabel1LP.fla, at (0,0). Name this instance "boundingBox_mc."

3. Select the stage and go through the Property inspector to the movie size button, and size the movie to "contents"(see Figure 10.7). Click OK.

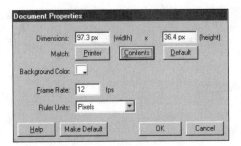

Figure 10.7   The Document Properties dialog.

The movie should now be tightly around the boundingBox_mc.

4. On the Assets layer, add a dynamic textfield, named "label_txt" (add this to the instance name field, not Var field, of the Property Inspector).

5. Name this layer "Assets," and add a new layer, "Actions."

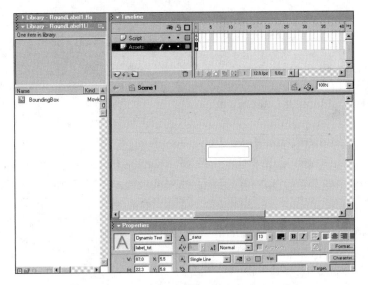

Figure 10.8   The state of the live preview so far.

6. In the Script layer, it's now time to add some code in the first frame:

```
function onUpdate() {
    label_txt.text = xch.labelText;
    label_txt.textColor = xch.textColor;
}
```

onUpdate *brings parameter values into the live preview.*

The preceding code uses an object that should be familiar to anyone who built custom UIs in Flash 5 Smart Clips—the xch object. This object is used as a transport mechanism that holds the component parameters you set.

So xch.labelText is the labelText parameter variable you set up in RoundLabel's component definition. onUpdate is a function called every time the component parameters are modified by the user, so in this case, you pull out both those values and apply them to the text field.

7. Save the .fla, then export it as RoundLabel1LP.swf. Now it's back to RoundLabel1.fla to hook the live preview onto the component.

And that's all! You've successfully built a live preview .fla.

Step 4: Attaching the Live Preview .swf to the Component

The last step is easy. Back in the original component RoundLabel1.fla, reopen the Component Definition dialog in the library (refer to Figure 10.6). Where it says "Live Preview," choose "set," and then choose to embed the .swf.

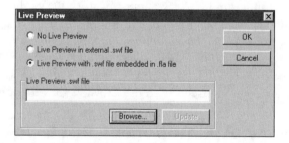

Figure 10.9   The Live Preview dialog.

Click Browse, and find RoundLabel1LP.swf, which you created in the previous step. After this has been added, click OK, and you are done. The live preview has been applied to the component on stage, and changing either parameter now affects its look on stage.

Be sure your live preview is turned on (Control, Enable Live Preview) to get the results shown here.

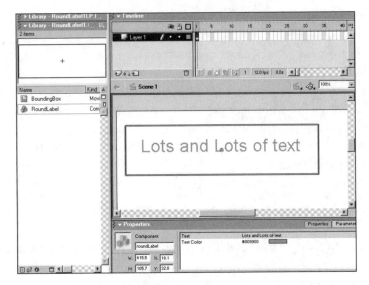

Figure 10.10   RoundLabel with a live preview.

There's really not much more to say about this story. We've shown the basics of passing parameter from the Property Inspector into the live preview, and how to hook it up. What we haven't done is made a round label—it is still conspicuously rectangular. This is a problem we'll grapple with shortly, but for now it's time to zoom out on the problem a little more and talk about how component design intersects with live preview construction.

Live Preview: A Component Inside Itself

Armed with the basic knowledge of how live previews work, we have to get back into a more conceptual discussion on the best way to make them. Think about the problem: You need to build an .swf that represents how the component looks at runtime. What would be the quickest way to make an .swf with that kind of content?

It's kind of pretty in its simplicity.

The answer is to make the component first, then put *the component itself* inside the live preview .swf. To manipulate the live preview, all you have to do is be sure the component has the right methods.

Component Parameters = Component Method Parameters

The key concept here is that the component should have a set of runtime methods for dealing with any configuration you could possibly make in authoring time, and probably a lot more. If you've properly defined a set of runtime methods, you've done the majority of the work it will take to set up your component parameters, as well as the live preview.

To me, methods are by far the most important part of a component. If I can manipulate a component dynamically (at runtime), then that component is useful in thousands more situations than it would be if all control was based in the component parameters. For instance, it's great to have a parameter that changes the text color, but if I have a method that changes text color, I can do this any time I need to while the .swf is running, not just at the initial state of the component in authoring time. There are a variety of other advantages:

- By having methods available for all your component parameters, all your component has to do to use them is feed the parameters to your methods in the component constructor. No extra work is needed to make the parameters affect the component.

- Similarly, by having the methods available, your live preview .swf (which contains an instance of the component) can use them to take those parameters from the xch object and configure the live preview component using those methods. This amounts to killing three birds with one stone.

- Also, centralizing all component functionality within the methods means bottlenecking the number of places things can go wrong. The Quality Assurance testing effort of a component can focus primarily on the methods; if they work, so will the live preview and component parameters. You have reduced the testing by nearly a third.

- Lastly, code is easier to maintain if it's all centralized. If you notice a bug in your methods and fix it, updating the code that fixes your parameters is done for free. Drop the fixed component into the live preview fla, re-export and embed it, and you've completely fixed your live preview as well. Not having to fix three places for every bug is a huge plus.

Unfortunately, there are likely exceptions to the optimized workflow shown here. For example, if using your method's results is way more work than is necessary for a live preview (recall, live previews need to instantiate quickly!), it might be your lot in life to have to build a "trimmed down" live preview that only represents the component instead of actually containing it. It's mostly a matter of common sense; if you're doing something extremely intensive or continuous, it's probably better left out. For example, a clock component that keeps accurate time is probably best left disabled at authoring time, because paying for constant updates can make authoring around the component a more painful experience. User discretion is advised.

But What About Sizing?

I seem to remember saying that WYSIWYG sizing was one of the most important and usable aspects of live preview. And it is. The great thing here is, like the component parameters, sizing is also done dynamically.

If you have a method, setSize, that takes in the width and height as parameters, which automatically lays out the component based on these settings, you're almost all the way there. Your component itself is much more usable, because it can build itself any size at any time, but again, it takes out most of the work you'd otherwise have to repeat three times. In the component's constructor, all it has to do is:

1. Look at its _width and _height to see how much the author stretched it at author time, and store them.

2. Scale itself back to normal size (this ensures that nothing is stretched within the component).

3. Call its own setSize method to lay itself out with the stored _width and _height.

As we've seen previously, before initializing, the component is really nothing more than a rectangular bounding box which happens to have a lot of code in it to build it into the thing it will become at runtime. Live preview gives you the chance to mimic this behavior on stage, again, using the component itself in an .swf and setting its runtime methods to configure it. For sizing, all the component in that .swf would need to know is how big the .swf had been stretched and use the component's setSize to tell it how to display. This is actually quite easily accomplished.

The live preview .swf is projected into the area the movie clip takes up on stage at authoring time, and that .swf's stage object is now exactly that size as well, because the live preview's stage size was fit to match the same contents size as the component had initially. Because the stage object has the ability to both listen for resize and report on its width and height, you really have all the tools you need to feed these details to the component. This is best served with an example, so it's time to finish the RoundLabel.

Building an Advanced Live Preview: Complete Methods

As stated time and again, the best way to make a good live preview is to make a component with good runtime methods. To do this, you need to decide on what functionality you want the component to have. To finish this example, let's support the following parameters (see Figure 10.11):

- Text and Text Color—These were in the original example
- Background Color
- Border Color
- Border Thickness
- Size—I like to think of this as a parameter, set by scaling the component rather than with the usual Property Inspector.

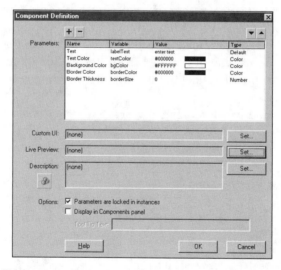

Figure 10.11 The component parameters for RoundLabel.

With these parameters firmly in mind (note the variable names—we'll be seeing these in the component code), it's time to set up methods in the component to handle these requirements.

Download RoundLabel2.fla from the book's web site to follow along.

We're going to dig into the component script of RoundLabel2.fla's. Open it and open the library (Window, Library), then double-click on the RoundLabel symbol in the library. Select the Actions layer and open the Actions panel (Window, Actions). Scroll down until you find the setSize method. There isn't much to it:

```
RoundLabelClass.prototype.setSize = function(w,h)
{
    this.width = w;
    this.height = h;
    this.drawBorder(w,h);
    this.attachMovie("TextSymbol", "text_mc", 3);
    this.text_mc._x = 3;
    this.text_mc._width = w-10;
    this.text_mc._height = h;
}
```

The RoundLabel component's setSize *method.*

This method has all the code you need to size the component at any time. The method stores the dimensions of the component as variables width and height (not the _width and _height that will stretch it), calls a function to draw the border based on those dimensions, and attaches a TextSymbol movie clip from the library to position and size it. If you look into this symbol (by double-clicking on its symbol in the library), you can see it's really no more than a textfield (named labelField) with Arial Black, which we'll be using to display the Text parameter.

The next method worth looking at is drawBorder:

```
RoundLabelClass.prototype.drawBorder = function(w,h)
{
    var r = h/2;
    var x1 = r;
    var x2 = w-r;
    var y1 = 0;
    var y2 = h;

    this.holder = this.createEmptyMovieClip("tmp", 1);
    this.holder.lineStyle(this.borderSize, this.borderColor);
    this.holder.beginFill(this.bgColor)
    this.holder.moveTo(x1,y1);
    this.holder.curveTo(0, y1, 0, r);
    this.holder.curveTo(0, y2, x1, y2);
    this.holder.lineTo(x2, y2);
    this.holder.curveTo(w, y2, w, r);
```

```
    this.holder.curveTo(w, y1, x2, y1);
    this.holder.lineTo(x1,y1);
    this.holder.endFill();
}
```

drawBorder's drawing API calls create the graphics for RoundLabel.

This method uses a bit of drawing API math that isn't really our focus (although you might note that we finally have round edges thanks to curveTo), but what's important is to notice that it uses this.borderSize, this.borderColor, and this.bgColor, which are all component parameter variable names. It also uses the dimensions of the component (w and h) to calculate the shape area. Essentially, this function draws the background and border using the parameters given. We'll be calling this method quite a bit.

So far we've covered only one method that the parameters directly set—setSize, which takes in the width and height. We still have to cover the other five, so let's start with the two text methods (because they're the easiest!):

```
RoundLabelClass.prototype.setText = function(txt)
{
    if (this.labelText!=txt) {
        this.labelText = txt;
        this.text_mc.labelField.text = txt;
    }
}
```

setText—a self-descriptive function name.

```
RoundLabelClass.prototype.setTextColor = function(col)
{
    if (this.textColor!=col) {
        this.textColor = col;
        this.text_mc.labelField.textColor = col;
    }
}
```

setTextColor—setting the color of the text.

There really isn't too much to say here. If the argument is a value new to the component, the method both stores the argument passed to it (in the same variable the parameter uses, to save space), and then sets up the textfield.

Three more methods to go. These methods all work in a similar manner to setTextColor method—save a state variable, then execute:

```
RoundLabelClass.prototype.setBackgroundColor = function(col)
{
    if (this.bgColor!=col) {
        this.bgColor = col;
        this.drawBorder(this.width, this.height);
    }
}

RoundLabelClass.prototype.setBorderColor = function(col)
{
    if (this.borderColor!=col) {
        this.borderColor = col;
        this.drawBorder(this.width, this.height);
    }
}

RoundLabelClass.prototype.setBorderSize = function(thick)
{
    if (this.borderSize!=thick) {
        this.borderSize = thick;
        this.drawBorder(this.width, this.height);
    }
}
```

setBackgroundColor, setBorderColor, setBorderSize—methods that call drawBorder.

You are now using drawBorder a fair amount. Because it does all the work of drawing, all you have to do is set one of the state variables (which drawBorder uses) and let it do its thing. Of note in these methods is that each of them makes sure only to redraw the graphics if the parameter has changed. Notice that each method makes sure the function argument is different from the current value before doing anything. This prevents the methods from wasting execution time for no reason.

The last thing to show in the component itself is making the constructor:

```
function RoundLabelClass()
{
    var w = this._width;
    var h = this._height;
    this._xscale = this._yscale = 100;
    this.boundingBox_mc._visible = false;
```

```
    this.setSize(w,h);
    this.setText(this.labelText);
    this.setTextColor(this.textColor);
}
```

The RoundLabelClass constructor.

With all the methods already doing most of the work, it's not surprising to see how little constructor code there needs to be. The only really interesting part is the first four lines. You write down the _width and _height of the component itself, which is its size after having been scaled on the stage at authoring time. You then remove all the scaling by setting it back to 100% in each dimension, and hide the bounding box. These steps are the essence of capturing the author time sizing of your component: using a bounding box to catch the author's scaling, undoing that scaling, and disposing of the bounding box. Lastly, call setSize to really start the process of building and laying out the component at the size specified. With this, we've covered all the component method code needed to *very* easily hook up live preview.

Creating the Live Preview .swf: An Anticlimax

Strangely, the process for creating the live preview for this component is substantially easier than the last one you made. Open RoundLabel2LP.fla and take a look (see Figure 10.12).

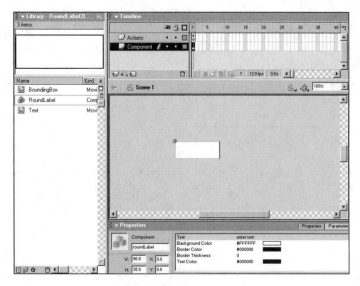

Figure 10.12   RoundLabel2LP.fla.

All you can see is the component and a code layer. The stage has been shrunk to fit the contours of the default component size, and that's about all. Let's look at the code. OnUpdate, a concept you've seen before, is in there:

```
function onUpdate() {
    roundLabel.setText(xch.labelText);
    roundLabel.setBackgroundColor(xch.bgColor);
    roundLabel.setBorderColor(xch.borderColor);
    roundLabel.setBorderSize(xch.borderSize);
    roundLabel.setTextColor(xch.textColor);
}
```

onUpdate *from the new RoundLabel2LP.fla.*

```
function onUpdate() {
    label_txt.text = xch.labelText;
    label_txt.textColor = xch.textColor;
}
```

The original **onUpdate**, *from RoundLabel1LP.fla*

The great thing here is that, instead of doing all the work by hand, the component methods (which handily match up one per parameter) take in the parameters from the xch object, and configure the component. The original code from RoundLabel1LP.fla needs to reach into the specific properties of the live preview to configure them. In the new example, there's no real thinking to do, which is always a plus. The methods of RoundLabel2.fla even make sure that they only do work when it's needed, executing them all for every update isn't a large detriment.

The interesting part of the code here is the pieces that figure out the size of the live preview .swf and size the live preview component to match it. There are two quick settings to set up to make scaling work:

```
Stage.align = "TL";
Stage.scaleMode = "noScale";
```

Two very small, but vital, lines of code.

The first line makes sure that the .swf is lined up at the top left corner of the component's bounding box as it scales. The second is important because it makes sure that scaling the live preview .swf doesn't stretch everything inside it;

instead, it grows the stage width and height (not the contents of the stage) to match the size of the stretched component bounding box (which is really just a rectangular symbol inside the component). With these details out of the way, it's relatively easy to size the component based on the stage size.

```
listen = new Object();
Stage.addListener(listen);

listen.onResize = function () {
    roundLabel.setSize(Stage.width,Stage.height);
}
```

Adding a listener object for sizing the live preview.

What's happening here is that you are adding a listener to the size of the Stage object, which calls `onResize` when the .swf size changes (in this case, when an author scales the component at authoring time). As can be seen, all `onResize` does is take the width and height of the .swf and tell the component to fill this same area.

Having these methods handy has made creating live preview a process that barely requires thought. And yet, the payoff is still pretty satisfying:

Looking in RoundLabel2.fla's main Timeline (with live preview enabled), you can see that the component responds to all component parameters and sizing as though it really was alive on stage (see Figures 10.13 and 10.14).

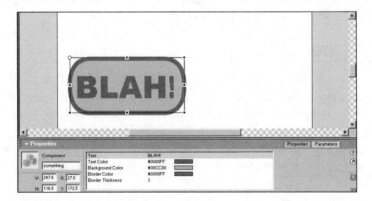

Figure 10.13 A big, ugly round label.

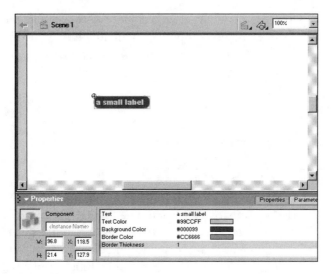

Figure 10.14   A smaller, more sedate round label.

Experiment with different sizes and colors. Although it's great to watch the component change live on stage, there's extra satisfaction in pressing Control-Enter to test the movie. If all has gone well, what you see at export should be nearly exactly what you've seen in authoring all along. In this way, live preview has created the illusion for your component that it was never *really* the plain old white rectangle filled with code that it truly is.

Conclusion

There's no doubt that live preview makes your component more tangible to developers using it; however what this feature really does best is to discourage an author from thinking about the component the same way he would about a movie clip he has authored himself. And as we've seen throughout the chapter, a well-designed component means that there isn't even much work in setting it up; in terms of bang for the buck, this feature really measures up well.

Perhaps what's most exciting about live preview, however, is the direction in which it points for the future of Flash components. For the first time, we've seen movie clips with some form of agency during authoring. A component author isn't just creating runtime content anymore; the *authoring experience* is beginning to come more to the fore. Starting with Flash 5's custom UI and following this progression through Flash MX's live preview, it's exciting to think what authoring time capabilities might start emerging in versions to come…

High-Level ActionScript

11

Debugging: Annoying Bugs and Where To Find Them

By Branden J. Hall

Bed Bugs Bite

When I was in college, I worked for one semester as a network technician for the university's dorm network. When students moved in at the start of the fall semester, the network techs had a desk in the lobby of each of the dorms and would wait for calls on our walkie-talkies from the tech support staff. Then we'd grab our toolkits and head up to the student's room and give him a hand getting on the LAN.

At first the job was pretty easy, but as soon as the folks at the support center realized that I seemed to always be able to get all my trouble tickets resolved quickly, I became one of the "go to" techs. Basically, anytime there was a problem that other techs couldn't solve, I was sent over to give it a shot.

My favorite one of these calls involved a student who had followed the directions to the letter, and his computer was online, but it was so slow you could probably have watched the 1s and 0s creep into his computer. Sending data out though, was fast. In vain I reinstalled the software and the network card a number of times and couldn't find any problem.

I then decided to check the jack in his room to see if that was faulty. When that didn't pan out I got the bright idea to trace his cable from the jack to the computer inch-by-inch. Low and behold, the smallest bit of his metal bed frame was sitting on the cable slicing neatly through one of the two receive wires inside. The metal in the bed was keeping the two parts of the wire connected, but the metal that the bed was made of provided enough resistance to let data through (incredibly slowly).

When all was said and done, I spent more than four hours trying to debug that student's network connection!

Introduction

Bugs have to be one of the leading causes of hair loss among programmers. They can be absolutely maddening when you don't even know what is causing them and everything you try seems to fail.

Part of the problem is that while computers have greatly progressed from the days where debugging meant removing moths that were attracted to the vacuum tubes, the actual art/science of debugging has not. In fact, debugging is still a skill that is mostly left up to individual programmers to sort out for themselves—even at universities. There are similarly few books that get into the topic of debugging, because frankly it is, such a messy topic. It's particularly amusing that debugging isn't discussed very much because it's what programmers *do* most of the time! Most standard estimates are that the average programmer spends 20% of his time actually coding and 80% debugging.

Bugs happen, and learning how to squish them is a skill that takes time to develop. However, if you know the debugging tools you have at your disposal, you'll become a better bug hunter and be able to spot and eradicate them faster. That's what this chapter is all about.

One important thing to note is that in general, object-oriented code is much easier to debug than procedural code. This is because in OO code you have separate distinct areas of control; therefore it's easy to find which object is acting incorrectly and thus where to focus your bug hunting. OOP also lends itself to much unit testing so that testing can be much more easily automated. One more reason to go OOP!

Compile-Time Bugs

The first type of bug that everyone runs into is a compile-time bug. A *compile-time bug* is also known as a *syntax error* and prevents your movie from working properly because some of your code isn't formatted according to ActionScript's syntax.

You can test the code you currently have in your Actions panel at any time by pressing the Check Syntax button located above the text area of the panel, or by pressing Ctrl+T (Command+T on a Mac) (see Figure 11.1).

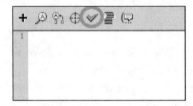

Figure 11.1 The Check Syntax button.

When you press this button, you'll get one of two responses: Either that your code is perfectly fine (from a syntax perspective), or your code has errors that you need to fix (see Figures 11.2 and 11.3).

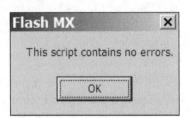

Figure 11.2 All syntax is correct.

Figure 11.3   There is some bad syntax in the code.

If you do have a syntax error, the Output panel will also open and give you information about the error. This text gives the exact scene, frame, and line of your error. The error explanation text has greatly improved with Flash MX, and now it even tells you what line your error is on, even when your code is held in an external .as file.

Syntax errors are by far the easiest type of bug to fix, but it can still be very frustrating to try to hunt down that one missing brace. One way to help yourself to not make syntax errors is to keep your code as neat as possible. Consistent indentation and brace placement is the key and Flash MX is your friend. The new auto format feature in the Actions panel can handle all your formatting needs and also is customizable. (See Figures 11.5 and 11.6.)

One type of syntax error that is particularly insidious occurs when you are missing curly braces. It's very tough to find and fix this sort of syntax error because, if you have numerous braces within other braces, Flash can't know where you meant the curly brace to go, only that one is missing.

To deal with this, it's best to write the closing brace when you write the open brace. This helps to prevent you from making a nasty bug that will drive you up the wall.

Another feature that helps out quite a bit while trying to hunt down syntax errors is Flash MX's new Reference panel (see Figure 11.6). Now you can look up the proper syntax for any action right in Flash. You can also place the cursor over any keyword in the Actions panel and press Shift+F1, and the Reference panel will open to the correct entry.

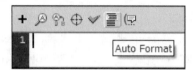

Figure 11.4 The Auto Format button.

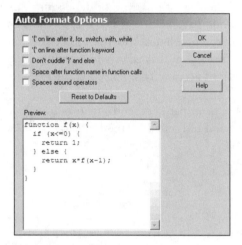

Figure 11.5 Customizing your auto format.

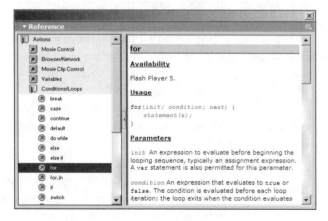

Figure 11.6 The new Reference panel.

Run-Time Bugs

Another type of bug is the *run-time bug*, which occurs when your code compiles okay but it doesn't work the way you want it to (it works the way you *told* it to!). This type of bug is also known as a *logic error*.

More than likely you will spend the majority of your time doing this type of debugging. The difficulty of this type of debugging can range from simple one-off errors (it should have been a 0, not a 1) to maddening my-whole-algorithm-is-wrong type problems. Also, the problem is rarely fixing a bug, it's finding it in the first place! If it takes you a couple of hours to find it, that one-off error might actually take you longer to debug than the algorithm error.

Finding bugs takes time, patience, and organization. A good guideline for finding bugs is the good old scientific method:

1. Observe.

2. Form a hypothesis.

3. Use the hypothesis to make predictions.

4. Test those predictions.

5. If your predictions, fail go back go step 2.

For example, say you wrote calendaring software and it wasn't working correctly. By observing it, you might notice that all the days were off by one. From this, you might hypothesize that there's a loop somewhere that's off by one. Given that hypothesis, you predict that the bug is in a particular section of code. You then go and look into that section of code and modify the loop and then test the software again. If the bug is still there, you'll have to try to form a new hypothesis, otherwise you squashed the bug.

There are a number of tools in Flash that have the explicit purpose of helping you form a hypothesis of where your bug is by allowing you to peer into your code as it's running.

One particular issue you may run into is that when you fix one bug, it might suddenly make 20 more appear. Often, I've found, a reason for this is because if I made a mistake once, I'm more than likely to have made it multiple times. So, when you fix a bug, you may want to go and search for other similar bugs.

The Always-Amazing Trace Function

The first and most revered of all bug-finding tools is the `trace` function. You pass to this function what you want to see, and it prints it to the Output window. It's usually best to not just spit out variables, but also format them in some way, for example

```
trace("foo: "+foo);
```

Now in the Output window it's clear what variable you are printing.

One issue developers run into when they start using `trace` is that when they try to trace an object, all they get in the Output window is

```
[Object object]
```

which is obviously not very informative. The way around this is to be sure you create a `toString` method for all your custom objects.

```
Employee = function(fname, lname, pos){
    this.fname = fname;
    this.lname = lname;
    this.pos = pos;
}

Employee.prototype.toString = function(){
    return("[lname: "+this.fname+" fname: "+this.fname+" pos:"+this.pos+"]");
}
```

*Creating a **toString** method for a custom object.*

Now you can simply trace any `Employee` object you'd like and it will print all that employee's info. Note that that even though it's compiled into the .swf, the `trace` action only works in the Flash authoring environment and not anywhere else. If you want to exclude the `trace` actions from the .swf creation process, check the Omit Trace Actions box in the Flash tab of the Publish Settings window. Be careful with this option though, because with it on, `trace` won't even work in the authoring environment.

Listing Variables and List Objects

Some other tools you have at your disposal are located in the Debug menu when you are testing a movie. The name of the first item, List Objects, is a bit of a misnomer, as it only prints a hierarchical list of the movieclips in your movie. List Variables, on the other hand, does exactly what it says (see Figure 11.7). Both items print their results to the Output window just like the `trace` action, although they erase anything previously printed there.

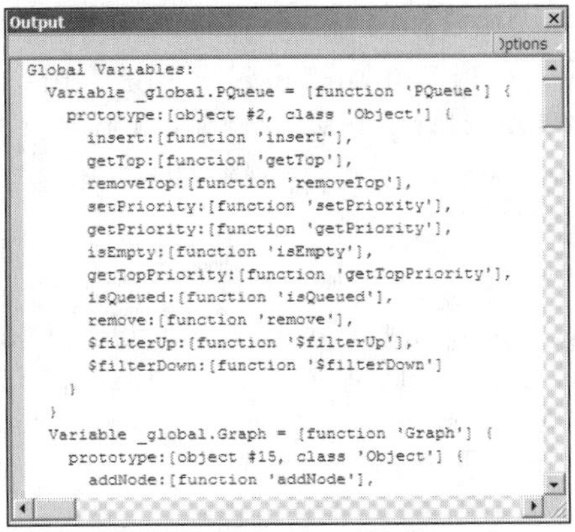

Figure 11.7 The results of List Variables.

The Integrated Debugger

Macromedia first introduced the Debugger with Flash 5. However, the debugger in that version of Flash had some severe limitations and was, for the most part, ignored by developers. Macromedia did learn from that experience, and the integrated Debugger in Flash MX is many times better and unless they don't know how to use it, developers don't have any excuse for not using it now!

To use the Debugger, select Debug Movie from the Control menu.

Overview of the Debugger

The Debugger allows you to do two main things. The first is to view all aspects of your movie at any point in the movie. This includes all movieclips and all variables within those clips. The second function is to stop your movie at specific lines of code to examine the state of the movie at that point.

The left side of the Debugger is concerned with examining the contents of the movie, while the right is dedicated to viewing and controlling when to start and stop code execution. (See Figure 11.8.)

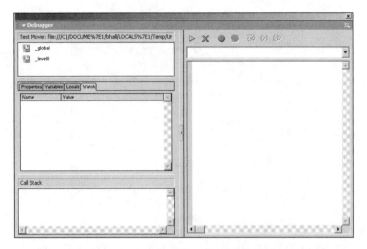

Figure 11.8 The Flash MX Debugger.

Code and Breakpoints

Inside of either the Actions panel or the Debugger, you can switch between all the code located in the current frame by selecting it from the drop-down menu at the top of the panel. This allows you to quickly flip between any code in that frame, whether it's on the main Timeline or buried 10 movieclips deep.

You also can add breakpoints to any line of the code in either panel. A *breakpoint* is a place where, when you are debugging your movie, the code should pause. Think of it like a pause button for your code. You create breakpoints by either right-clicking on any line and selecting Set Breakpoint in either the Actions or Debug panel or by selecting a line and pressing the stop sign button in the Debug panel.

When you test a movie, it is actually stopped so that you can flip through the code and find spots where you might want to add breakpoints. To start the movie, click the green Play button. If you later want to forget about debugging and just get back to fiddling with the movie directly, click the red X. The next button adds breakpoints and the one after that removes all of them from your movie. The next three buttons though are a bit more complex: Step Over, Step In, and Step Out.

Figure 11.9 Working with the code window in the Debugger.

Say you had the following code:

```
1 function doSomething(begin, end){
2   while (begin < end){
3     ++begin;
4   }
5   trace("done function");
6 }
7
8 doSomething(0, 10);
9 trace("done movie");
```

Now, if you place a breakpoint on line 8 and then tell the Debugger to run the movie, it would stop on line 8 and wait for your input.

If you clicked the Play button, the movie would continue to play and because there are no other breakpoints, the movie plays, traces its two messages to the Output window, and exits.

If you were to click the Step In button though, the movie would play but stop on 2, inside the doSomething function. This is because the Step In button enables you to step into a loop or call what Flash would normally skip over. If you continue to click the Step In button you will walk through, line by line, every other action in the movie.

If, while doing this, you need to exit one of the loops you are stepping through, click the Step Out button. This pops out of the loop and takes the Debugger to the next breakpoint.

If you are stopped at the beginning of a function or loop and want to just skip over it and not examine it at all, click the Step Over button (though that code will still execute).

These three buttons give you a lot of control over how you step through a movie while debugging. Be sure you take some time to play with them on your own.

Movie Structure Pane

The Movie Structure pane in the top left of the Debugger shows you the structure of your movie from a movieclip perspective (see Figure 11.10). The top-level nodes in this tree include _global, as well as all the levels in your movie (_level0, _level1, and so on). After you select one of the items in this pane, you can view its variables in the variables pane below.

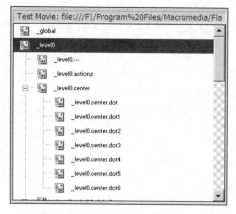

Figure 11.10 The Movie Structure pane of the debugger.

Variables Pane

The Variables pane allows you to view all the variables and properties of the currently selected movieclip in the Movie Structure pane above it (see Figure 11.11). It also allows you to pull out variables you would like to track and look inside a currently running function to see what variables are in there.

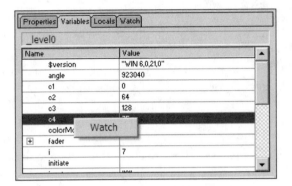

Figure 11.11 The Variables pane of the debugger.

To view the data inside or about a particular movieclip in your movie, you need to first select that clip in the Movie Structure pane and then select the Variables or Properties tab of the Variables pane, depending on which you are interested in.

With all these ways to find variables in your movie, you'll often want to isolate a few variables that you want to track. You can do this by adding these variables to the Watch tab. If you select the variables, you then have the option to right-click (Ctrl-click on the Mac) on any item in the list and select Watch. This adds the variable to the Watch tab. If you do this, a small icon appears next to the variable to denote that it is being watched. You can then remove the watch on it by right-clicking on it again or by going to the Watch tab and right-clicking on it there. This is a handy way to pull out the exact variables you are interested in as you step through your movie.

If your movie is currently stopped at a breakpoint, you can also select the Locals tab, which displays all the variables local to the place where your code is currently stopped. You can similarly add any of these variables to your watch list.

Call Stack Pane

The Call Stack pane allows you to view the current call stack if your code is stopped at a breakpoint (see Figure 11.12). The *call stack* is a list of all the functions that were called in order for your code to get where it is. This is helpful in making sure all the correct functions are getting called in the right order without having to step through them one by one.

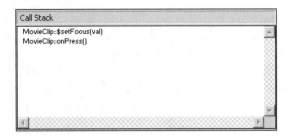

Figure 11.12   The Call Stack pane.

Using the Debugger

Now that you know how all the buttons work, how do you use them to help you debug?

Here's a general methodology that's worked well for me:

1. Before you do anything, develop a test plan. Write down exactly what your movie should do at each and every point—what the input should be, what the output should be, and so on. Be sure you include your input "illegal" values. Never assume anything about your users. Remember, even if you build it idiot-proof, they'll just build a bigger idiot.

2. Now, without opening the Debugger, walk through your movie and check against your test cases. Just write down what you find rather than trying to immediately fix the problem. Too many times I've "fixed" one problem only to have that fix break something else.

3. Now that you have a good sense of what's wrong with your movie, look for patterns in the errors. Is the same type of error happening all the time? Are some errors intermittent? If so, can you find a pattern to when the error pops up? Because good debugging mimics the scientific method, this is the hypothesis part.

4. Once you have an idea on what's going wrong, start up your movie, but this time with the debugger running (Control, Debug Movie). Before you start running the code, dig around in it and find the area where you believe the bug is originating from. Now spread a few break-points around in this point, particularly anywhere a function is getting called or there's an if statement. Also be sure you place at least one breakpoint before the code that you believe is messing up, then start the code running.

5. Now interact your movie as needed until your code hits your first breakpoint. At this point, dig around in the Movie Structure pane and find any and all movieclips where the variables you are interested in live. Find these variables in the Variables or Locals tab and then add them to your Watch tab.

6. Once you've found all of the variables, keep an eye on start-stepping through your code using either the Step In button or by just clicking the Continue button and letting the code stop at the next breakpoint. Either way, keep an eye on the variables in your Watch tab. You should be able to find the spot where they are changing to "bad" data. You may need to refine your search a few times by adding more breakpoints or by stepping through the code line-by-line, but once you find the error, simply jump out of test movie mode and go fix the code.

Keep following these steps until your movie is debugged. You may also want to have someone else test your movie to spot problems. Remember, many eyes makes bugs shallow, so the more people you can have testing your code the better (within reason, of course).

Remote Debugging

One of the most useful, yet least used features of the Flash debugger is remote debugging. With remote debugging you can run the movie in a browser yet still be able to step through the movie's code in the Debugger. In addition, the movie can be running on a different computer than the Debugger!

The first thing you have to do to enable remote debugging is to locate the most recent version of the debug plug-in. The version that comes with Flash MX is located in the Players folder of the application, but this is probably not an up-to-date version. Be sure you check Macromedia's site to see if there is a new version available. Install this plug-in wherever the user that will actually be testing the movie is. For example, if you have a client that keeps breaking your movie but you can't figure out why, you can have the client install the Debugger player and try to break the movie while you receive all the debug information on your machine.

After you have the Debugger installed, you need to publish your movie so that it supports remote debugging. To do this, open the Publish Settings window, select the Flash tab, and check the Remote Debugging box and be sure you type in a password (see Figure 11.13). If you don't have a password, anyone who has the Debugger player can look at the debugging info about your movie. Now publish your movie.

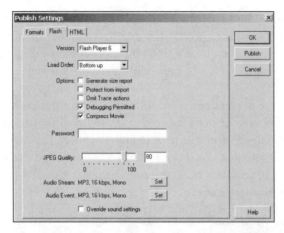

Figure 11.13 Enabling remote debugging in Publish Settings.

When you publish the movie, you'll notice that you get three files, an .swf, an HTML, and an .swd. The .swd file contains all the debugging information, so when you upload the files to a server to test, you must include this file as well.

Now that everything is set up on the client and server end, you need to set up your Flash environment to accept remote debugging information. Open up the debugger (Window, Debugger) and then click on the menu in its upper-right corner. From this menu, select Enable Remote Debugging. Now your debugger can receive information from a remote debugging session.

You can now begin to debug remotely! Browse to the HTML file that includes the .swf that you want to debug on a machine that is running the debugger plug-in. When you do this, a window will pop up asking you where you want the debugging information sent (see Figure 11.14).

Figure 11.14 The Remote Debug window.

If you are running the Flash environment on the same system from which you are testing, just choose localhost, otherwise have the person who is running the movie enter your computer's IP address. Now the plug-in will send a password challenge to the computer that's receiving the debug information (see Figure 11.15).

If you enter the correct password, all of the debug information will now be sent to the instance of the Flash environment you have running and will appear in the debugger. You can now debug as you would normally.

It can be a bit awkward to work in both a browser and the debugger at the same time though; you may need to come up with a special panel layout in Flash to do this most efficiently.

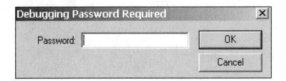

Figure 11.15 Password challenge for remote debugging.

Conclusion

Even in the modern world of web development, debugging is just as much an art as it is a science. It will take you time to develop good debugging skills, but by learning the tools that Flash MX offers, you will definitely have a leg up.

At first debugging will be a messy, arduous task, but over time, and with the use of strict methodology, it will get easier and more manageable. In particular, the use of object-oriented programming will make debugging much, much easier.

Debugging is one of those skills that you must learn.

12

Blurring the Line

By Samuel Wan

Chopsticks and the Spork

The chopstick is probably one of the most underestimated technologies in human history. Those two wooden sticks combine to form an amazingly versatile tool, and yet three quarters of the world population doesn't use chopsticks simply because they haven't learned the technique.

With a decent pair of chopsticks, you can pick up scalding hot items, twirl noodles into bite-sized rolls, skewer your food like a fork, or scoop rice like a spoon. Experienced users can even apply a scissoring force on the sticks to slice and dice all kinds of foods. (According to kung-fu movies, chopsticks also come in handy for defending yourself against dangerous waiters.)

On the other hand, specialized tools such as the fork and spoon have their own advantages, and combining them into a single product does not guarantee success. Consider that the English empire perfected the art of specialized utensils and cutlery, while great minds of our age later came up with what has become a one-liner at comedy clubs: the spork. (If you haven't heard of the spork spoon/fork, you haven't heard enough jokes.)

A versatile tool like the chopstick requires some knowledge of how to use it correctly. In other cases, being aware of different tools will prevent you from combining the wrong ones. As developers, it's important for us to understand how movieclips in Flash evolved to serve many purposes, while objects such as the textfield were designed for specific tasks.

Introduction

There are three basic building blocks used in constructing interactive Flash projects: movieclips, buttons, and textfields. These three objects are unique because you can access them as both "visual objects" in the Flash editor, and as "virtual objects" through the ActionScript language.

First of all, they are visual objects because you can use drawing tools in the Flash editor to create movieclips, buttons, and textfields on the stage. You can also refer to them as virtual objects because they're also accessible as objects in ActionScript, with a full complement of methods and properties. All three objects can capture user input through the triggering of event-handlers, which we'll discuss in more detail later. Graphic symbols could be considered the fourth building block, except that they're neither interactive nor dynamically accessible through ActionScript for reasons I'll explain later.

If you're an experienced Flash developer, then the basic purposes of movieclips, buttons, and textfields probably seem obvious. Even so, be careful not to underestimate the significance of added features in Flash MX. All three building blocks have an expanded set of features that can improve the way we work in Flash.

Blurring What Line?

This chapter bears the title "Blurring the Line" because the differences between movieclips, buttons, and textfields have suddenly blurred into each other in Flash MX. They now support many overlapping behaviors that you can access through ActionScript. The differences between them have blurred so much that it's difficult to know when to use the appropriate object.

For example, movieclips, buttons, and textfields did not have many common properties in Flash 4 and Flash 5, so people invented standard techniques that are widely used today. Actually, you might better describe these standard techniques as "workarounds" or "hacks." Designers would nest buttons or textfields inside movieclips to gain more control through the movieclip's ActionScript methods and properties.

The properties in the following list were only available for the movieclip object in Flash 5, but they're now supported by buttons and textfields as well:

- Position: _x, _y
- Dimension: _width, _height
- Scaling: _xscale, _yscale
- Mouse position: _xmouse, _ymouse

Creating and repositioning textfields dynamically required some sleight-of-hand in Flash 5 to combine the behaviors of textfields with movieclips. This technique involved several complex steps:

1. Create a movieclip symbol that contains a dynamic textfield.
2. Give the movieclip an external linkage ID.
3. Write code to dynamically attach the movieclip from library to stage.

   ```
   attachMovie("field", "myfield", 1);
   ```

4. Write code to reposition the movieclip and assign a string value to the textfield inside.

   ```
   myfield._x = 100;
   myfield._y = 100;
   myfield.textvalue = "Hello World"
   ```

In Flash MX, the entire task is performed in two lines of code:

1. Create an empty textfield with position and dimension arguments, and give its *text* property a string value.

   ```
   createTextField("myfield", 1, 100, 100, 200, 30);
   myfield.text = "Hello World";
   ```

Not only do the new ActionScript objects require less code, but they also offer more functionality. In the textfield example, it's possible to create a textfield of any size without having to predefine a textfield inside another movieclip. Better textfield manipulation is just one of the consequences of more powerful Flash MX objects. There are other ways in which the overlapping features of movieclips, buttons, and textfields will change the way Flash projects are built.

The earlier strategy of mixing elements to combine their behaviors is no longer necessary in many cases. In fact, you can create and modify both movieclips and textfields with pure ActionScript, without having to draw any elements on the screen. Whether you want to build something with nothing but the ActionScript code would really depends on the nature of the project. The main point is that "workaround" techniques from earlier versions of Flash can be completely discarded in favor of a cleaner, more efficient approach toward building interactive projects.

Although graphic symbols can be considered the fourth building block of Flash, graphic symbols have never been accessible from ActionScript. They offer few, if any, benefits compared to movieclips. A graphic symbol is basically a movieclip that doesn't have the resource requirements (CPU, memory) of supporting movieclip behaviors or ActionScript commands, beyond simple goto and stop actions.

Most often, graphic symbols are only used to manage graphics in the Flash library and organize animation in the Timeline. However, graphic symbols that contain animation will only play the animation as the parent Timeline allows. This drawback makes the graphic symbol unsuitable as a standalone animation container because it cannot display and control animation within a single keyframe. In terms of interactive programming, graphic symbols are rarely used because of their static nature. There's simply not much to say about graphic symbols in a book about ActionScript.

Coverage of Textfields

Even though this book contains another chapter about textfields, comparing textfields to movieclips and buttons gives you a better perspective on when and how to use them. This chapter focuses on changes in programming strategies due to expanded ActionScript behaviors for textfields. Chapter 13, "Textfield Mangling," focuses more on specific features of the object, including deeper techniques on textfield manipulation and formatting.

Building Blocks for Interface Programming

Interface programming in Flash MX can be broken down into three main topics: interactivity, functionality, and structure. *Interactivity* refers to how an interface can react to user input via mouse, keyboard, microphone, and so on. *Functionality* describes the tasks performed by the interface. *Structure* refers to the outward appearance and internal organization of interface elements, such as the visual "look" and internal guts of a scrollbar or listbox.

I've created three tables to clarify the comparisons between movieclips, buttons, and textfields. Here's a brief description of each table:

- Table 12.1 compares the event-handling capabilities of each object. Event-handlers can detect user input, such as mouse-clicks or keystrokes, and then execute specific code when a particular type of event occurs. Event-handling is the key ingredient for defining interactive behavior.

- Table 12.2 compares the methods of each object. Methods are actions that an object can perform, either on itself, or on something else.

- Table 12.3 compares all the properties available in all three objects. Properties give us access to such attributes as position, size, and transparency. Note that some of the properties do not belong to a specific class, but rather exist more or less in the global space: _focusrect, _highquality, _quality, _soundbuftime, and _url.

Table 12.1   **Compare Event-Handlers**

	MovieClip	Button	Textfield
	onData		
	onDragOut	onDragOut	
	onDragOver	onDragOver	onScroller
	onEnterFrame		
	onKeyDown		
	onKeyUp	onKeyUp	
Event-Handlers (invoked on event)	onKillFocus	onKillFocus	onKillFocus
	onLoad		
	onMouseDown		
	onMouseMove		
	onMouseUp		
	onPress	onPress	
	onRelease	onRelease	
	onReleaseOutside	onReleaseOutside	
	onRollOut	onRollOut	
	onRollOver	onRollOver	
	onSetFocus	onSetFocus	onSetFocus
	onUnload		
			onChanged

Table 12.2 **Compare Object Methods**

	MovieClip	Button	Textfield
METHODS			addListener
	attachMovie		
	createEmptyMovieClip		
	CreateTextField		
	duplicateMovieClip		
	getBounds		
	getBytesLoaded		
	getBytesTotal		
	getDepth	getDepth	getDepth
			getNewTextFormat
	getURL		
	globalToLocal		
	gotoAndPlay		
	gotoAndStop		
	hitTest		
	loadMovie		
	loadVariables		
	localToGloabal		
	nextFrame		
	play		
	prevFrame		
			removeListener
	removeMovieClip		
			removeTextField
			replaceSel
	setMask		
			setNewTextFormat
			setTextFormat
	startDrag		
	stop		
	stopDrag		
	swapDepths		
	unloadMovie		

MovieClip Drawing API
beginFill
beginGradientFill
clear
curveTo
endFill
lineStyle
lineTo
moveTo

Table 12.3 **Compare Object Properties**

MovieClip	Button	Textfield	Textfield Specific Properties
_alpha	_alpha	_alpha	autoSize
_currentframe			background
_droptarget			backgroundColor
enabled	enabled		border
focusEnabled			borderColor
_focusrect	_focusrect		bottomScroll
_framesloaded			embedFonts
_height	_height	_height	hscroll
hitArea			html
_highquality	_highquality	_highquality	htmlText
	_quality	_quality	length
_name	_name	_name	maxChars
_parent	_parent	_parent	maxhscroll
_rotation	_rotation	_rotation	maxscroll
_soundbuftime	_soundbuftime	_soundbuftime	multiline
tabChildren			password
tabEnabled	tabEnabled	tabEnabled	restrict
tabIndex	tabIndex	tabIndex	scroll
_target	_target		selectable
_totalframes			text
trackAsMenu	trackAsMenu		textColor
_url	_url	_url	textHeight
useHandCursor	useHandCursor		textWidth
_visible	_visible	_visible	type
_width	_width	_width	variable
_x	_x	_x	wordWrap
_xmouse	_xmouse	_xmouse	
_xscale	_xscale	_xscale	
_y	_y	_y	
_ymouse	_ymouse	_ymouse	
_yscale	_yscale	_yscale	

You'll also find a PDF of each table in the chapter files on the book's web site, and I encourage you to print the tables as a convenient reference while reading this chapter.

Quick Review About Methods and Properties

In case you skipped the first part of this book that introduced OOP concepts, I'll briefly clarify the difference between methods and properties. Because ActionScript doesn't enforce encapsulation like other OOP languages such as Java or C++, both methods and properties can be used to set and get properties of an object. The target property can either represent a variable containing some value, or an attribute of the object, such as a movieclip's rotation.

You can set an object's internal variable author like this:

```
book.author = "Sam and Branden";
```

Or you could define an object's setter method and call it like this:

```
book.setAuthor = function(name)
{   this.author = name;
}
```

Making changes to special properties within the movieclip, button and textfield types of objects can also affect their appearance or behavior. Sometimes you have to set a property's value directly, and other times require a method call. For example, the following code moves the _x and _y properties of a button to the coordinates (100, 200):

```
button._x = 100;
button._y = 200;
```

This method call changes another property of a movieclip—the depth property:

```
myClip.swapDepths(anotherClip);
```

In the swapDepths example, the parameter, anotherClip, tells the myClip movieclip to swap depths with anotherClip. Parameters change some detail about how a method performs a task. Both methods and properties can set or get attributes of a movieclip, such as its position, transparency, or instance name. However, a method allows parameters to customize how the set or get task is performed.

There's no obvious pattern that dictates when an ActionScript object's attributes are directly set via properties, or indirectly via methods. As a general rule, methods are defined for actions that require more than one parameter, while properties are typically used to access object attributes with a single primitive data type.

If you skipped the first few OOP chapters and you're having difficulty understanding methods, properties, and event-handlers, this is a good time to go back and read those chapters. We know it happens sometimes because we tend to read ahead too.

Part I: Interactivity with Movieclips Versus Buttons

In the first part of this chapter, we'll explore different strategies for building interactive elements. Buttons are the most basic element of interactivity, but it's really the behavior of buttons that we're interested in using. All three building blocks (movieclips, buttons, and textfields) support button-like behaviors in some way, so we'll be looking at how they can be used in interactive programming.

When the user clicks the mouse, rolls it over a button, or rolls away from a button, a "button event" has occurred. Movieclips, buttons, and textfields all have event-handlers, and you can see a comparison of their availability in Table 12.1. The event-handlers shown in Table 12.1 are arranged horizontally by type of event. Any event not supported by an object has a shaded box to indicate a missing event-handler.

Movieclips and Buttons

The first observation you can make from Table 12.1 is that the movieclip object supports all the same events as the button object. However, the button object does not support most of the movieclip events. You would be right if you guessed that movieclips can behave like buttons in Flash MX, but buttons cannot behave like movieclips!

But wait, movieclips and buttons supported similar events in Flash 5 too— didn't they? In fact, movieclips and buttons share common event-handlers in Flash MX, but movieclips also have other mouse-aware event-handlers not available in buttons: onMouseDown, onMouseMove, and onMouseUp. It gets a bit confusing when you try to differentiate between the onPress event-handler common to buttons/movieclips, and the onMouseDown event-handler, which is only available to movieclips.

The Legacy of Clip Events and Button Events

You have to go back to Flash 5 to clarify the reason behind the confusing overlap in event-handlers. In Flash 5, movieclips supported a set of events called "clip events." The name "clip event" describes how event-handlers had to be defined for each movieclip instance by selecting the movieclip on the stage and then opening the Actions panel. The ActionScript code for clip events wasn't written inside a timeline keyframe, but stored in the Actions panel off of the movieclip instance. As a result, most of the code for event-handling was written for a specific movieclip instance on the stage.

Flash 5 Legacy: Clip Events

Figure 12.1 shows an example of clip events in Flash 5. The Actions panel contains the clip events for a movieclip instance, selected to the left of the panel. This movieclip behaves like a button in the sense that it detects when the mouse is pressed down and released. However, using movieclips as buttons in Flash 5 created several major problems:

First of all, the mouseDown and mouseUp clip events won't automatically detect whether the mouse cursor was positioned on top of the movieclip when the events occurred. The user could click anywhere on the stage and still trigger the event-handlers, which defeats the whole purpose of using a movieclip as a button. One solution was to add collision-detection code to compare the mouse cursor's position with the movieclip's area. Unfortunately, this solution involves an awkward bit of additional programming that wastes an extra cycle of CPU resources:

```
onClipEvent (mouseDown)
{
   var hit = this.hitTest(_parent._xmouse, _parent._ymouse, true);
   if(hit)
   {
      this.gotoAndStop("down");
      trace("movieclip was pressed");
   }
}
```

*An **onClipEvent()** event-handler for the **mouseDown** event, written in Flash 5.*

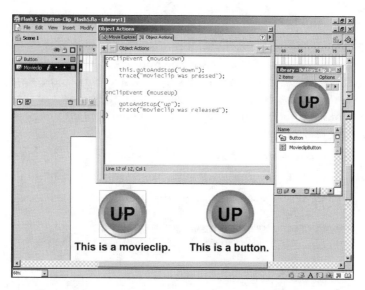

Figure 12.1 Detecting mouse events with a Flash 5 movieclip.

Secondly, another disadvantage of using movieclips as interface elements was their lack of automatic state control. A button has three keyframes for each mouse-driven state: up, over, and down. A movieclip has no such automation, so you'd have to write code for each event to tell it to go to the appropriate keyframe.

The third problem was that movieclips don't have ActionScript commands to change the mouse cursor from an arrow into a pointing hand. This became a problem if the cursor hovered over a movieclip acting as a button, because the user had no indication about whether he or she could click on the movieclip.

The source file for both Figures 12.1 and 12.2 is available as the file "01_Flash5_Example.fla" as part of the downloadable files for this chapter. It's saved as a Flash 5 file, but you can still open it with Flash MX.

Flash 5 Legacy: Button Events

Figure 12.2 shows an example of button events written in Flash 5. Here, the Actions panel is opened after selecting the button on stage. Regular buttons support a different set of event-handlers, and these event-handlers are only triggered if the mouse cursor is positioned within the hit area of the button. A button consists of four keyframes, three of which contain the graphics for each of its three states:

- `Up`—Mouse is released or away from the button
- `Over`—Mouse is hovering over the button, but not pressed
- `Down`—Mouse is pressed down over the button

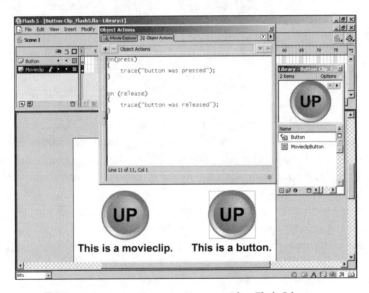

Figure 12.2 Detecting mouse events with a Flash 5 button.

The fourth keyframe is the `Hit` keyframe. Graphics contained within the `Hit` keyframe are used by the button to check for overlapping with the mouse cursor. If the mouse cursor isn't positioned within the shape of the button's `Hit` keyframe contents, then the button's event-handlers won't activate.

In Flash 5, buttons had a huge disadvantage over movieclips because buttons didn't share any of the useful functionality offered by movieclips. For example, you couldn't define an `onClipEvent(enterFrame)` handler for a button to execute code continuously. You also couldn't create animation inside a button due to its four-keyframe structure, though it's common for designers to place movieclip animations into the keyframes of the button states.

In terms of Flash applications, Flash 5 buttons presented a significant obstacle for disabling buttons and indicating their enabled/disabled/selected/ unselected states. Most often, developers simply put buttons inside a movieclip and moved the movieclip to different keyframes to enable/disable buttons.

Better Code Placement in Flash MX Versus Flash 5

Macromedia always makes sure that newer versions of Flash players are backward compatible. Therefore, Flash MX supports the writing of event-handlers directly onto instances of movieclips and buttons, the same way as Flash 5. This approach probably makes more sense to newer Flash users because the event-handler is directly linked with the object that owns it. For anyone beyond the beginner's level, this approach scatters the code too much, making it difficult to use.

Although this brief review of Flash 5 movieclips and buttons helped clarify why clip events and button events exist in Flash MX, remember that just because you can write events directly onto a movieclip instance or button instance doesn't mean you should! Instead, try to define all your event-handlers within the keyframe.

Here's an example of an event-handler for a movieclip's `MouseDown` event, written as an `onClipEvent()`. The only way to write this code in Flash 5 and Flash MX is to Option-click or right-click on the movieclip to open the Actions panel:

```
onClipEvent(mouseDown)
{   trace("Mouse was pressed");
}
```

*An **onClipEvent( )** event-handler, written in Flash 5 style.*

A better way is to define the event-handler from within a keyframe. Flash MX event-handlers follow a similar naming convention, adding an "on" prefix to the name of the event, such as `onMouseDown` or `onRollOver`. You can define the event-handler inside the movieclip's keyframe:

```
this.onMouseDown = function()
{   trace("Mouse was pressed");
}
```

*An **onMouseDown** event-handler defined in Flash MX from inside the movieclip's keyframe.*

You can also define the event-handler by referencing the movieclip instance from another timeline:

```
container.innerMovieclip.onMouseDown = function()
{   trace("Mouse was pressed");
}
```

*An **onMouseDown** event-handler defined in Flash MX from a timeline outside the movieclip.*

Most advanced Flash MX developers avoid writing event-handlers directly onto instances, because Flash MX provides a better alternative by allowing you to define event-handlers for an object from inside a keyframe. Because you can access any object and define its event-handlers from a keyframe, you can now move most of your code into a few important keyframes. This organization makes the code much easier to locate and edit. The code also becomes easier to understand because you can read related code by scrolling up and down in the Actions panel, rather than hunting through event-handlers scattered among different instances.

Many advanced ActionScript programmers store all their code entirely inside the first keyframe of the main Timeline. It's a very tidy approach, but certain scenarios, such as building components, require ActionScript to be stored in the movieclip's own Timeline.

What's a Button Movieclip?

If you refer to Table 12.1, you'll see that the movieclip object now supports all the button event-handlers as well. We've already shown that button event-handlers are more appropriate for detecting mouse events against a specific hit area, but buttons are missing much of the functionality from movieclips. So, the next logical step is to explore how to use a movieclip as a button to gain the best of both worlds. With Flash MX, you can have your movieclip cake and eat the button frosting too!

Adding button behaviors to a movieclip is simply a matter of defining a button event-handler inside a movieclip. Take a look at Table 12.1 again; any event-handler listed in the Button column can be defined for a movieclip to activate button-like behaviors. These movieclips are commonly known as button movieclips, even though they're just movieclips.

For the rest of this chapter, the term "button movieclip" refers to a movieclip whose button behavior is activated because one of its button event-handlers has been defined in ActionScript.

So how do we define these event-handlers from inside a keyframe? Let's walk through a quick example.

A Simple Button Movieclip

Open the file 02_FlashMX_SimpleButtonClip.fla for an example of activating button behaviors in a movieclip. In the new demo file, you'll see the same blue button from the previous Flash 5 example. All the clip events from the movieclip have been deleted so that you can start from scratch.

Select the movieclip with your mouse, and give it an instance name of BigButton in the Property Inspector. Now that it has an instance name, you can start using ActionScript to define BigButton's event-handlers. Select the empty keyframe in the Script: layer of the main Timeline, and open the Actions panel. Insert the following code into the keyframe:

```
BigButton.onRollOver = function()
{
}
```

onRollOver event-handler defined for the BigButton movieclip.

The snippet of code simply defines onRollOver as a function in BigButton. Because BigButton is actually a movieclip, it recognizes that a button event-handler has been defined, and then activates the button behavior. Press Ctrl-Enter or use the Control, Test Movie command in the pull-down menu to test this movie. Run your mouse cursor over the movieclip, and notice how the mouse cursor turns into a pointing hand cursor whenever it rolls over the movieclip.

That's all! The event-handler doesn't even have to be defined. As long as the movieclip has as a function declared with the same name as any of the listed event-handlers, the movieclip will start behaving like a button, even if the function has an empty definition (that is, even if the function doesn't do anything).

A Complete Button Movieclip

You know from Table 12.1 that movieclips support all the event-handlers of buttons, but what about the four special keyframes? Movieclips also support the three button states and hit area, but in a slightly different manner. To define states for up, over, and down, we'll have to make some small additions to the BigButton Timeline. If you want to skip ahead to the final result, check out the file 03_FlashMX_CompleteButtonClip.fla.

1. Using the previous example file, double-click on the BigButton movieclip to edit its contents.

   The movieclip should only have two layers at this point: Text and Graphics. Create two more layers, named Script: and Labels. You could put all your ActionScript inside the keyframes of the Labels layer, but separating script from other layers makes your code easier to manage.

2. Drag your mouse vertically across all the layers at frame 5, and press F6 to create new keyframes at frame 5. Repeat the same step at frame 10.

   Now, you should have three columns of keyframes at frames 0, 5, and 10 (see Figure 12.3). These three columns of keyframes represent the up, over, and down states of the button movieclip. A movieclip activated as a button recognizes those keyframes as proper states if you give them special frame labels.

   In the Labels layer, give the first keyframe a label name of _Up, name the next keyframe _Over, and name the last keyframe _Down. Be sure you use an underscore for the first character of the frame label! Otherwise, the movieclip won't recognize those keyframes as button states.

3. The final step is to change the contents of each keyframe so that the user sees some indication about the state of the button movieclip, as the mouse rolls over or presses down on it.

   In the final demo file, 03_FlashMX_CompleteButton.fla, I've simply changed the textfield to reflect the state of the button movieclip.

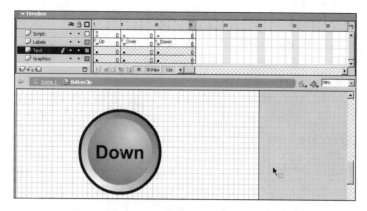

Figure 12.3   Create four keyframes for the button movieclip.

If you test the movie at this point, you see that the movieclip starts to play through all the keyframes automatically, until the mouse rolls over the movieclip. Remember, the button movieclip is still just a movieclip, so it will start playing through the timeline by default. You have to add a `stop()` command in the first keyframe of the Script: layer. Every time a button event-handler is triggered, the movieclip executes the equivalent of three possible `gotoAndStop` methods:

```
onRelease, onReleaseOutside, onRollOut, onDragOut, gotoAndStop("_up")

OnRollOver, gotoAndStop("_over")

onPress, onDragOver, gotoAndStop("_down")
```

Now the button movieclip has three keyframes for each button state, but you are still missing a keyframe for the hit area of a button. The hit area for a button movieclip is created by defining the `movieclip.hitArea` property as a reference to some movieclip instance inside the main movieclip. You can also assign an instance name of `hitArea` to the intended movieclip if you want to define the `hitArea` by default. The `hitArea` movieclip remains active even if you set the movieclip's alpha transparency to 0 or set its `_visible` property to `false`. Remember that a button movieclip is still just a movieclip with button behaviors, so the button movie clip's Timeline can contain any number of movieclip instances to serve as a hit area.

A Complete Button Movieclip with *hitArea*

Let's continue with the BigButton example to define a `hitArea` property. If you want to see the final result, check out the file 04_ButtonClip_HitArea.fla.

1. First, clear out all the keyframes in the Graphics layer, except for the first keyframe. You can select any part of the movieclip to act as a `hit area`, but it has to be a movieclip instance first. Select the blue sphere, press F8 to convert it into a movieclip, and give the new movieclip an instance name of "innerSphere." Select the outer gray ring, convert it into a movieclip, and give the new movieclip and instance name of "outerRing."

2. Now you've got two movieclips inside the BigButton movieclip, so all you have to do is choose one movieclip and assign a reference to it as the `BigButton.hitArea` property. Add the following code into the main timeline:

    ```
    BigButton.onRollOver = function()
    {
    }
    BigButton.hitArea = BigButton.innerSphere;
    ```

    BigButton's *hitArea changes when mouse rolls over.*

3. If you test the code, you'll see that the button movieclip only senses the mouse cursor when the cursor hovers over the area of the inner sphere movieclip. Try changing the last line of code to target the outerRing movieclip:

    ```
    BigButton.onRollOver = function()
    {
    }
    BigButton.hitArea = BigButton.outerRing;
    ```

    Set the **BigButton**'s **hitArea** *to the outerRing movieclip.*

Now the button movieclip is only sensitive to the mouse cursor over the outerRing movieclip's shape. If the `hitArea` property hasn't been declared, then the entire contents of the button movieclip will act as the default hit area.

Interesting Techniques with *hitArea*

The hitArea property gives you an incredible amount of control over the hit area of a button movieclip. For example, open the file 05_Shift_HitAreas.fla to see two changing hit areas. Here, BigButton's innerSphere movieclip animates with a shape tween, and the shape tween constantly changes the hit area of the button movieclip.

The other button movieclip to the right contains a dynamic textfield with the Show Border Around Text option enabled. The textfield has the instance name "label," and code in the main timeline defines the label button's hit area:

```
LabelButton.onPress = function()
{   trace("Label Button was pressed");
}
LabelButton.hitArea = LabelButton.label;
```

Movieclip uses a textfield as the hit area.

A Note on Reusability

Until now, we've defined the hit area in the keyframe of the Timeline that contains the movieclip/button movieclip. The ActionScript for setting the hitArea property can also be stored inside the first keyframe of the button movieclip. This defines the hit area for the movieclip even if it's not activated by any defined button event-handlers. Such an approach gives all instances of the movieclip a default hit area, and you can always override the property by redefining the hitArea reference at any time.

If you're just looking for a simple customizable button, I highly recommend using either the Push Button component, or the Icon Button component. The Push Button component comes with Flash MX software as part of the Flash UI Components Set, and the Icon Button component can be freely downloaded from http://www.macromedia.com/exchange as part of the Flash UI Components Set 2.

Toggling Hand Cursors for Buttons and Movieclips

So far, we've demonstrated that defining a button event-handler on a movieclip activates button-like behaviors in the movieclip. One of these button behaviors is the ability to change the mouse cursor to a hand cursor when the mouse hovers over the button movieclip. It's possible to disable the change to a hand cursor by setting a useHandCursor property to false. This property is available for both buttons and movieclips.

The example file, 06_ToggleHandCursor.fla, demonstrates how to use one button to toggle the useHandCursor property. The button on the left is a button movieclip that contains two keyframes, "on" and "off" with corresponding text labels. It has an instance name of "toggle." The button on the right is the same BigButton movieclip from previous examples. It has the same instance name of "BigButton." Figure 12.4 shows the Timeline of the LabelButton movieclip.

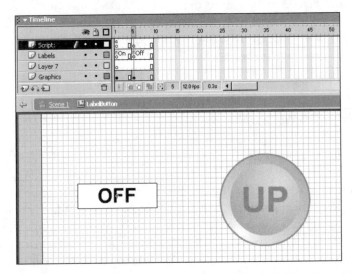

Figure 12.4 Timeline for the Toggle movieclip in 06_ToggleHandCursor.fla.

Aside from a stop() command in the first keyframe of both button movieclips, all the code for this example is stored inside the first keyframe of the main Timeline:

```
toggle.onRelease = function()
{
    var isFirstFrame = (this._currentframe == 1)
    this._parent.BigButton.useHandCursor = !isFirstFrame;

    if(isFirstFrame)
    {
        this.gotoAndStop(5);
    } else {
        this.gotoAndStop(1);
    }
}

bigButton.onRelease = function()
{   trace("You clicked on Big Button");
}
```

Code for the file 06_ToggleHandCursor.fla.

The first part of the code defines a "release" event-handler for the Toggle button movieclip. Clicking on the Toggle button movieclip triggers this event-handler to assign a `True` or `False` Boolean value to a variable called `isFirstFrame`, depending on whether the movieclip is on frame 1. The value of `isFirstFrame` is then assigned to the `useHandCursor` property of the `BigButton` button movieclip. Note that all code inside a movieclip's event-handler definition actually exists inside the movieclip's scope. So, the reference to this actually refers to the movieclip.

```
this._parent.BigButton.useHandCursor = !isFirstFrame;
```

If the movieclip is playing at the first keyframe, set `useHandCursor` to `false`, otherwise set it to `true`.

Depending on the value of the `isFirstFrame`, the button movieclip will toggle back and forth between frame 1 and frame 5, switching the text label "On" and "Off."

Try running the example and you'll notice that the code toggles the mouse cursor's ability to change into a hand cursor when rolling over the big button (see Figures 12.5 and 12.6).

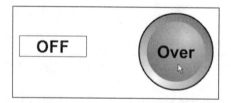

Figure 12.5 Mouse hovering over button with hand cursor disabled.

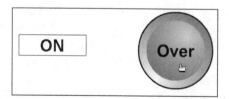

Figure 12.6 Mouse hovering over button with hand cursor enabled.

Scoping Confusion with Button Event-Handlers

There's an interesting story about how the previous snippet of code references the BigButton button movieclip. Note how the reference to BigButton is prefaced with the syntax `this._parent`.

```
this._parent.BigButton
```

Because the code defines an event-handler function for the toggle movieclip, the keyword `this` refers to the object that contains the event-handler. Here, the keyword `this` refers to the toggle movieclip. The keyword `_parent` refers to the parent Timeline of the toggle movieclip, which contains both the `toggle` movieclip and the BigButton movieclip.

There's something we should explain about how ActionScript handles scoping for functions (thanks to Andreas Heim for clearing this up). Let's see what happens if you define a function within one scope, such as _root, and then execute it as a reference from another scope.

```
identity = "main timeline";
this.releaseHandler = function()
{    trace(this);
    trace("First try: " + identity);
    trace("Second try: " + this.identity);
}

foo.identity = "Inside the movieclip";
foo.onRelease = this.releasehandler;
```

*Define **releaseHandler** function in the main Timeline, execute from inside the foo movieclip.*

In the hypothetical example shown here, all the code exists on the main Timeline. You start by defining a variable named `identity` with a value of `main timeline`. Then, you define a function named `releaseHandler`. You also define a property named `identity` within the foo movieclip. Then, you take a movieclip with an instance name of `foo`, and assign its `onRelease` event-handler as a reference to the main Timeline's `releaseHandler()` function.

If you run the code, you'll see three trace statements in the Output window after clicking on the foo movieclip button:

```
_level0.foo
First try: main timeline
Second try: Inside the movieclip
```

The first `trace` statement outputs the value of `this`, which refers to the Timeline in which the `releaseHandler()` method is defined. As you can see from the output `_level0.foo`, clicking on the button executes the function within the scope in which it was originally defined.

The second `trace` statement outputs the value of the `identity` variable. Even though this code is executed by the `foo` movieclip, the function will retrieve variables within the scope in which it's defined (in this case, the main Timeline).

If you want to make any references within the scope of the object that called the function, you have to prefix the reference with `this`. The third `trace` statement will output the value of the `foo.identity` property because you forced the variable reference `this.identity` to look up the property in the calling object. In this case, `foo` has called the function, so the reference `this.identity` forces the function to look up a variable named `identity` within the calling object of `foo`. Without the `this` prefix, the function would look in the main Timeline, rather than inside the movieclip.

When To Disable Hand Cursors

Try using your mouse to interact with a web browser. Scroll up, drag the scroll tab around, or press any of the window buttons. You'll see that the mouse cursor keeps its arrow icon. Now, try moving the mouse over any hyperlink on a web page, and you'll notice that the mouse cursor changes into a hand cursor.

The mouse cursor is a consistent feature in most user interfaces, including operating systems and graphical applications. Most of the time, standard user interface elements like scrollbars, menus, and buttons do not use hand cursors. The Flash UI components (scrollbars, listboxes, and so on.) also apply the `useHandCursor` property to disable hand cursors, so that the Flash UI components have a more familiar look and feel. Switching to a hand cursor is most appropriate for indicating the purpose of a hyperlink, or any kind of graphics in a document that will change the focus of the document viewer. If the hand cursor is disabled, a pop-up tool tip can provide the user with valuable cues for navigating the interface.

There might be other situations that call for the hand cursor to be disabled, so keep this feature in mind when you build your next project! If you need to disable hand cursors for all buttons or all movieclip-buttons, there's a little-known technique that involves setting the `prototype.useHandCursor` property for the `Button` and `MovieClip` classes. For example, you can disable hand cursors for all buttons:

```
Button.prototype.useHandCursor = false;
```

*Set the **useHandCursor** property of the **Button** class prototype so that all instances of the **Button** class will not show a hand cursor.*

And you can disable hand cursors for all movieclips:

```
MovieClip.prototype.useHandCursor = false;
```

Disable hand cursors for all movieclips.

Enabling/Disabling Movieclips and Buttons

Finally, there's also a property for completely disabling and re-enabling the button-behaviors of both movieclips and buttons. The name of this property is simply called `enabled`. By setting the `enabled` property to `false`, you can disable not only the event-handlers and hand cursors, but also stop the ability to switch between the _up, _over, and _down keyframes.

Give it a try by changing the `useHandCursor` reference to `enabled` in the previous example code:

```
toggle.onRelease = function()
{
    var isFirstFrame = (this._currentframe == 1)
    this._parent.BigButton.enabled = !isFirstFrame;

    if(isFirstFrame)
    {
        this.gotoAndStop(5);
    } else {
        this.gotoAndStop(1);
    }
}

bigButton.onRelease = function()
{   trace("You clicked on Big Button");
}
```

*The toggle button movieclip enables and disables the **useHandCursor** property of the BigButton movieclip.*

Conclusion of Part I: Movieclips Versus Buttons

As you can see from the examples discussed so far, the movieclip object can do all the tasks that the button object can do, once its button behaviors are activated. On the other hand, the button doesn't support a complete timeline or some of the movieclip methods. There's very little reason for using buttons in Flash MX, because button movieclips offer all the features of both objects.

Beginners might find the four-keyframe structure of buttons more convenient, and beginners might also prefer writing code directly onto the button instance in the style of Flash 5. As projects grow increasingly complex, however, the capability to centralize code and leverage the full power of movieclips becomes a more attractive way to build Flash projects.

Part II: Interactivity with Textfields and *ASFunction*

Since Flash 5, textfields have supported HTML formatting, and one of the supported HTML tags is the anchor tag. The capability to create hyperlinks inside textfields can come in handy for document-style content, where you'd want to put URL links directly into the text. We'll spend more time talking about the HTML capabilities of Flash MX in Chapter 13, "Textfield Mangling," so we're more interested in discussing how textfields can behave like buttons and movieclips.

In DHTML, anchor tags also have the capability to hook into JavaScript event-handlers. For example, a hyperlink in DHTML might trigger an alert box through the `onClick` event:

```
<A onClick="alert('New Riders published this book')";>Publisher</A>
```

The hyperlink itself can trigger a JavaScript function call instead of a URL:

```
<a href="JavaScript:alert('New Riders published this book')">Publisher</a>
```

Not many Flash programmers take advantage of the fact that Flash 5/MX supports the latter technique of calling a JavaScript function inside an anchor tag's `href` attribute. This technique offers several advantages when used correctly, and we'll discuss a few scenarios in the next section.

Introducing the *ASFunction*

In the same way, Flash MX textfields support anchor tags with an event-handler that is similar to the onClick event-handler in JavaScript/DHTML. The Flash MX event-handler for hyperlinks is called asfunction, and it only accepts two parameters separated by a comma:

1. The name of the function to be called.
2. A string value passed to the function.

To see an example of asfunction() in action, open the file 08_simple _ASFunction.fla. This file contains two dynamic textfields on the main timeline, with the instance names textfield_1 and textfield_2. When you select either textfield and look at the Property Inspector, you'll see that the textfield has multiline enabled, renders text as HTML, and shows the border around the text.

The first keyframe of the Script: layer on the main Timeline contains the following code:

```
link1 = "<a href='http://www.google.com'><u>Website</u></a> ";
link2 = " - <a href='asfunction:moreinfo,google'><u>Description</u></a>";

textfield_1.htmlText = link1 + link2;

function moreinfo(message)
{
    textfield_2.htmlText = "You clicked on the link " + message;
}
```

*Create HTML anchor tags that will call the **moreInfo( )** function.*

In this code, we've defined two kinds of HTML anchor tags as string variables. The link1 variable contains a regular hyperlink, which takes the user to www.google.com when clicked. The link2 variable contains an asfunction hyperlink, which consists of two parts: the name of the function and the string argument. In this case, an href attribute of asfunction:moreinfo,google calls the function moreinfo() with the argument of google. Note that there's no space between the comma and either parameter.

In this example, the name of the function is moreinfo, and the string argument is google.

Clicking on the hyperlink calls the moreinfo(message) function (see Figure 12.7). After it's called, the moreinfo(message) function receives google as the value for its message argument, and displays a message in the other textfield.

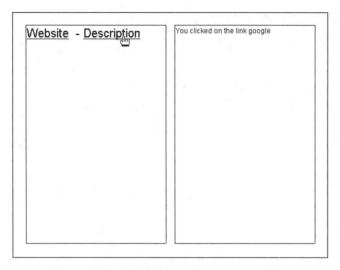

Figure 12.7 Clicking on an ASFunction hyperlink.

Advanced *ASFunction* Techniques

Hyperlinks with the ASFunction event-handler are not as powerful as buttons or movieclips because they only handle the click event. There's no provision for sensing whether the mouse has rolled over the hyperlink, unlike the onMouseOver event-handler for DHTML/JavaScript.

On the other hand, the ASFunction feature can make the generation of list menus very easy and lightweight. The process involves creating an index of pointers in an array, and using those index numbers as references in the ASFunction hyperlink. We highly recommend using the listbox or combobox components for scenarios that require listed menu items, but this technique works well if you want to embed a list of links in the middle of a text document.

Open the file 09_Advanced_ASFunction.fla for a demonstration (see Figure 12.8). The purpose of this Flash movie is to display a list of search engines with two hyperlinks. The first hyperlink goes directly to the website. The second hyperlink, labeled "more info," causes the second textfield to display more information about the search engine. Try it and click on the links!

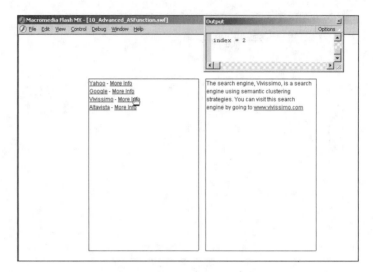

Figure 12.8 Advanced `ASFunction` Demo.

This technique works with any kind of recordset or external data, but we'll use a constructor to generate data objects in this case. The first part of the code simply defines a constructor called `SearchEngine`, and accepts the name, url, and description as parameters:

```
//Constructor for an object that holds data
//about search engines
function SearchEngine(name, url, description)
{
    this.name = name;
    this.url = url;
    this.description = description;
}
```

A simple constructor that creates an object describing a search engine.

The second part of the code actually creates instances of the `SearchEngine` class, and pushes each data object into an array with the variable name of `list`.

```
//Create an array of SearchEngine objects
list = new Array();
list.push(new SearchEngine("Yahoo", "www.yahoo.com",
    "an index of sites on the internet."));
list.push(new SearchEngine("Google", "www.google.com",
    "the most popular search engine."));
```

```
list.push(new SearchEngine("Vivissimo", "www.vivissimo.com",
        "a search engine using semantic clustering strategies"));
list.push(new SearchEngine("Altavista", "www.altavista.com",
          "one of the earliest search engines"));
```

An array of **searchEngine** *objects.*

The third part of the code clears out `textfield_1`. Then, it loops through the list array to populate the textfield with a list of links:

```
//Clear out the textfield
textfield_1.htmlText = "";

//Loop through
for(var i = 0; i < list.length; i++)
{
    var site = list[i];
    var link1 = "<a href='http://" + site.url + "'><u>" + site.name + "</u></a>";
    var link2 = " - <a href='asfunction:moreinfo," + i + "'><u>More
Info</u></a>\n";
    textfield_1.htmlText += link1 + link2;
}
```

Clear the **textfield 1** *and repopulate with HTML hyperlinks.*

Pay special attention to the `asfunction` tag being constructed within the first loop of the code (line 30 in your Actions panel editor):

```
var link2 = " - <a href='asfunction:moreinfo," + i + "'><u>More Info</u></a>\n";
```

An anchor tag that calls the **moreInfo( )** *function.*

You'll notice that the `asfunction` calls the same function, `moreinfo`, but now it's passing the index number of the list array as the loop runs through the list array's contents. The `asfunction`'s limitation of a single function argument makes it awkward for passing multiple values, so we've created a workaround by simply passing an index to an array element. The index number acts as a key to the entire data object array, to be retrieved and reformatted by the `moreinfo` function into a message for the second textfield:

```
//Display more information about a search engine
function moreinfo(index)
{
    trace("index = " + index);
```

continues

```
//Grab the name, url, and description from the info object
var name = list[index].name;
var url = list[index].url;
var description = list[index].description;

//Create the output message with HTML formatting
str = "The search engine, " + name + ", is " + description;
str += ". You can visit this search engine by going to ";
str += "<a href='http://" + url + "'><u>" + url + "</u></a>";

//Send the output message to the textfield
textfield_2.htmlText = str;

} // moreinfo
```

The **moreInfo** *function populates textfield 2 with more information about a selected search engine.*

Again, we'd like to answer a common question: No, `asfunction` hyperlinks do not have an event-handler for mouse-over events. One possible solution only works with single-line textfields, which brings us to the next topic, mixing textfields and movieclips. We'd like to answer another common question: Dynamically generated anchor tags in Flash MX will not automatically show as underlined text like the default HTML formatting in web browsers. To indicate an active hyperlink, you'll have to manually add some `<u></u>` underline tags, or change the font's color, bold, or italic with HTML tags.

Textfield Collision Detection

If you look at Table 12.3, near the beginning of this chapter, you'll see that textfields now share the same positioning, resizing, and rescaling properties as movieclips. However, a textfield does not have any of the button event-handlers that a movieclip or button would offer, or any of the powerful movieclip methods for getting bounds with `getBounds()` or performing collision detection with `hitTest()`.

It's possible to add mouse event listeners to a textfield with the intention of giving it button-like behaviors (assuming you have a dynamic textfield on stage with an instance name of `myfield`). For example, check out the following code from the file 10_CollisionDetectionWithTextfields.fla:

```
Mouse.addListener(myfield);
myfield.onMouseDown = function()
{
    //Collision detection
```

```
var mouseX = this._xmouse;
var mouseY = this._ymouse;
if(mouseX <= this._width && mouseX >= 0 &&
   mouseY <= this._height && mouseY >= 0)
{
   trace("Clicked on myfield");
}
}
```

Add the `myfield` *textfield as a listener for mouse events.*

Mouse click detection poses a problem with the textfield object, because it has neither `getBounds()` nor `hitTest()` for collision detection. The textfield object also does not support hand cursors or keyframes for button states (`_up`, `_down`, `_over`). So, you have to write your own code to detect whether the mouse is overlapping with the textfield area when clicked, taking advantage of the fact that textfields have `x`, `y`, `width/height` and `Mouse` position properties:

```
var mouseX = this._xmouse;
var mouseY = this._ymouse;
if(mouseX <= this._width && mouseX >= 0 &&
   mouseY <= this._height && mouseY >= 0)
{
   trace("Clicked on textfield");
}
```

Collision detection between the mouse and the textfield to see if the mouse cursor overlaps with the textfield area.

A simple solution would nest the textfield inside a button or a movieclip symbol. (An even simpler solution would be to use the Push Button component from the Flash UI Component set.) Right now, discussing how to mix textfields with movieclips and buttons will help uncover some important tips.

Problems with Nesting Textfields Inside Buttons

Nesting a textfield inside a button can lead to some confusion because the button does not contain a real timeline. Therefore, referring to a textfield inside a button only works by referring to the textfield's variable name within the scope of the Timeline that contains the button. Referring to the instance name of the textfield will not work in any scope if the textfield exists inside a button.

Check out the file 11_TextfieldInsideButton.fla. Here, we have a button with an instance name of "button." The button contains a textfield with an instance name of "textfield" and a text variable name of "textvariable." Three different lines of code attempt to set the value of the textfield inside the button, but only one approach works:

1. You cannot set textfield value by referring to `textfield.text` in button, because all the button's contents exist within the scope of the main Timeline.

    ```
    button.textfield.text += "Attempt One";
    ```

2. Even though all contents are in the scope of the main Timeline, you still cannot refer directly to the nested textfield in the button:

    ```
    textfield.text += "Attempt Two";
    ```

3. The only way is to refer to the textfield's variable name, in the style of Flash 5 ActionScript:

    ```
    textvariable += "Attempt Three";
    ```

Again, scoping problems encountered with nested textfields inside buttons are just another example of the button's legacy functionality, left over from Flash 5 technology. It's also another reason for avoiding buttons in Flash MX and sticking to the more versatile button movieclip.

General Problems with Nested Textfields

Certain scenarios call for embedding textfields inside a movieclip or button symbol. When you've nested a dynamic textfield inside a button movieclip or a regular button, there are times when you might want to change the alpha, masking, distortion, or rotation of the movieclip/button. The textfield will not react predictably if you try to make any of those three changes, unless the font outlines are embedded with the Flash movie.

For example, setting the alpha property of a movieclip or button below 100% will not change the alpha of the inner textfield. The text simply shows up in its default color. To enable alpha settings for the textfield, embed the font outlines by selecting the textfield in the movieclip/button, press the Character button in the Property Inspector, and choose one of the embed font options.

The textfield also renders in default size and font if you try to distort the container movieclip, or rotate it with either ActionScript or the Rotation tool. If the movieclip or button is masked, the textfield will not show up at all in the Flash player. Again, the solution to all these problems is to embed font outlines for the textfield. Because non-embedded fonts use the operating system (Windows, Mac OS) to render system fonts, Flash is not able to manipulate them. Therefore, you have to embed a font for Flash to gain control over the rendering of text as vectors.

Conclusion of Part II: Interactivity with Textfields

As shown in Table 12.3, textfields now support all the positioning, dimension, scaling, visibility, and mouse position properties. These properties were only previously available for the movieclip in Flash 5.

Even though textfields support many of the movieclip's properties, it has limited functionality in terms of interacting with the user via mouse. We'll discuss more advanced ways to enable keyboard interactivity with the textfield in the next chapter on the Textfield object. As a navigation element, however, textfields are mostly limited to hyperlinks and `asfunction` calls. The `asfunction` provides a useful feature for placing large amounts of click-handling links within a large body of text. Aside from the `asfunction`, however, textfields do not work well as interactive labels, for which movieclips or the Flash UI button components are more appropriate.

Conclusion

Hopefully, this chapter has given you a better sense of the subtle nuances between all three Flash MX objects. Feel free to compare the events, methods, and properties of all three objects by printing out the tables from the chapter files.

Based on the limitations and features we've covered so far, it's safe to say that the movieclip object offers the most benefits by far, and should be used whenever possible instead of buttons. When compared to movieclips, buttons don't offer much more than a subset of the movieclip's capabilities. On the other hand, movieclips offer all the benefits of the button symbol, on top of all the control features of the movieclip object. Button symbols might appear more intuitive than button movieclips, but using buttons will paint you into a corner if you want more functionality from the button that is only available in movieclips. On the other hand, the versatility of button movieclips make them the most important building block in a Flash developer's knowledge base.

Last but not least, the textfield has also grown in versatility and power, but it often lacks the interactive features found in buttons and movieclips. Textfields are better suited for the formatting and display of textual information. In the next chapter, we'll discuss textfield manipulation techniques, and continue addressing some of the ideas from this chapter, such as pop-up tool tips and dynamically created/positioned textfields.

13

Textfield Mangling

By Samuel Wan

Text Is King

Note: This personal anecdote was written by Branden Hall.

When I was in high school, I was part of the journalism club. I'm not quite sure why I decided to join, but I've always been very happy that I did. You see, unlike most other high school newspapers, we handled every part of production except for the actual printing, and even then we were at the plant when the paper was printed.

This means that as a section editor, I got to do a lot of different jobs. Sure I did editing, but I also spent a lot of my time working on layout. My problem was that I would get so enamored with laying out my pages in a "cool" way I would often accidentally chop off stories and have to fix the problem at the last minute—usually at the expense of my "cool" layouts.

Because the kind of mistakes I was making were becoming more and more common with the editors, our advisor got some books on newspaper writing and layout. She then spent a few weeks working through it with us. The one lesson I will never forget from one of those books was that before everything else, the text is king. This fact, it turns out, is true in many mediums—especially the web where text can both be read and manipulated. It doesn't matter how cool your site or application is—if the text isn't usable, you are sunk.

Introduction

Text is how, for the most part, we communicate on the web. Because of this, it's simply not possible to overstate the importance of the textfield object in Flash MX. In this chapter, you will learn just about everything there is to know about textfields. This includes focus/selection, formatting, and dynamic creation and manipulation of textfields.

Text on the Web

Before we dive into the new Flash MX `TextField` object, I'd like to put things in perspective by discussing the role of text on the web. In using the word "text," I'm not referring to books, paragraphs, or even sentences. I'm actually referring to "text" as a standard for encoding information according to a predefined character set.

The Value of Text-Based Information

If you're reading this book, then you're already familiar with at least one character set: the Roman alphabet. Other character sets include Chinese characters, Japanese characters, and so on. These are all standard sets of characters which large groups of people (sometimes billions of people) have agreed to use for encoding, storing, and sharing nonverbal information.

Standard character sets, such as the alphabet, can make information very valuable if many people can read that character set. If we had written this book with Egyptian hieroglyphics, nobody would be able to read our book except for a few Egyptologists. A book written in hieroglyphics would have little value for anyone else. However, we've written this book in clear English, so the value of this book increases with the number of people who can read English. In other words, a standard becomes more valuable as more people start to use it; modern economists refer to this phenomenon as the "Network Externality Effect."

However, standards have a hidden cost. If we ever wanted to translate this book into Japanese, we would have to rewrite every word as a Japanese symbol, which would take a lot of time and resources. Most programming books are written in English, and the cost of translating a book into less widely used languages sometimes outweighs the benefits. As a result, many technical books are written in English and not translated into other languages. Economists refer to this phenomenon of sticking with the most popular standard as the "Lock-In Effect." The cost of switching to a different standard is known as the "Switching Cost."

At this point, we've covered the following concepts:

- **Network externality effect.** The value of a standard increase, with number of people who subscribe to that standard.

- **Lock-in effect**. People tend to stick with the current popular standard.

- **Switching cost**. Switching to another standard requires time, effort, and other resources.

> For more information on computer character sets, read the article "A Brief History of Character Codes" by Steven J. Searle at `http://tronweb.super-nova.co.jp/characcodehist.html`

Alternatives to HTML: Usefulness Is Important!

So why are we bringing economics into a chapter about Flash MX textfields? Well, consider how the World Wide Web began with a text-based markup language known as HTML. The web evolved on top of HTML, and new web technologies evolved in parallel. Today, most web sites still display information in HTML format.

A lot of human effort has gone into developing superior alternatives, and most of these superior technologies are somehow related to XML. However, HTML has developed such a strong network effect that the act of switching to another standard is too costly for both consumers and software developers. Something will eventually replace HTML. Maybe a group of separate technologies will replace HTML in separate situations. For example, it's plausible that the Flash .swf format could become standard for web application interfaces.

Be careful, however, in assuming that visual interfaces will overthrow the central role of text on the web. Java applet programmers made the same mistake, and probably so did many people with other technologies. We have to understand that people won't adopt a technology until its usefulness outweighs the costs of adopting the technology. You can judge a technology's usefulness based on its ability to solve problems, and when it comes to the Internet, solving problems mostly involves the handling of text-based information. If you can develop Flash applications that manipulate text information better than HTML applications, then your services will become more valuable to other people. That's the bottom line on the importance of learning ActionScript for textfields.

Advantages of Flash MX Textfields

I've argued that Flash applications can be more valuable than HTML applications if they can handle text more flexibly and efficiently. So let's talk about some specific advantages of textfields in Flash MX. If you're going to use Flash MX instead of HTML for a complex interface, there are several categories of features you can exploit:

- Interactivity with event-handling
- Dynamic formatting
- Dynamic creation, resizing, and positioning
- Basic HTML formatting
- Scrolling

For the rest of this chapter, we'll go through each of these categories and talk about the most useful ActionScript techniques you can perform with the `TextField` object.

Interactivity

There are two ways to interact with an HTML web page: You can either reload the page after every click and render the page differently with server-side script, or you can use JavaScript to change the content of the web page. Interactivity through server-side scripts is incredibly inefficient because the browser has to reload the entire contents of a web page at every step. JavaScript manipulation (that is, DHTML) involves a lot of complex scripting with forms or layers nested deep inside the Document Object Model.

Chapter 12, "Blurring the Line," provides some perspective on how textfields compare with other Flash MX objects such as movieclips and buttons. If you haven't read that chapter yet, you might want to go through the last half of the chapter to get a sense of when and where to use textfields.

Flash has a huge advantage over HTML in terms of interactivity because the event-handling system is much more versatile, and the user can receive instant feedback through animation or sound. The `TextField` object supports four important event-handlers: `onSetFocus`, `onKillFocus`, `onScroller`, `onChanged`. The problem is that these events are JavaScript based; hence you have to deal with numerous differences between browsers, not to mention people who have JavaScript turned off.

onSetFocus and *onKillFocus*

The first two events are used to trigger code when a textfield gains or loses keyboard focus. Both dynamic textfields and input textfields can gain focus in three ways:

1. The user selects the textfield with a mouse-click.

2. Some ActionScript code calls the `Selection.setFocus(field)` method with "field" being a reference to the textfield's instance name.

3. The user presses the Tab key until the textfield gains focus.

Once an input textfield gains focus, the user can start typing into the textfield. Even though a dynamic textfield can gain focus and allow text highlighting/selection, only the input textfield accepts keystroke entries at runtime.

> Flash MX input textfields support cutting, copying, and pasting. You can cut, copy, or paste either by right-clicking on a textfield for options, or by using the standard keyboard shortcuts: Ctrl+X, Ctrl+C or Ctrl+V on a Windows PC and Command+X, Command+C or Command+V on a Macintosh.

Event-handlers for gaining or losing focus come in handy for many situations. For example, you can build an intelligent form to provide tips to the user, depending on which textfield the user's working in. Open the file 01_Focus.fla for this chapter, and we'll go through an example of a smart form.

Introducing a Smart Form Field

In the file 01_Focus.fla, there are two layers: one for ActionScript and one containing all the textfields. This Flash movie represents an online application form to get into a cooking school. Textfields in the left half of the form are input textfields, so that the user can type into them. The big textfield to the right is a dynamic textfield with the name output_txt, and it displays tips about the input field currently in use. Try running this example file and click on the Name input field. As soon as the cursor appears, a hint on the right-side panel suggests what to type into the machine (see Figure 13.1).

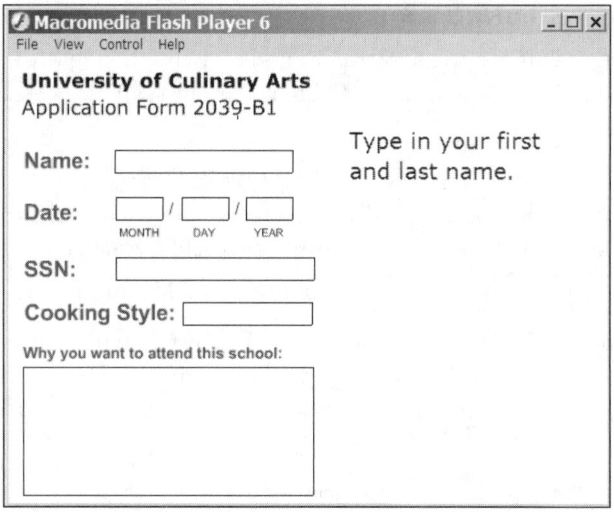

Figure 13.1   A hint shows up when the cursor focuses on the name_txt textfield.

Each textfield in this movie has an instance name ending with the characters "_txt". As I mentioned in Chapter 1, "Starting Off on the Right Foot," the Actions panel will pop-up hints if you use a special naming convention. In this case, ending any variable with "_txt" will pop up a list of methods and properties for the `TextField` object.

The first textfield next to the Name label has an instance name of name_txt. Let's take a look at the code to handle the onSetFocus event for this textfield. Open the Actions panel for the first keyframe, and check out the ActionScript:

```
function show(message){
        output_txt.text = message;
}
name_txt.onSetFocus = function()
{
        show("Type in your first and last name.");
}
name_txt.onKillFocus = function()
{
        show("");
}
```

Here, we've created a show function that receives a message parameter, and assigns the message value to the text of the output_txt textfield object. When you click on the name_txt textfield, it receives focus, and the setFocus event-handler is triggered:

```
name_txt.onSetFocus = function()
{
        show("Type in your first and last name.");
}
```

Once triggered, the event-handler calls the show function with the message Type in your first and last name. If you're new to Flash MX, you'll notice that we're passing a string value to output_txt.text, rather than simply setting the value of output_txt. In earlier versions of Flash, textfields had variable names instead of instance names, and changing the value of a variable would change the contents of the textfield.

In Flash MX, however, textfields are complete objects rather than variables, so the text property provides access to the contents of the textfield. You can still give the textfield a variable name by typing in a name in the Var field of the Property Inspector. However, using variable names to control a textfield will only give you control over the content of the field, while an instance name gives you control over all the textfield objects' methods and properties.

The final event handler defined, onKillFocus, is triggered when the textfield no longer has keyboard focus and the cursor disappears and fires before a new onSetFocus is triggered. This event handler calls the show("") function and passes it an empty string to clear the output panel.

```
name_txt.onKillFocus = function()
{
        show("");
}
```

A Complete Smart Form

If we had to define new event-handlers and hints for every textfield in this form, the ActionScript code would grow very long, and typing in all the code would be a tedious chore. As usual, anytime you find yourself performing a repetitive task, a better solution probably exists.

Open the file 02_CompleteFocusHandlers.fla. Test this movie, and try clicking into different textfields. You'll notice that all the textfields will pop up hints now. Believe it or not, it only took a few lines of code to define event-handlers and hints for all the textfields!

```
function show(message)
{
    output_txt.text = message;
}


//Create an associative array of textfield instance names
//and hint messages.
hintList = [];
hintList["name_txt"] = "Type in your first and last name.";
hintList["month_txt"] = "Type in the 2-digit month of your birthdate. For example,
➥type in '03' for March.";
hintList["day_txt"] = "Type in the 2-digit day of your birthdate. For example,
➥type in '20' for the 20th";
hintList["year_txt"] = "Type in the 4-digit year of your birthdate. For example,
➥type in '1978'.";
hintList["ssn_txt"] = "Type in your social security number. Use numbers and dashes
➥between groups of numbers.";
hintList["style_txt"] = "Please specify the cooking style you'd like to major
➥in.";
hintList["essay_txt"] = "Please describe your reasons for applying to this school,
➥and your aspirations as a chef.";


//Loop through all the elements in the array
for(var n in hintList)
{
    //Use the hash key to create a reference to the textfield
    var fieldRef = this[n];

    //Define a hint property in the textfield with the value
    //of the hintList element.
    fieldRef.hint = hintList[n];

    //When the textfield gains focus, trigger the show function
    //with the message of the textfield's hint property
    fieldRef.onSetFocus = function()
    {
        show(this.hint);
    }
    //When the textfield loses focus, clear the output
     fieldRef.onKillFocus = function()
    {
        show("");
    }
}
```

This strategy allows you to apply similar event-handlers for multiple textfields in a few lines of code. The first lines of code consist of the same `show(message)` function. The next few lines of code define an associative array called `hintList` (refer to the data-structures chapter for more explanation).

The `hintList` associative array, also known as a "hash table," uses the instance names of textfields as the hash keys, and each corresponding hash value contains the actual hint message. For example, the following line of code creates an element in `hintList` with the value of `Type in your first name and last name`, and it uses a hash key of `name_txt`. Therefore, you can say that

```
hintList["name_txt"] = "Type in your first and last name.";
```

Next, a for-loop runs through all the hash keys in the `hintList` array, and defines a local variable as a reference to the corresponding textfield. The variable `fieldRef` will point to a different textfield after each loop:

```
for(var n in hintList)
{
    //Use the hash key to create a reference to the textfield
    var fieldRef = this[n];
```

The loop also defines a property in the textfield called `hint`, and assigns to it the hint message in the `hintList` array. As the `fieldRef` variable points to each new textfield, you can define event-handlers for `fieldRef`, and thus define event-handlers for all the textfields:

```
    //When the textfield gains focus, trigger the show function
    //with the message of the textfield's hint property
    fieldRef.onSetFocus = function()
    {
        show(this.hint);
    }
    //When the textfield loses focus, clear the output
    fieldRef.onKillFocus = function()
    {
        show("");
    }
}
```

Note the use of the reference `this` in the line `show(this.hint)`. The keyword `this` creates a reference to the object containing the `onSetFocus` event-handler, which is the textfield, and `this.hint` refers to the textfield's hint property defined earlier.

> If you're having trouble using hotkeys to toggle between the Text tool and the Selection tool in Windows, here's a quick tip: Press T for text tool, create a textfield on the stage. Press the Escape key to deselect the textfield (you're still in Text tool mode). Then, if you press the Escape key again, the editor's focus will move into the Property Inspector's font selection box. So be sure you only press Escape once, and then press V to switch to the Selection Arrow tool.

Setting Input Restrictions

Form control in regular HTML requires a lot of JavaScript programming and some nightmarish wrestling with the Document Object Model. It's especially difficult to control the number of characters and types of characters allowed in a textfield.

Fortunately, the Flash MX `TextField` object supports three important properties for setting input field restrictions:

- `maxChars`
- `restrict`
- `password`

Let's start with the `maxChars` property. In the application form, the Month and Day textfields should only accept up to two numbers. You are going to add code to the previous example file, 02_CompleteFocusHandlers.fla, but if you want to see the final code, you can skip ahead to 03_InputRestrictions.fla.

Open the file 02_CompleteFocusHandlers.fla and then open the Actions panel for the first keyframe. You'll add three new lines of code at the bottom of the existing code:

```
//Limit number of characters
m_txt.maxChars = 2;
day_txt.maxChars = 2;
year_txt.maxChars = 4;
```

Okay, so you've set a limit to the number of characters for these three textfields. Try testing this movie to see for yourself! But the instructions say that the user should only enter numbers, so we'll add three more lines of code to restrict the input to numbers:

```
//Restrict input characters
month_txt.restrict = "0-9";
day_txt.restrict = "0-9";
year_txt.restrict = "0-9";
```

The `restrict` property also accepts ranges and exclusions (there are too many details to mention here, check out the Reference panel for more information):

```
month_txt.restrict = "0-9";
```

The `restrict` property restricts input characters to the characters stored in its string value. In this case, input is restricted to the characters 0 to 9. The SSN_txt textfield for social security number should also restrict itself to numbers and dashes:

```
ssn_txt.restrict = "0-9\\-";
```

The SSN_txt textfield should allow the "–" (dash character), but the dash character is used to define ranges, such as 0-9. So, you have to add two backslashes to indicate explicitly that you're allowing the "–" character, rather than simply using it to denote a range of characters (see Figure 13.2).

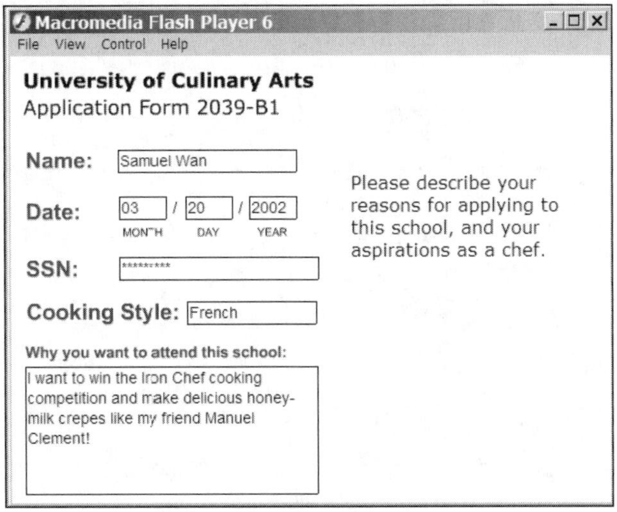

Figure 13.2 Restricted input characters and password masking.

If users don't want other people to see their social security number, you can also set the password property to `true`, so that input characters are shown as "*" characters.

```
ssn_txt.password = true;
```

ActionScript doesn't support regular expressions for form validation. If you're interested in using `regexp`, Pavils Jurjans has written a `RegExp` class in ActionScript. Pavils has made the `RegExp` class available on his web site, `http://www.jurjans.lv/flash/`, along with other interesting textfield-related projects.

Highlight Focus

Before we move on to other event-handlers, I have one more usability trick to show you. In huge forms with lots of textfields, sometimes it's difficult to find your cursor, or to figure out which textfield you're working in. We can modify the `onSetFocus` and `onKillFocus` events to toggle the background color of a textfield, to indicate which textfield is currently active (see Figure 13.3).

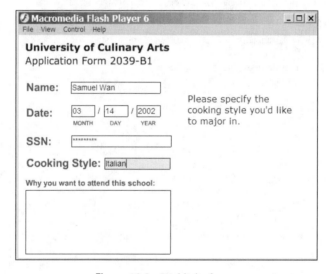

Figure 13.3　Highlight focus.

Here are the modified event-handlers:

```
fieldRef.onSetFocus = function()
{   show(this.hint);
    this.backgroundColor = 0xaaff00;
}
//When the textfield loses focus, clear the output
fieldRef.onKillFocus = function()
{   show("");
    this.backgroundColor = 0xffffff;
}
```

Simply add one line of code to the `onSetFocus` event-handler, which sets the background color of the textfield to a bright green.

```
this.backgroundColor = 0xaaff00;
```

The `backgroundColor` property accepts hexadecimal numbers, identical to HTML colors `#AAFF00`, except for the prefix `0x` instead of `#`. Then, set the background color back to white in the `onKillFocus` event-handler.

```
this.backgroundColor = 0xffffff;
```

So far, we've been able to do things with forms that would require much more effort in DHTML/JavaScript. Let's push the interactivity even further with the `OnChanged` event-handler.

onChanged **Event-Handler**

The `onChanged` event-handler is a function defined in a `TextField` object, and triggered every time the user makes a change to the textfield. For example, open the file 05_onChanged.fla and test the movie. Making any changes to the Cooking Style textfield will cause a reflected text to appear in the big output textfield.

Open the Actions panel for the first keyframe and you'll see some new ActionScript at the bottom of the code:

```
//On Changed Event Handler
style_txt.onChanged = function()
{
    output_txt.text = this.text;
}
```

As in previous event-handlers, you simply have to define the event-handling function and wait for it to be triggered by user input. In this case, the `onChanged` event-handler will grab the text contents of the current textfield, and assign it to the `output_txt` textfield. Try typing some letters into the `style_txt` textfield, and use the delete and backspace keys to change the contents (see Figure 13.4).

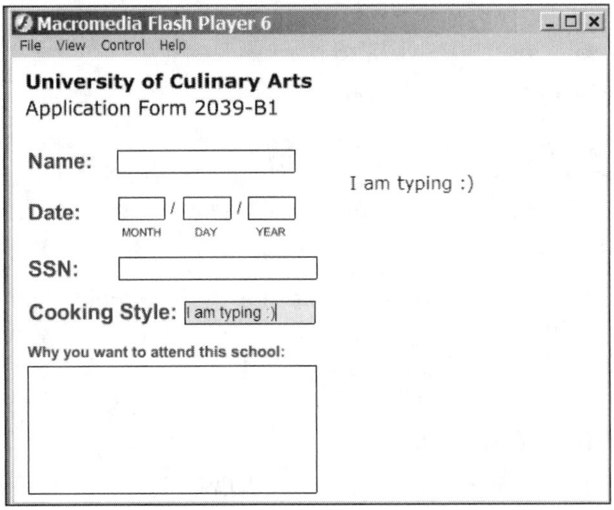

Figure 13.4   OnChanged reflection.

onChanged Event Handling and the *Selection* Object

Now that you can trigger events with user input, you can expand into some advanced techniques to make the textfield even more useful. The first technique introduces the Selection object's getCaretIndex() method.

The Selection object provides access for deciding which textfield has the cursor. In other words, the Selection object allows you to select which textfield will gain focus with ActionScript. It's also a singleton object in the sense that you can't create multiple instances, because the cursor can only focus on one textfield at a time.

The Selection object also has several powerful but little-known methods dealing with the text cursor. You can use the Selection.getCaretIndex() method to retrieve the current position of the text cursor. Two other methods, getBeginIndex() and getEndIndex(), allow you to calculate the span of selected text. I'll explain these last two methods in more detail later.

Right now, let's try grabbing the current position of the cursor. With the example 05_onChanged.fla, adjust the onChanged event handling code like this:

```
style_txt.onChanged = function()
{
    output_txt.text = this.text + newline + newline
            + "CURSOR POSITION: "
            + Selection.getCaretIndex();
}
```

When the user makes any changes to the textfield contents, the event-handler triggers code to send its contents to the `output_txt` textfield. However, this code also adds two carriage returns (`newline`), and then appends the current position of the cursor in the textfield.

```
+ "CURSOR POSITION: "
+ Selection.getCaretIndex();
```

You'll notice that the `Selection` object exists globally, so you can call its methods from any object, in any scope. Now give it a try! Test the movie and type some text into the Cooking Style textfield. Try the Delete and Backspace keys as well.

Use the arrow keys to move your cursor around (see Figure 13.5). Notice how the `onChanged` event-handler doesn't capture arrow keys? That's because you're not making any changes to the textfield contents, just moving the cursor around.

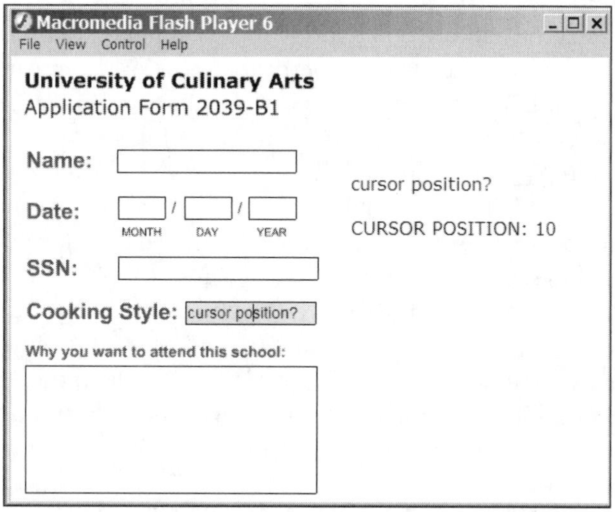

Figure 13.5 Cursor position.

To solve this problem, you'll have to add this textfield as a listener to the Key object. Then, re-route the Key object's onKeyDown event–handler to trigger the onChanged event–handler, so that it's also sensitive to arrow keys:

```
//On Changed Event Handler

style_txt.onChanged = function()
{
    output_txt.text = this.text + newline + newline
                + "CURSOR POSITION: "
                + Selection.getCaretIndex();
}
style_txt.onKeyUp = function()
{
        this.onChanged();
}
Key.addListener(style_txt);
```

Advanced Textfield Example: Simple Word Completion

The onChanged event–handler only works for user input; if you write ActionScript to change the .text property, the onChanged command will not trigger. Regardless, you can use the onChanged event–handler in many imaginative ways to make Flash textfields more useful!

Open the file 07_WordCompletion.fla and test the movie in your Flash editor. Type "French" into the Cooking Style textfield. Did you notice that the textfield tried to guess what you were typing? Press Backspace until you reach the letter "f", and start typing "usion" to spell "fusion." Now the textfield will guess what you're typing even before you've completed the word!

This feature is called word completion. It's possible to implement in DHTML/Javascript, but it's even easier in Flash MX. Open the Actions panel for the first keyframe, and scroll all the way down to the bottom. This file contains some new code for word completion:

```
//Word Completion
styleList = ["french", "fusion", "japanese", "jamaican", "indian", "indonesian",
➥"italian", "cajun", "creole"];
style_txt.onChanged = function()
{
    //Calculate the last position of "real" characters
    //and then check for word match.
    if(Key.getCode() == Key.BACKSPACE || Key.getCode() == Key.DELETEKEY)
    {
        //Erase all "suggested" characters
        //during backspace and delete
        lastPosition = Selection.getCaretIndex();
```

```
        this.text = this.text.substr(0, lastPosition);
    }
    else
    {
        //Check for word match up to the last "real" position
        lastPosition = Selection.getCaretIndex();
        var matchFound = false;
        var capturedText = this.text.substr(0, lastPosition).toLowerCase();
        for(var i = 0; i < styleList.length; i++)
        {
if(capturedText == styleList[i].substr(0, lastPosition))
        {
this.text = styleList[i];
            matchFound = true;
        }
    }

    //If word match isn't found, then remove
    //any "suggested" characters
    if(matchFound == false)
    {
this.text = this.text.substr(0, lastPosition);
    }
    } // if-else
} // onChanged
```

Let's break down the code into smaller pieces for explanation. The first line of code defines an array called styleList, which contains a list of different cooking styles:

```
styleList = ["french", "fusion", "japanese", "jamaican", "indian", "indonesian"];
```

Some of these styles have similar spellings, so that you can test how well the code completion feature really works. The next piece of code defines the onChanged event-handler and assigns the current location of the cursor to the index variable:

```
style_txt.onChanged = function()
{
    //Calculate the last position of "real" characters
    //and then check for word match.
    if(Key.getCode() == Key.BACKSPACE ¦¦ Key.getCode() == Key.DELETEKEY)
    {
        //Erase all "suggested" characters
        //during backspace and delete
        var lastPosition = Selection.getCaretIndex();
        this.text = this.text.substr(0, lastPosition);
    }
```

If the Backspace or Delete keys were pressed, the code should clean up any suggested characters, and only leave the characters between the first character and the current cursor position. (Try out the demo and you'll see why we need to add this behavior.)

If neither Backspace nor Delete was pressed, then the only possible change is the addition of a character, so it's time to check for a word match! First, grab the current cursor position and store the value inside the lastPosition variable:

```
else
{
    //Check for word match up to the last "real" position
    var lastPosition = Selection.getCaretIndex();
```

The lastPosition variable keeps track of where the user's input ends, and where the suggested completion characters begin. Next, the local variable matchFound gains a default value of false, and it only becomes true if one of the words in styleList match the user's input. As you loop through the styleList array, you only compare the same number of characters typed by the user with an equivalent sequence of words in the styleList array.

```
var matchFound = false;
var capturedText = this.text.substr(0, lastPosition).toLowerCase();
for(var i = 0; i < styleList.length; i++)
{
    if(capturedText == styleList[i].substr(0, lastPosition))
    {
        this.text = styleList[i];
        matchFound = true;
    }
}
```

If the algorithm finds a word–match, then you overwrite the textfield with the whole word. If the word match isn't found, then the matchFound variable still has a false value, and the code that follows will clean up any suggested characters leftover from previous word-matches:

```
//If word match isn't found, then remove
//any "suggested" characters
if(matchFound == false)
{   this.text = this.text.substr(0, lastPosition);
}
```

Keep in mind that the cursor remains in the same index, so if the user types in another character that causes the entire word to mismatch, then the next execution of this onChange event-handler will clean up extra suggested characters.

The code-completion feature only took 12 simple lines of code! Not only does it help suggest cooking styles in the application form, but it also makes the form-filling task a lot easier and user-friendlier. You can apply the onChanged event-handler to many other scenarios. Just use your imagination!

As a bonus to this chapter, I've attached another demo. You'll find the file on the web site for this book under the name xilhouette.zip. The Xilhouette editor (see Figure 13.6) will visualize XML nodes as you type XML data into the textfield.

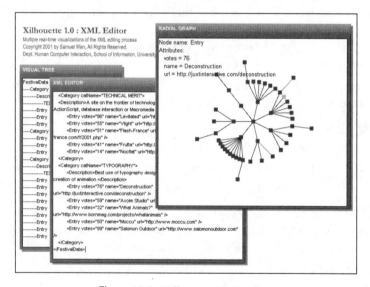

Figure 13.6 Xilhouette XML editor.

The visualization model is based on the Radial Layout algorithm from the research paper "Nicheworks: Visualization of Very Large Graphs," by Graham Wills at Bell Labs (1997). Thanks to Professor Mirel at the University of Michigan for her guidance with this demo.

.talk about a more advanced version of code-completion later in book, and code for this version is available on the book's web site. But need to cover the next group of important techniques: Text formatting ..id selection.

The *TextFormat* Object

The TextFormat object enables programmers to create a data object that defines multiple style properties of a textfield. After the object is created and style properties are defined, you can apply all the styles in the object to a textfield by using the TextField.setTextFormat() method. The usage of TextFormat objects is straightforward and well-documented in the Flash MX ActionScript Dictionary, so I will only provide a brief example before moving on to more interesting concepts. You'll find a helpful list of text format properties in the Reference panel. Also, TextFormat objects with a variable name ending in _fmt. generate a list of suggested properties in the Actions panel.

The formatting of a textfield involves five simple steps:

1. Create a textfield (either by hand, or by using the createTextField method which we'll discuss later).

2. Give the textfield an instance name.

3. Create a new TextFormat object by calling its constructor.

4. Define properties for the TextFormat object.

5. Set the textfield format using setTextFormat().

Open file 08_SimpleTextFormatExample.fla for a quick example (and a really lame joke). In this demo, there is a textfield with an instance name of field_txt. Open the Actions panel for the first keyframe. Here, you'll see code corresponding to the formatting steps from the previous paragraph:

```
//Create a new TextFormat object
format_fmt = new TextFormat();

//Define properties for the object
format_fmt.font = "verdana";
format_fmt.size = 18;
format_fmt.italic = true;
format_fmt.bold = true;
format_fmt.leftMargin = 60;
format_fmt.rightMargin = 60;

//Apply TextFormat object to the textfield
field_txt.setTextFormat(format_fmt);
```

TextFormat objects can be reapplied to other textfields as well. For example, you could copy and paste the field_txt textfield, give it a new instance name of field2_txt, and apply the same object:

```
//Apply the same TextFormat object two textfields
field_txt.setTextFormat(format_fmt);
field2_txt.setTextFormat(format_fmt);
```

Export Font Symbols

Although the TextFormat object allows you to specify a font, the font will not appear in another user's browser or Flash player unless the user has that font installed. To make dynamic font selection possible on all platforms, Flash MX supports the creation of embedded font symbols.

Figure 13.7 shows the New Font command in the Library panel's pull-down menu. To export fonts for use with TextFormat objects, create a new font symbol, and specify both the font symbol name and the actual font (see Figure 13.8). It's a good idea to use the same name for your symbol and font to keep your library assets organized.

Then, select the Linkage option for the font symbol by right-clicking on it in your Library panel for Windows users, or by command-clicking on it for Mac users. Give the font symbol the same linkage name as your font name, but without spaces or special characters. We suggest adding the suffix "font" to the linkage identifier, such as "GaramondFont," to make later ActionScript code easier to read (see Figure 13.9).

After you've created several linked font symbols, you can reliably specify those fonts for the font property of TextFormat objects.

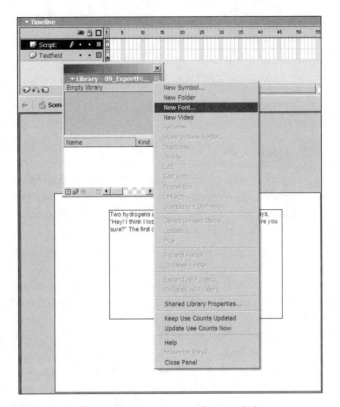

Figure 13.7 Create new font symbol.

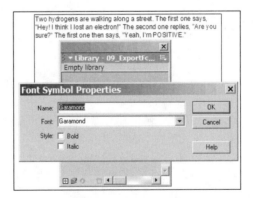

Figure 13.8 Define symbol.

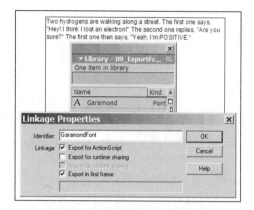

Figure 13.9 Export for ActionScript.

Selection.getBeginIndex() and *Selection.getEndIndex()*

This section explains the `Selection` object's `getBeginIndex()` and `getEndIndex()`. You can select a span of characters in a textfield in two ways. First, you can hold down the mouse button and drag across a piece of text. The second way is to move the cursor to a starting point with arrow keys, and then hold down the Shift key while moving the cursor left or right with the arrow keys. You are probably familiar with these other selection methods as nearly every other text editing program works this way.

Flash MX textfields can capture the beginning and ending of a selection span through the `Selection` object's `getBeginIndex()` and `getEndIndex()` methods. Like arrays, the `Selection` indexes start at 0 instead of 1.

Figure 13.10 shows an example of a textfield with a selection span over the word "typing." The selection span has a beginning index of 11, and an ending index of 17.

Obviously, the method `Selection.getBeginIndex()` would return a value of 11, and `Selection.getEndIndex()` would return a value of 17.

You can also use `Selection.setFocus()` to set focus to another textfield, and then use `Selection.setSelection()`. Open the file 10_FormatSelection.fla for an example. There's a lot of code in the first keyframe of this example, but ignore all that for now. Scroll down to the bottom of the code and you'll see the following two lines that control focus and selection:

```
//Set focus and make a selection, just as an example
Selection.setFocus(editor_txt);
Selection.setSelection(10, 30);
```

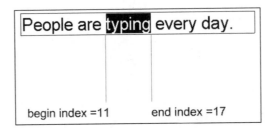

Figure 13.10   Selection span with begin index and end index.

These two methods are called from the `Selection` object, and they're focused on the textfield with an instance name of `editor_txt`. Once a selection is made, you can use the `beginIndex()` and `endIndex()` methods to retrieve the starting and ending indexes of the selection span:

```
//Get the beginning and end indexes of the selection
trace("Begin Index = " + Selection.getBeginIndex());
trace("End Index = " + Selection.getEndIndex());
```

Flair Design Pattern, Selection, and Textfields

If you've tried to do anything with selected text in a textfield, you've probably run into problems with focus. For example, pressing another button to call a function to manipulate selected text will often result in nothing happening at all.

Here's the main problem:

Let's say that you've written a function to underline the selected text. The function requires you to get the `beginIndex` and `endIndex` of a selection span, and then make changes to all characters between those indexes. Keep in mind that you can only get `beginIndex` and `endIndex` from a textfield if it has focus. However, the textfield will lose focus the moment you press another button to execute your function.

According to OOP design conventions, you should extend the textfield object to add functionality to it, but trying to subclass a textfield in Flash will lead to major problems. Some ActionScript programmers would point out that the `Object.registerClass` method, combined with `attachMovie`, provides a way to subclass movieclips with a parameterized constructor. However, textfields cannot be subclassed like movieclips because you can't use `Object.RegisterClass` with textfields (they don't support export linkages as library symbols). For this reason, class extension and inheritance are not appropriate for adding new functionality to textfields.

We found an answer for both extending textfield functionality *and* detecting text selection properly. The answer is to apply a mixture of the Decorator and Factory design patterns into a new pattern we call the "Flair design pattern." I will discuss the implementation of several Flairs, but will not discuss the general strategy Flairs in this chapter. The concept is beyond the scope of this chapter; you should read Chapter 4, "Practical OOP: Welcome to the Real World," for a detailed explanation.

Formatting Selected Text—Flair Design Pattern

If you select some text and then click on another button to manipulate selected text, the textfield will have already lost its selection indexes. The answer is to create an object that listens for any keyboard or mouse events that might take focus away from the textfield. The object should then extend the textfield's functionality by manipulating the selected text in some way. We call this "adding some flair" to the textfield, because it's a lightweight extension of the textfield object that doesn't interfere with its regular operations.

Applying the Flair design pattern is the best strategy we've found for creating such an object. To demonstrate, we've created an example that allows the user to underline selected portions of text (see Figure 13.11). Let's go through the creation steps first. Be sure you've opened the Actions panel on the first keyframe of the file 10_FormatSelection.fla.

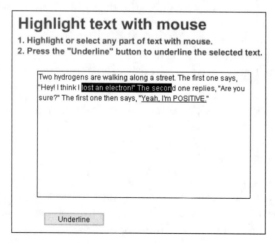

Figure 13.11 Allow user to underline selected portions of a textfield.

First, make sure that the `TextFlair` object exists in the `_global` scope. This object acts as the main global container for smaller Flair objects.

```
//Make sure the parent class exists
if (_global.TextFlair == null)
{   _global.TextFlair = new Object();
}
```

Then, create an `UnderlineFlair` object inside the `TextFlair` container, and also set a shortcut variable `r` to reduce keyboard typing while programming:

```
// Define the enhancer object as an object of the TextFlair object
// library, and create a shortcut variable "r" to reduce keyboard typing.
r = _global.TextFlair.UnderlineFlair = new Object();
```

Now define the `snapOn` method, which is used to add a Flair to any targeted textfield. The `snapOn` method acts as an initialization method, in the sense that it creates all of the necessary properties, methods, and event-handlers:

```
// snapOn - add completion flair a textfield
//--------------------------------------------------------------
// txtObj: the textfield to enhance
r.snapOn = function(txtObj)
{   // Create an enhancer object inside the textfield
```

Inside the `snapOn` method, we've defined a new object within the textfield, called `$underlineFlair`. We refer to this object as the "inner Flair" object, which contains all the properties, methods, and event-handlers.

```
    txtObj.$underlineFlair = new Object();
    txtObj.$underlineFlair.txtObj = txtObj; //self-reference to textfield
```

> Note that in the code shown above, the `txtObj` variable refers to the `textfield`. The `$underlineFlair` object exists inside the `textfield` object, and we'll refer to this object as the "inner Flair" object. We'll refer to the `_global.TextFlair.UnderlineFlair` object as the "outer Flair" object.

The second line of the preceding code defines a reference inside the `inner Flair` to the textfield that contains the `inner Flair` object. So from now on, anytime you execute code within the scope of the `$underlineFlair` object, the reference `this.txtObj` will actually refer to the textfield object containing `$underlineFlair`. For those who want a Flash-friendly comparison, the `$underlineFlair.txtObj` reference behaves a lot like the movieclip's `_parent` property, except that it points to a textfield.

Once the inner flair object has been defined, add it as a listener to the Mouse object in the code that follows. The reason for adding `$underlineFlair` as a mouse listener is because you need to capture any events that could possibly indicate that a text selection has been made. When you select text with the mouse, the `mouseUp` event always signals that a selection has just been made:

```
//Add a listener from the inner object to the textfield
Mouse.addListener(txtObj.$underlineFlair);
```

The purpose of the listener registration is to listen for a `MouseUp` event, so you link the inner Flair's `onMouseUp` event-handler to the outer Flair's `onMouseUp` event-handler. This allows you to create multiple Flairs and have them all use the same method; consequently, you can save memory space, remove redundant code, and centralize all the functional code in a single global object:

```
// Link methods and event handlers from the inner object to this object
txtObj.$underlineFlair.onMouseUp = this.onMouseUp;
txtObj.$underlineFlair.underlineSelection = this.underlineSelection;
} // snapOn
```

Note that you are also defining a reference of `underlineSelection` from the inner `Flair` to the outer `Flair`. This reference also acts as a link for a method called `underlineSelection()`, which we'll define later. That's it for the `snapOn` method.

The `snapOff` method acts as a de-initializer. It removes the inner `Flair` object and unregisters all event listeners associated with the inner Flair object.

```
// snapOff - remove enhancements from textfield
//-------------------------------------------------------------
// txtObj: the textfield to de-enhance
r.snapOff = function(txtObj)
{   Mouse.removeListener(txtObj.$underlineFlair);
    delete txtObj.$underlineFlair;
} // snapOff
```

In the `snapOn()` method, we linked the inner Flair's `onMouseUp` event-handler to the outer Flair's definition of the same method. If the inner Flair calls the `onMouseup` method, the code will execute within the scope of the inner Flair object.

```
// onMouseUp - Capture mouse event in case selection was made.
//--------------------------------------------------------------
r.onMouseUp = function()
```

continues

```
    {
        // If currently focused on this textfield, a selection
        // might have been made
        if(eval(Selection.getFocus()) == this.txtObj)
        {   this.beginIndex = Selection.getBeginIndex();
            this.endIndex = Selection.getEndIndex();
        }
    }
```

The onMouseUp method acts as a mouse event-handler for any textfields that have an UnderlineFlair snapped on. You want to capture the indexes of the selection span anytime the mouse is released (after dragging to highlight some text). However, there's the possibility that the user had activated the mouse on another textfield or another movieclip, so you need to make sure you're not capturing the wrong selection indexes.

The code shown previously tests if the textfield currently has focus. The method, Selection.getFocus(), returns the target path of a textfield, movieclip, or button as a string value. For example, _level0.editor_txt would be the returned string for Selection.getFocus() if the cursor was blinking in the editor_txt textfield. In order for the inner Flair object to test whether this textfield currently has focus, you can evaluate the target path string into an object reference using the eval() statement, and test for equality with the txtObj reference to the textfield:

```
    if(eval(Selection.getFocus()) == this.txtObj)
```

If the textfield currently has focus, then you can record the beginIndex and endIndex of the Selection object as beginIndex and endIndex properties in the inner Flair object:

```
        this.beginIndex = Selection.getBeginIndex();
        this.endIndex = Selection.getEndIndex();
```

Now we'll move on to the underlineSelection method, which takes several steps to underline any text currently selected in the textfield:

```
    // underlineSelection - Underline currently selected text
    //-----------------------------------------------------------
    r.underlineSelection = function()
    {
        trace("underline selection");
        var tempTFO = new TextFormat();
        tempTFO.underline = true;
        this.txtObj.setTextFormat(this.beginIndex, this.endIndex, tempTFO);
    }
```

The first step is to create a temporary `TextFormat` object named `tempTFO`. Then, set the underline property of `tempTFO` to `true`.

In earlier examples, you applied a `TextFormat` object to a textfield simply by using the `setTextFormat(formatObject)` method. However, the `setTextFormat()` method also supports two additional arguments for the beginning and ending of a selection span. Therefore, you can apply `tempTFO` to the textfield within its selection indexes by supplying the innerFlair's last recorded positions for `beginIndex` and `endIndex`. Remember, the `onMouseUp` listener recorded the last index positions.

At this point, you're finished defining the `UnderlineFlair` object. In a real-world situation, the code would exist in an external text file named UnderlineFlair.as to keep the code conveniently packaged in a portable location.

The only remaining code is to snap on the Flair extension to the textfield, in this case, `editor_txt`:

```
TextFlair.UnderlineFlair.snapOn(editor_txt);
```

Then, make the pushbutton component call a function named `editorUnderline()`. This function calls the `underlineSelection()` method of the textfield's inner Flair object, `$underlineFlair`.

```
function editorUnderline()
{   this.editor_txt.$underlineFlair.underlineSelection();
}
```

Not only have you solved the problem of textfield selection focus, you've also established a reusable object that can be applied to any number of other textfields as well. If the `UnderlineFlair` object were defined in an external text file, the actual code used for modifying a textfield wouldn't take more than a few lines:

```
#include "UnderlineFlair.as"

TextFlair.UnderlineFlair.snapOn(editor_txt);

function editorUnderline()
{   this.editor_txt.$underlineFlair.underlineSelection();
}
```

You'll find a version of the `UnderlineFlair` example as file 10_FormatSelection _ExternalPackageVersion.fla, with the external ActionScript file UnderlineFlair.as.

In this example, you've created a packaged object named UnderlineFlair, which can be snapped onto any textfield. This Flair object gives a target textfield the capability to underline any text selected by the mouse, through an underlineSelection() method. Extending the behavior of a textfield with more functions is nice, but the Flair design pattern can also add behavior to handle textfield events.

The next example provides a similar demonstration of the Flair design pattern applied to textfields. The difference between both examples is that we'll add some behavior for handling the onChanged event, instead of simply adding an extra function.

Ransom Generator—Advanced Textfield Event-Handling

Old, classic movies used to feature kidnappers who left behind ransom notes with cut-and-pasted letters from different magazines and newspapers. In this example, we'll demonstrate the use of the Flair design pattern with event-handling to build a Ransom Note generator.

Open the file 11_RansomFlair.fla and try testing the movie. Type some characters into the textfield and see how the font size and font face change randomly with each new character input (see Figure 13.12).

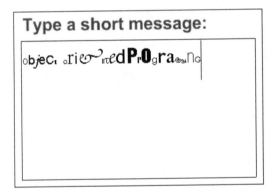

Figure 13.12   Random formatting of each new character input.

Now, take a look at the ActionScript code in the first keyframe. You'll notice that the code structure looks similar because we're building the same kind of Flair object with snapOn() and snapOff() methods. The main differences exist in the snapOn() method definition, and the onChanged event-handler.

```
// snapOn - add completion flair a textfield
//----------------------------------------------------------------
// txtObj: the textfield to enhance
r.snapOn = function(txtObj)
{   // Create an enhancer object inside the textfield
    txtObj.$ransomFlair = new Object();
    txtObj.$ransomFlair.txtObj = txtObj; //self-reference to textfield

    //Add a listener from the inner object to the textfield
    txtObj.addListener(txtObj.$ransomFlair);

    // Register event-handler from the inner flair object
    // to this flair object
    txtObj.$ransomFlair.onChanged = this.onChanged;

    //Get the font list and store into variable to optimize future retrievals
    txtObj.$ransomFlair.fontList = TextField.getFontList();
} // snapOn
```

In this case, the inner Flair is called $ransomFlair instead of the earlier
$underlineFlair that we defined inside the textfield object. We're also adding
the inner Flair object as a textfield listener instead of the Mouse listener,
because we want to capture the textfield's onChanged event.

An additional line of code stores the list of fonts available in the user's operating system as an array in the $ransomFlair object, for faster retrieval later:

```
//Get the font list and store into variable to optimize future retrievals
txtObj.$ransomFlair.fontList = TextField.getFontList();
```

To handle user input, the outer Flair object defines an onChanged method.
called by the inner Flair object. Remember, the inner Flair object has a variable reference to the outer Flair object's onChanged method, so the onChanged
method will execute within the scope of the inner Flair (that is, $ransomFlair)
whenever the $ransomFlair.onChanged() event-handler is called.

```
r.onChanged = function()
{
    var tempTFO = new TextFormat();
    tempTFO.size = 8 + Math.random() * 30; // automatically converts to integer
    var fontChoice = Math.round(Math.random() * this.fontList.length)
    tempTFO.font = this.fontList[fontChoice];
    this.txtObj.setNewTextFormat(tempTFO);
}
```

Again, create a temporary `TextFormat` object called `tempTFO`. Then, randomly set the value of the `tempTFO`'s size property. The `fontChoice` variable also receives a random number within the size of the `fontList` array, which was defined in the `snapOn()` method. Using the `fontChoice` variable, you can choose a random font from the `fontList` array.

```
this.txtObj.setNewTextFormat(tempTFO);
```

The last line of code in the `onChanged()` event-handler sets the temporary `TextFormat` object to the textfield. However, we're using the `setNewTextFormat()` method instead of `setTextFormat()`, so that any new input will use the style of the `tempTFO` object. It's important to keep in mind that `setTextFormat` applies only to text that is already in the field, while `setNewTextFormat` will apply to any new text that is added to the field but won't affect the text already in it.

With the `RandomFlair` object defined, what do you need to apply this `Flair` to a textfield? Just one line of code:

```
TextFlair.RansomFlair.snapOn(editor_txt);
```

Again, you could save the `Flair` object's definition as an external ".as" file, so that the actual code needed to reuse this object would look like the following two lines:

```
#include "RandomFlair.as"

TextFlair.RansomFlair.snapOn(editor_txt);
```

At this point, you have built an `UnderlineFlair` object that extends any textfield with an `underlineSelection()` method, and a `RandomFlair` object that extends any textfield by randomizing the format of input characters. One `Flair` object adds a function, the other `Flair` object adds behavior to handle textfield events.

Of course, why not build a bigger `Flair` object that handles multiple kinds of formatting of selected text, while allowing the user to edit text and make selections with mouse or Shift+arrow keys? In the next example, you'll take the ActionScript strategies applied here, and create a simple text editor with much more powerful formatting capabilities.

A Simple Text Editor Built In Flash

Before you build a text editor in Flash, let's review the concepts you'll use for this example:

- **Flair design pattern**—Extending the behavior of a Flash object, such as a textfield, with a Flair object. The Flair object creates an inner Flair object inside the target textfield, and allows the inner Flair object to use defined behaviors in the global Flair object. If you haven't read the earlier OOP chapters, you can go back for a more detailed explanation of the concept.

- `Selection` **object methods**—The `Selection` object allows you to control the keyboard focus, retrieve reference to a currently focused object, set selection spans, retrieve selection span indexes, and add listeners for `Selection` changes.

- `TextFormat` **object**—New instances of the `TextFormat` object can be applied to textfields to change the style of the entire textfield, or small parts of the textfield.

- `TextField` **event listeners**—The `TextField` object also supports event listeners for changes made to a textfield's contents, and for focus changes.

Open the file 12_SimpleTextEditor.fla and test the movie. You can select portions of the text with the mouse, or by holding down Shift and pressing the arrow keys to highlight with the text cursor. After a selection is made, you can change different style properties by clicking on the buttons, or by choosing different fonts and font sizes. The upper-right buttons also allow you to extract the selected text, or to extract the entire text with HTML formatting.

While not a complete text editor, Figure 13.13 shows the true power of the textfield when combined with solid object-oriented ActionScript programming. The demo contains 239 lines of code, but most of the fundamental concepts have been explained in previous examples. Rather than walking through every little detail, I'll discuss the more important concepts found in the `SelectionFormatFlair` object, and explain how they're implemented in ActionScript.

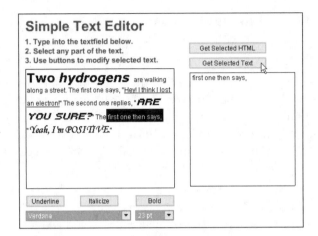

Figure 13.13   A simple editor built in Flash MX.

SelectionFormatFlair Object Definition

The snapOn method for the SelectionFormatFlair object works similarly to previous examples of the Flair design pattern. To add selection formatting capabilities to a textfield, the object's snapOn(textfield) method is called, with a textfield reference as the method parameter.

This snapOn() method differs from earlier examples in the number of methods linked from the innerFlair object ($selectionFormatFlair) and the outerFlair object:

```
// Register methods from the original flair object
txtObj.$selectionFormatFlair.enableSelDetect = this.enableSelDetect;
txtObj.$selectionFormatFlair.disableSelDetect = this.disableSelDetect;
txtObj.$selectionFormatFlair.detectSelection = this.detectSelection;
txtObj.$selectionFormatFlair.setFormat = this.setFormat;
txtObj.$selectionFormatFlair.getFormat = this.getFormat;
txtObj.$selectionFormatFlair.getSelectedText = this.getSelectedText;
txtObj.$selectionFormatFlair.getSelectedHTML = this.getSelectedHTML;
txtObj.$selectionFormatFlair.regainFocus = this.regainFocus;
```

Also, the snapOn() method adds the innerFlair object as a listener to the Selection object. The snapOn() method then defines an onSetFocus event-handler for the innerFlair object. This event-handler disables selection detection for the textfield that just lost focus, and enables selection detection for the textfield that just gained focus:

```
// Let the textfield listen to changes in selection focus,
// so that it can activate/deactivate enhanced listeners
Selection.addListener(txtObj.$selectionFormatFlair);
txtObj.$selectionFormatFlair.onSetFocus = function(oldFocus, newFocus)
{   if(oldFocus == this.txtObj)
        this.disableSelDetect();
    else if(newFocus == this.txtObj)
        this.enableSelDetect();
}
```

So when a textfield gains focus, the method `enableSelDetect()` executes to activate several event listeners in the textfield. The event-handlers listen to the `Key`, `Mouse`, and `Textfield` events. Keystrokes and mouse clicks are important because they indicate the possibility that the selection of text has just occurred. Textfield events are important because any changes made to the textfield changes the selection span:

```
sff.enableSelDetect = function()
{   // Add onChanged listener and link its event handler to this object
    this.txtObj.addListener(this);
    this.onChanged = this.detectSelection;

    // Add Key listener for arrow keys and link to this object
    Key.addListener(this);
    this.onKeyDown = this.detectSelection;
    this.onKeyUp = this.detectSelection;

    // Add mouse listeners in case the person is using the
    // mouse cursor to make text selections
    Mouse.addListener(this);
    this.onMouseDown = this.detectSelection;
    this.onMouseUp = this.detectSelection;
} // enableSelDetect
```

When any of these event-handlers are triggered, they redirect the execution of code to another method called `detectSelection`. The `detectSelection()` method captures the `beginIndex` and `endIndex` positions of a selection span, if any text is currently highlighted in a textfield:

```
sff.detectSelection = function()
{   // Note: This function executes inside the scope of
    // the caller, txtObj.$selectionFormatFlair.
    this.beginIndex = Selection.getBeginIndex();
    this.endIndex = Selection.getEndIndex();
}
```

Upon losing focus, the textfield should disable its event listeners. It's impossible to make selections in a textfield if the textfield doesn't have focus. Therefore, the textfield can remove event listeners to prevent the detectSelection() method from capturing a selection span (beginIndex and endIndex) that doesn't exist:

```
sff.disableSelDetect = function()
{   Mouse.removeListener(this);
    Key.removeListener(this);
    this.txtObj.removeListener(this);
}
```

The SelectionFormatFlair object revolves around its core method, setFormat(). This method accepts two possible "sets" of arguments:

- Format Property Name, Format Property Value
- TextFormat Object

The first set of arguments enables you to set any format property of selected text in the textfield. This approach provides quick formatting of selected text. The other option is to pass a single TextFormat object as the argument. This approach allows you to reuse a more complex set of styles to format your selected text.

```
sff.setFormat = function()
{   // Get current textformat of selected text, and create
    // a temporary textformat object to make changes
    var currentTFO = this.txtObj.getTextFormat(this.beginIndex, this.endIndex);
    var tempTFO;
    this.regainFocus();

    //Figure out whether parameters are name/value pair or TextFormat object
    if(arguments[0] instanceof TextFormat)
    {   tempTFO = arguments[0];
    }
    else if(arguments.length == 2)
    {   var propName = arguments[0];
        var propValue = arguments[1];
        tempTFO = new TextFormat();

        // Toggle textformat properties that are boolean,
        // Otherwise write the new textformat property values
        if(typeof(currentTFO[propName]) == "boolean")
        {   if(currentTFO[propName])
                tempTFO[propName] = false;
            else
                tempTFO[propName] = true;
            this.txtObj.setTextFormat(this.beginIndex, this.endIndex, tempTFO);
```

```
        return tempTFO[value];
    }
    else
    {   tempTFO[propName] = propValue;
        this.txtObj.setTextFormat(this.beginIndex, this.endIndex, tempTFO);
        return tempTFO[propValue];
    }
  }
} // setFormat
```

Once called, the setFormat() method also returns a TextFormat object that describes the formatting styles of the selected piece of text.

You might have noticed a reference to the regainFocus() method near the top of the setFormat() method definition. The regainFocus() method returns focus to a textfield, and resets the selection span to its previous indexes.

Here's the reason why the regainFocus() function plays an important role: When the user clicks on one of the formatting buttons, the textfield loses focus, causing the selection indexes to disappear as well. Fortunately, event listeners registered by the enableSelDetect() method record beginIndex and endIndex values at every event, and disable listening on losing focus. So, the internal properties of beginIndex and endIndex always store the last known values of the selection span. Using these recorded values, the regainFocus() method simply restores the focus and selection span to the textfield, so that you can click on multiple formatting buttons without having to reselect the text:

```
sff.regainFocus = function()
{   Selection.setFocus(this.txtObj);
    Selection.setSelection(this.beginIndex, this.endIndex);
}
```

Nobody wants to select text, click a button, and select the same text again—that behavior would not be consistent with standard word processors. Thoughtful enhancements such as the regainFocus() method can go a long way in creating a fun, intuitive user experience, especially when dealing with textfields. When you create Flash movies with complex text interaction such as large forms, or even a text editor, be sure you conduct some basic usability testing, preferably with another user as the test subject. I recommend a practical book on usability testing by Jeffrey Rubin, entitled *Handbook of Usability Testing*. Also check out Jakob Nielsen's original text, *Usability Engineering*.

HTML Support In Flash MX

Flash MX supports a small subset of the tags in the HTML 1.0 specification.
The supported tags are limited, but they do offer some flexibility in formatting
the content of textfields.

This table lists all of the HTML tags and their supported attributes:

Table 13.1

HTML Tag	Supported Attributes
`<a>`	`href="URL"`
	`target="Target"`
`<b>`	
` `	
`<font>`	`color="#xxxxxx"`
	`face="Font Name"`
	`size="Size"`
`<i>`	
`<li>`	
`<p>`	`align = "left", "right", or "center"`
`<textformat>`	`align = "left", "right", or "center"`
	`blockindent = "number"`
	`bold = "true" or "false"`
	`bullet = "true" or "false"`
	`color = "#xxxxxx"`
	`font = "font name"`
	`indent = "number"`
	`italic = "true" or "false"`
	`leading = "number"`
	`leftMargin = "number"`
	`rightMargin = "number"`
	`size = "number"`
	`tabStops = "number"`
	`target = "target"`
	`underline = "true" or "false"`
	`url = "url"`
`<u>`	
`&lt;`	special character <
`&gt;`	special character >
`&amp;`	special character &
`&quot;`	special character "
`&apos;`	special character '

The Macromedia web site also provides an excellent summary of HTML formatting in one of the technotes:

`http://www.macromedia.com/support/flash/ts/documents/htmltext.htm`

HTML Limitations and Restrictions

Textfields support formatting with HTML tags, but only under specific circumstances and with special restrictions (see Figure 13.14). Most of the requirements for setting up HTML support are well documented in the technote mentioned earlier and in the documentation. The more important requirements are listed here:

- Textfield must be of a dynamic or input type.
- Embed the font to make sure the user can see all fonts specified by the font tag.
- Embed the font to be sure the textfield shows up inside a movieclip with alpha transparency, or in a masked layer.
- Enable the textfield's HTML setting either by setting the `textfield.html` property to `true`, or by toggling the "<>" button in the Property Inspector.
- Send text with HTML tags into the `TextField.htmlText` property instead of the `TextField.text` property.

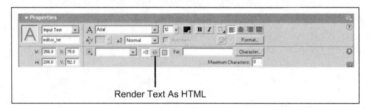

Render Text As HTML

Figure 13.14 A button in the Property Inspector for rendering a textfield's text as HTML-formatted text.

Open the file 13_demo_HTML.fla, and then open the Actions panel in the first keyframe. This file contains a dynamic textfield with the instance name `field_txt`. By default, the textfield has HTML disabled in the Property Inspector.

The following code enables the textfield's HTML rendering, and then passes an HTML formatted string to the `field_txt.htmlText` property (see Figure 13.15).

```
field_txt.html = true;
field_txt.htmlText = "<u>Lorem ipsum dolor sit amet.</u>";
```

Lorem ipsum dolor sit amet.

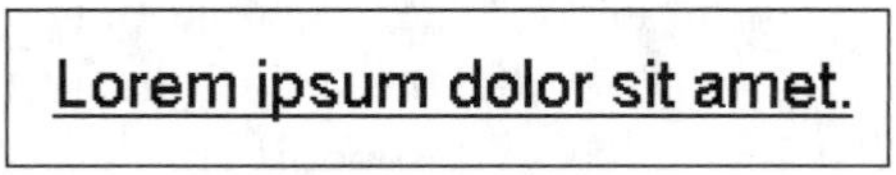

Figure 13.15 Textfield properly configured to display HTML formatted text.

If the `field_txt.html` property were `false`, then the HTML tags would appear in the textfield at runtime. If the HTML formatted string were sent to the `field_txt.text` property instead of `field_txt.htmlText`, then the HTML tags would also show up at runtime (see Figure 13.16).

<u>Lorem ipsum dolor sit amet.</u>

Figure 13.16 Textfield not properly configured. The HTML tags also show up at run-time.

You can retrieve pure text without formatting by getting the value of the `TextField.text` property. Otherwise, the `TextField.htmlText` property returns a string containing the HTML tags as well as the actual text.

```
trace(editor_txt.text);
trace(editor_txt.htmlText);
```

TextFormat and HTML

As demonstrated in earlier examples, applying a `TextFormat` object to a textfield changes the style of the textfield. But what happens when you try to apply `TextFormat` and HTML to the same textfield?

If the `TextField.html` property is set to `true`, the textfield can support both `TextFormat` and HTML formatting. Otherwise, the textfield will only display regular text. The textfield converts any applied text format object into the equivalent HTML tags. Additional styles not supported by HTML are converted into a nonstandard `<TEXTFORMAT>` tag.

Consider this ActionScript from the example 14_HTML_TextFormat.fla:

```
field_txt.html = true;
field_txt.htmlText = "<u>Lorem ipsum dolor sit amet.</u>";

tfo = new TextFormat();
tfo.underline = false;
tfo.italic = true;
tfo.size = 20;
tfo.font = "Garamond";

field_txt.setTextFormat(tfo);
trace(field_txt.htmlText);
```

The second-to-last line of code applies the new text format object to the field_txt textfield. Then, a `trace` statement sends the value of the textfield's `htmlText` property to the output screen. Try testing this code and you'll see the following string:

```
<TEXTFORMAT LEADING="2"><P ALIGN="LEFT"><FONT FACE="Garamond" SIZE="20"
➥COLOR="#000000"><I>Lorem ipsum dolor sit amet.</I></FONT></P></TEXTFORMAT>
```

The value of the `htmlText` property contains the original text, the HTML tags, and a nonstandard TEXTFORMAT tag. Apparently, you can only retrieve HTML-tagged strings from the `TextField.htmlText` property if the `TextField.html` property is set to `true`. If the `html` property is set to `false`, then the `htmlText` property will only return the text content without any additional formatting tags:

```
field_txt.html = false;
trace(field_txt.htmlText); // outputs "Lorem ipsum dolor sit amet."
```

External HTML in Flash MX Textfields

It is possible to preserve HTML formatting from externally loaded text files. For example, the file pc_html.txt contains text marked with HTML tags:

```
<a href="www.samuelwan.com"><u>Samuel Wan's Website</u></a><br>
<a href="www.waxpraxis.org"><u>Branden Hall's Website</u></a><br>
<i>Italicized and sometimes <b>bolded.</b></i><br>
<font face='Garamond' size='20'>Garamond font used here.</font><br>
```

The demo file, 15_LoadExternalFiles.fla, contains a dynamic textfield with an instance name of output_txt. The following code creates a LoadVars object, and then sends the raw text received by the LoadVars object to the textfield:

```
function finished(raw)
{   output_txt.html = true;
    output_txt.htmlText = raw;
}

output_txt.html = true;
output_txt.htmlText = data;

data_lv = new LoadVars();
data_lv.container = this;
data_lv.onData = function(raw)
{   this.container.finished(raw);
}
data_lv.load("unix_html.txt");
```

Note that the variable container inside the XML object refers to the scope in which the XML object resides. In this case, the xmlObject.container property refers to the _root Timeline, which contains the xmlObject. Once the external file has loaded into the XML object, the onLoad function executes within the scope of the XML object, calling the _root.finished() method through the container reference.

XML CDATA and HTML Formatting

I'll briefly mention XML CDATA text nodes here, but the topic is beyond the scope of this chapter. For more information on the use of XML object, and loading external data, read Chapter 14, "Talking Back—Server Integration," by Andreas Heim.

XML documents support a formatting tag called CDATA, which tells the XML parser to ignore any reserved characters within the CDATA tag. Because the XML parser in Flash also recognizes CDATA, you can write HTML-formatted text inside a CDATA node and still preserve the formatting when loading the XML data into Flash.

Check out the example, 16_LoadXML_CDATA.fla. This file loads an external XML file, but each message node in the file contains text wrapped by a CDATA tag. The CDATA tag preserves the inner HTML tags, so that the Flash XML parser does not convert them into XML structures (see Figure 13.17).

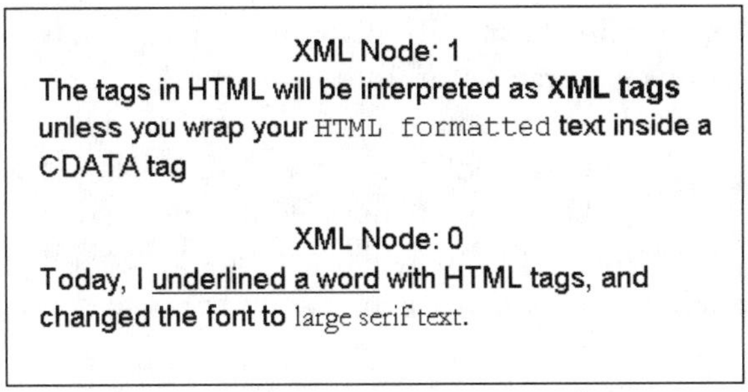

```
+-------------------------------------------------------+
|                                                       |
|                   XML Node: 1                         |
|   The tags in HTML will be interpreted as XML tags    |
|   unless you wrap your HTML formatted text inside a    |
|   CDATA tag                                           |
|                                                       |
|                   XML Node: 0                         |
|   Today, I underlined a word with HTML tags, and      |
|   changed the font to large serif text.               |
|                                                       |
+-------------------------------------------------------+
```

Figure 13.17   HTML formatting inside a CDATA text node in an XML file.

Carriage Returns in HTML and XML

Carriage returns in a text document may cause double-spacing when sent to
an HTML-enabled textfield. This problem can occur with both HTML and
XML files.

Unwanted double-spacing will occur if your text files are saved as PC text
files, rather than Unix text files. Windows and DOS systems use a carriage
return character, followed by a line feed character, to denote the end of a line.
On Unix systems, the end of a line is denoted by a single line feed character.
Flash recognizes both, so textfiles created in PC will actually cause two line
breaks to appear in the textfield. Mac OS computers end a line with a single
"\n" line feed character, so text files created on the Mac should not produce
any double-spacing errors for rendering external HTML formatted text—
though this does depend on the editor you use.

To clarify further, anyone creating text on a PC will have lines of text
that end with an "\r" carriage return, followed by an "\n" line feed. The "\r"
carriage return corresponds to the ASCII code 13, and the "\n" line feed
corresponds to the ASCII code 10. A carriage return moves the cursor to the
first position in the current line. A line feed will move the cursor to the next
line. Unix text files only use line feeds.

You can observe the difference in PC versus Unix textfiles by modifying
which text file to load in example 16_LoadXML_CDATA.fla. Both
unix_html.txt and pc_html.txt contain the same HTML-formatted text,
but are saved as PC and Unix text formats. Change the last line from

```
xmlObject.load("unix_html.txt");
```

to

```
xmlObject.load("pc_html.txt");
```

You'll notice the extra line breaks. To solve this problem, higher quality text editors such as Textpad, UltraEdit, or EditPlus should give you an option to save as PC or Unix file format. You can also find various DOS-to-Unix text format conversion utilities online for free. If you already have many PC-formatted text files on a Unix server and need to convert them quickly, many Unix shells support a simple PC-to-Unix text file converter named dos2unix. For more information, type **man dos2unix** on any Linux telnet session.

Creating and Manipulating Textfields Dynamically

Creating and manipulating textfields has evolved into a straightforward process thanks to the expanded methods and properties of the textfield object in ActionScript. Chapter 12, "Blurring the Line," provides a good comparison of the three objects. More importantly, the `TextField` object now supports most of the positioning, resizing, and rescaling capabilities that used to be limited to movieclips. If you haven't read that earlier chapter yet, now might be a good time to go through it to get a sense of the important differences and similarities between movieclips and textfields.

For the rest of this chapter, we'll use pure ActionScript instead of creating any textfields by hand, to demonstrate the power of the `TextField` object. The first important topic is the `createTextField()` method:

```
myMovieClip.createTextField (instanceName,depth,x,y,width,height)
```

Any movieclip, including the main Timeline, can create textfields through the `createTextField()` method. This method works the same way as the `createEmptyMovieClip()` and `attachMovie()` methods, except that it creates new textfields instead of new movieclips. Be sure you supply all six arguments to the `createTextField()` method, otherwise it won't work! To see the actual size of your textfield while programming, try setting the `background` and `border` properties to `true`, so you can see the outline of the textfield at runtime.

```
myTextField.background = true;
myTextField.border = true;
```

Each new textfield exists within the virtual depth shared by dynamically created movieclips. As a result, textfields have a `getDepth()` method and can be passed as a target argument to the movieclip's `swapDepth(target)` method. Check out the file 17_SwapDepths_WithTextfield.fla for a working example:

```
clip.swapDepths(button);       //works
clip.swapDepths(textfield);      //works
//button.swapDepths(clip);       //doesn't work
//button.swapDepths(textfield);   //doesn't work
//textfield.swapDepths(button);   //doesn't work
//textfield.swapDepths(clip);      //doesn't work
```

Textfields also have _x and _y properties for positioning, and _width and
_height for resizing without distortion. Textfields also support the _xscale and
_yscale rescaling properties, but those two properties simply resize the textfield
based on percentages of its original dimensions and will distort the text if the
fields have fonts embedded. (The only way to distort a textfield is to place
the textfield inside a movieclip.)

Elastic Textfields with *autoSize*

The position and dimension properties certainly come in handy if you need to
define a textfield's layout only once. But what about textfields whose contents
are constantly changing? Fortunately, the autoSize property defines how the
textfield will resize to accommodate the addition or removal of text.

There are four autoSize modes:

none	Textfield behaves normally, doesn't resize.
left	Textfield is left aligned and expands to the right.
right	Textfield is right aligned and expands to the left.
center	Textfield expands left and right equally. New lines expand downward, and the origin of the textfield is the center of its upper border.

The file 18_AutoSize.fla contains a live demonstration of all four kinds of
auto-sizing textfields expanding simultaneously. Try testing the movie now.
As you can see, the direction in which a textfield expands really depends on
its autoSize property. The three auto-sized textfields start with a width and
height of 1 pixel, but they expand both horizontally and vertically to fit their
content. The fourth textfield, which has an autoSize value of none, doesn't
resize, so it must have fixed dimensions to show its contents.

Tool Tip Example—Creating Elastic Textfields

One of the more obvious possibilities for combining dynamically created textfields with auto-sizing is to build tool tips, which are small blocks of text that appear near your mouse cursor when it's hovering over a button. Check out the file 19_ToolTip.fla for a simple example.

```
buttonclip.onRollOver = function()
{
   this.createTextField("tooltip_txt", 1, this._xmouse, this._ymouse, 1, 1);
   this.tooltip_txt.background = true;
   this.tooltip_txt.border = true;
   this.tooltip_txt.autoSize = "left";
   this.tooltip_txt.text = "hey";
   this.onMouseMove = function()
   {
      this.tooltip_txt._x = this._xmouse + 15;
      this.tooltip_txt._y = this._ymouse + 15;
      updateAfterEvent();
   }
}

buttonclip.onDragOut = buttonclip.onRollOut = function()
{
   this.tooltip_txt.removeTextField();
   this.onMouseMove = null;
}
```

Conclusion

As you can tell by now, the TextField object is one of those things that appears to be straightforward, but in practice is quite complex. Between formatting, selection, and dynamic creation and modification, there's a lot to understand about textfields. And, unlike other complex objects, you can't ignore textfields—you always need to work with text!

14

Talking Back—Server Integration

By Andreas Heim

Live and Learn

Just as Flash 4 hit the shelves in 1999, Shockwave asked us at Smashing Ideas if we could do a chess game in Flash that would be played via email. Sure, we said, and soon I was working on my first project that involved Flash-Server talk. I sure ran into a lot of walls and dead ends, and a lot of loose ends had to be tightened up, but in the end it all worked out. About six months later, Shockwave Email Chess finally launched and quickly became very popular.

2000 was the year of the Sydney Olympics, followed by the Paralympics. Flash 5 with XML support had just been released and we were asked to create a rich media web site for the Paralympics webcast, the largest successfully attempted webcast so far—10 days, 12 hours a day, 3 simultaneous live video streams. Working with XML in Flash was a new challenge for the team and me. But after six weeks of barely any sleep and a flooded apartment, the site went live just in time for the opening ceremonies. Time to hit a bar in Sydney and celebrate. Oh did I say Sydney? Yes, at the end of those six weeks I wound up down under—the client wanted us to work on site. Now if you asked me what was more exciting—learning XML or spending two weeks in Australia—the answer would be the latter.

Yet, this crash course in XML has proven to be helpful over and over again. Working with a new technology (or at least new to you) can mean a lot of hurdles, with unforeseen obstacles showing up right in the moment you needed them the least.

Macromedia has done a lot to make your life easier with Flash MX, and that includes Flash-server communication. But this ease won't just fall in your lap—you have to discover it, after which you'll wonder how you ever lived without it. This chapter will help you avoid some of the obstacles that we ran into when trying to make Flash and servers understand each other.

Introduction

An entire third of this book is dedicated to components—and in particular, the Flash UI components have been deconstructed for you. You will probably use them a lot to build user interfaces for applications. A user interface by itself is nice and dandy, but to come to life it will need data. For the most part you don't want to store that data within your Flash movie. You can't modify it any more without publishing the movie again.

The data you want to display may likely already exist in an electronic form: a simple text file, an Excel spreadsheet, an XML document, or maybe even in a relational database. In some cases you could copy and paste the data into Flash, convert it into ActionScript data by converting certain things (such as inserting a backslash (\) before all double quotes (") so that the quotes are considered part of text instead of marking the end of a string), and then adding some code. If you want to make changes, you may have to make them in the original file and in Flash, or go through the entire process again— a cumbersome process you really want to avoid.

Be glad that there are better ways of bringing data into Flash, and be glad you have this chapter to explain them. Although Flash has been able to interact with servers since version 4, the subsequent releases increased this capability. Now with MX, you have a variety of choices. You can:

- Pass variables to Flash when the movie loads.
- Send and receive variables with the LoadVars class.
- Send and receive XML-formatted data with the XML class.
- Create persistent connections using the XMLSockets class.
- Communicate with web services using Flash Remoting.

Unfortunately I won't be able to cover persistent connections with XML sockets here. It is an interesting technology, but hasn't changed since Flash 5. If you want more information, however, you can find an introduction in *ActionScript the Definitive Guide* (O'Reilly) by Colin Moock.

Starting Up—Passing Variables from the Embedding HTML Page

Chronologically speaking, the first time a server has the capability to send information into a Flash movie is if variables are passed through the HTML page that hosts the Flash movie.

There are two slightly different ways in which variables can be passed to Flash through the HTML page. You can either append them to the URL of the Flash movie, or you can set a special parameter call `FlashVars`. This latter option is new in Flash MX.

Passing Variables with the Movie's URL

Since Flash 4, it has been possible to pass variables to a Flash movie by adding a URL-encoded query string to the movie path like this:

For Internet Explorer in the object tag:

```
<param name=movie value="yourMovie.swf?userName=Andreas+Heim">
```

And for Netscape in the embed tag:

```
<embed src="yourMovie.swf?userName=Andreas+Heim">
```

Then in yourMovie.swf, the `userName` variable is set to Andreas Heim. As you can see, the variable value has been converted, and the plus has been replaced with a space—the Flash player does this decoding for you. Because a URL only allows certain characters to be used, other characters—like the space—need to be encoded.

There are two problems with this method of passing variables. One is that if you want to be on the safe side, you should limit the overall length of the URL to 256 characters. (Many browsers will drop the part of the query string that exceeds this length.) There is only so much information you can pass within that limitation. The other problem is that if you change anything in this string, the browser will download the .swf again, instead of using a cached copy. You can use this to your advantage to force the browser to not cache a file, but most of the time it will not be the behavior you want.

Passing Variables Using the *FlashVars* Parameter

Most of you have learned to work around these problems, so it's easy to miss that Flash MX introduces `FlashVars`. You can now separate the movie's URL and the variables you pass to the movie by specifying a special `FlashVars` parameter with the variables as value:

For Internet Explorer:

```
<param name=movie value="yourMovie.swf">
<param name=FlashVars value="username=Andreas+Heim">
```

And for Netscape:

```
<embed src="yourMovie.swf" FlashVars="username=Andreas+Heim">
```

Now the .swf can be cached, even if you change the variables. The format in which the variables are stored stays the same—they are passed as a URL-encoded query string, but they are sent separately from the movie's URL. The `FlashVars` method does not have the same length limitations as the original URL variables method. You can pass up to 63KB worth of data through `FlashVars`. That should be enough to get you started.

So far you have a one-way communication—the server may pass some initial variables to a Flash movie. This is often used for information such as several ids and URLs to where to get the real data or to where to submit data. Typical ids are user id, application or game id, transaction id, and data id. Although you can now pass much more data to Flash on startup, you probably still want to keep the amount fairly low, so that your Flash application can load quicker. Yes, you want all data available right away, but you also need to give your user a visual feedback as quickly as possible. To achieve that it is probably not a good idea to start off with a huge chunk of data to download.

Flash can still pick up the remainder of the data. A lot of the required data may depend on user interaction. Loading and sending data from Flash allows you to react to user interaction, and also the use of different formats. We'll start with using the `LoadVars` class.

Loading Variables with the *LoadVars* Class

Before jumping into the all-new `LoadVars` class, I want to take a step back in the past. Most of what you now can do with `LoadVars` was already possible with previous versions of Flash, but in a different way.

The Past: Sending Out Movieclip Variables with *loadVariables* and *getURL*

Flash has been able to send out the variables of a movieclip to a server since version 4 with the `loadVariables` and `getURL` actions. The server receives those variables exactly like variables sent from a form in HTML—as URL-encoded query string. And like HTML forms, you can choose between GET and POST as the sending method. While `getURL` forces a page refresh, `loadVariables` is able to receive an answer from the server. It expects the same format as when sending the variables out, again a URL-encoded query string. Upon receipt, Flash decodes the string and sets Flash variables. In Flash 5 an `onClipEvent(load)` or `onClipEvent(data)` handler would then be called.

The way to use this is a bit cumbersome. First, you need to create a movieclip container in which to set the outgoing variables. And before MX you couldn't do this on-the-fly. You had to place the event handler "on" the movieclip, something you couldn't do dynamically either. And lastly, if you used the Flash 5 way of receiving variables, the outgoing and incoming variables had to be in the same movieclip:

```
mcInbox.loadVariables ("http://yourdomain.com/cgi-bin/giveMeData.cgi", "POST");
```

Now, the variables in `mcInbox` get sent to the server, and the response goes back to it as well. Naming it `mcInbox` is actually a bit misleading due to this double role—but in this case it is there to indicate that the main purpose is to receive data from the server.

Relief in the Present: The *LoadVars* Class

Guess what? Finally, all this pain has come to an end. Flash MX introduces the `LoadVars` class, giving you object-oriented access to `loadVariables` functionality and more. And it's quite easy to use.

1. First, create an instance of `LoadVars`:

    ```
    score_lv = new LoadVars ();
    ```

    For this imaginary project, you want to post a score to a scoreboard. So name the new object `score_lv`. The suffix `_lv` is an abbreviation for `LoadVars`.

2. Next, specify the variables you want to send out:

```
score_lv.userName = "wiz";
score_lv.score = 33500;
```

3. To send out the information in `score_lv`, call the `send` method:

```
score_lv.send ("postScore.cgi");
```

This assumes there is a postScore.cgi CGI-script located in the same folder as your Flash movie.

4. If you look at the documentation of `LoadVars.send` in the Reference panel, it tells you that you can also specify a target, or more exactly a target window:

```
score_lv.send ("postScore.cgi", "_self");
```

In the downloadable files for this book, you will find the script postScore.cgi. Instead of a scoreboard, it prints out the variables sent to it, and some additional information. Such a script is useful during the development process to make sure your Flash application sends out the correct data. To use the script, your server has to support Perl CGI scripts. The folder you place it in needs to be enabled to run CGI scripts; often you will find a standard cgi-bin folder. Finally, you need to be sure postScore.cgi can be executed, by setting the proper file permissions. Because this is different for every operating system, I won't go into more detail here.

Now the `send` method acts like a `getURL` action: The call goes out to the specified browser window and displays the server output. In this case it replaces the current page where the Flash movie lives.

The third optional parameter is the sending method. You can specify either `GET` or `POST` (the default is `POST`).

If you don't specify the sending method, a `LoadVars` object will always send using POST. Always? Actually, not quite always. From the standalone player and the test-movie player, Flash can't send via POST. And although previous versions would then just not send the variables at all, the Flash 6 standalone and test-movie players will send requests as GET, even if you specified POST.

5. In most cases you probably want to see if your request was received properly, but without going to a different HTML page. Here is how you can accomplish this with the sendAndLoad method instead of send:

```
scoreResult_lv = new LoadVars ();
scoreResult_lv.onLoad = function (success) {
  trace ("success: " + success);
  trace ("result is in: " + this.result);
}
score_lv.sendAndLoad ("postScore.cgi", this.scoreResult_lv);
```

This first defines another LoadVars instance that is meant to receive the result of posting a score. Then you define an onLoad handler for it that gets called when data arrives. There is one argument that gets passed to onLoad: success. It is a Boolean variable that indicates whether the load action succeeded, but no further detail is available. We assume that postScore.cgi returns a variable called result and traces it. Lastly, you use the sendAndLoad method of score_lv and tell it to send the server response straight to scoreResult_lv.

It is important that you define onLoad *before* you call sendAndLoad. Otherwise it's possible that the server response arrives before onLoad is defined, and thus never gets called.

Receiving Non-URL-Encoded Data

Now a problem is that a lot of servers are not set up to return a response in the format Flash expects. While it is very common to send variables as URL-encoded query string to a server, the server usually spits out some HTML as result, not a query string.

Flash on the other hand first receives this server response and then parses it into name-value pairs, before the onLoad handler is called. If you have worked with the XML class in Flash 5, you may know that with the XML class, you can intercept the parsing. This is the same for LoadVars. When a LoadVars object receives the server response, first an `onData` handler is called, which takes care of the parsing before `onLoad` is called. If the server response is not the query string that Flash expects, you can define the following `onData` handler instead of the `onLoad` handler:

```
scoreResult_lv.onData = function (rawResult) {
  trace ("raw server response:" + newline + rawResult);
}
```

Now it's up to you to make sense out of the raw result. As with `onLoad`, be sure you define `onData` before you make a server call.

This also can be useful if you want to bring in regular formatted text. Because Flash MX understands Unicode, you could store your text in UTF-8 format in a text file, and then use the `load` method of a `LoadVars` object to bring it in:

```
myText_lv = new LoadVars();
myText_lv.onData = function (rawResult) {
    trace ("text file contents:"+ newline + rawResult);
}
myText_lv.load ("unicode_test.txt");
```

The `load` method doesn't send out any variables to the server.

A couple more things you might find useful about the `LoadVars` class:

- It supports `getBytesLoaded` and `getBytesTotal` methods. This means you can show the load progress. This makes sense particularly if you load a larger file. If you're not familiar with these methods, you may want to take a look at Chapter 7, "Building Your First Component."

- Every instance has a `contentType` property. By default it is *application/ x-www-urlform*. If the server expects a different content type, you can set it accordingly before sending anything.

- The object that receives the response when you do a `sendAndLoad` doesn't necessarily have to be an instance of `LoadVars`. For example, if the response is in XML form, you can use an XML object instead.

Taking a Look at the Bigger Picture

Now that we've discussed how to use the LoadVars class, let's step back from the code, review what LoadVars is good for, and take a look at where the problematic areas are.

- LoadVars is an object-oriented class that offers loadVariables functionality and more.

  It removes the need for workarounds required with loadVariables. It also allows you to read the loaded data raw, using the onData handler as described previously. Because of all that, I expect loadVariables to be deprecated in a future version of Flash.

- You can use LoadVars to submit form data.

  You can set up a form in Flash and use LoadVars to submit the data the user entered. This way you can replace any regular HTML form with Flash. Variables get sent out the same way as the form would do it.

- LoadVars is backward compatible.

  The format is compatible back to Flash 4, so any backend written to send data to Flash 4 or 5 using loadVariables, doesn't have to be modified to use it with Flash 6 LoadVars.

- LoadVars can save you download time.

  A URL-encoded query string is a fairly compact format. That means you can achieve quick send and load times because not much overhead data has to be transmitted. On the other hand, the XML format discussed next, is significantly larger in file size. For low bandwidth connections, the LoadVars format might be your better choice. Often however, the benefits of XML will weigh more than the larger file size.

Unfortunately, there are some problematic areas that the transformation from loadVariables to LoadVars couldn't help with:

- The way of receiving variables as URL-encoded string is really not common practice.

  You can't just hook into an existing backend this way, it needs to be written or modified for Flash. With the focus of web development in general being on standardizing ways of data exchange mainly through XML, I don't think URL-encoded strings have a bright future.

- It is hard to send or receive complex data structures this way.

  The query string works fine for name-value pairs, but as soon as you want to transfer more, you have to write code on both ends that transforms your data structures into a string and then back into the original structure. These processes are called serialization and deserialization. For example you could represent a simple two-dimensional array like this: "o¦x¦x,o¦o¦x,x¦x¦o". As you can see, creating this string is not really something you want to do all the time, neither is re-creating the array structure.

- URL-encoded query strings are difficult to debug.

  They are hard to read for our human eyes. Not only is everything put into a single line, but also characters get encoded, and more complex data structures need an extra encoding level. By just glancing at such a string, it is almost impossible to tell whether it is correct, and even harder to tell what exactly it actually contains. Not surprisingly, this makes debugging much more difficult.

XML Class

You say you want standards? You want to be able read your data? Welcome to the world of XML. Seeing the problems with getting data into Flash with the `loadVariables` approach, Macromedia included XML support with Flash 5. From the beginning, the XML class was built in an object-oriented manner, so there was no need to change much in how to use it for Flash MX. Let's take a glance at why XML is such a great feature to have in Flash:

- XML is a universal format. Many server technologies are able to output XML data; some databases are even organized using XML. Flash can directly hook into such systems.

- By using XML data, you can use the same data source and display it in many different ways and technologies. For example, if a web site was built with an HTML interface using XML as data source, you can transform it to a Flash interface with only a small effort on the server side.

- You can open an XML file and read it. This is indeed helpful when debugging. You can even write and maintain your own XML files without too much trouble.

Support for XML was all the way there in Flash 5, but it had one severe usage limitation: performance. It was so slow that just loading a larger file could freeze your browser. Your choices were to use smaller XML files or to buy everyone a faster computer. The latter usually not being an option, developers spend a fair amount of time making sure XML data would come in Flash-digestible junks and optimizing every piece of code dealing with XML in Flash; workaround time that probably could have been better spent creating things.

Flash MX solves this problem once and for all. The XML class has been turned into a native class. This means all the processor intensive code now runs in C++, not in ActionScript. That doesn't change the way you have to deal with XML, it is just a lot faster. You don't even have to change your code.

Creating an XML Object

One thing that hasn't changed though, is that Flash has a nonvalidating XML parser. This means Flash just reads in what you tell it to read and doesn't test it against anything. It only tries to make XML-sense out of it. If there is an error in your XML document, for example, a closing tag is missing, Flash will simply stop parsing afterward, and your XML object will only include the nodes found before the error.

In Chapter 3, "Event Wrangling: When To Do What," you saw how to create an XML object, and how to set up an onLoad callback handler. You also saw how to set a reference to a timeline in the XML object so that the timeline can receive the data. We make use of the same concept here, but also show you how to access the data in the XML object. Take a look at the following code:

```
desDev_xml = new XML ();
desDev_xml.ignoreWhite = true;
desDev_xml.onLoad = function (success) {
  if (success) {
    trace ("desDev loaded: " + this.firstChild.nodeName);
  }
  else {
    trace ("desDev load FAILED");
  }
}
desDev_xml.load
("http://www.macromedia.com/desdev/resources/macromedia_resources.xml");
```

First, you create a new XML object called desDev_xml. You make sure white space is ignored by setting ignoreWhite to true. Then you define the onLoad handler before you load the Macromedia Designer and Developer (desDev) news feed (macromedia_resources.xml).

When you enter this code into a new movie and test the movie, you should see the following in the Output window:

```
desDev loaded: macromedia_resources
```

If you take a look at the actual XML feed, you will see it looks somewhat like this:

```
<?xml version="1.0" ?>

<macromedia_resources
xmlns:macromedia_resources="http://www.macromedia.com/desdev/resources/
➥macromedia_resources.dtd">
  <resource type="Tutorial">
    <title>Macromedia Flash MX Application Development Center Update</title>
    <author>Macromedia</author>
    <url>http://www.macromedia.com/desdev/mx/flash/</url>
    <product name="Macromedia_Flash" />
  </resource>
</macromedia_resources>
```

How does this look inside Flash? Think of it as a linked and nested list. Linked means that every item in the list knows which item is before it and which item follows it, this is expressed in the properties previousSibling and nextSibling. Nested means that an item may not only have siblings, but also children, and a parent. An item in such a linked list is called a *node*.

Everything has to start somewhere—so there is a root node at the level of the XML document itself. A valid XML document has only one node at the document level, in this case <macromedia_resources>. Because the document is considered a node, this node is a child node of your XML object, and you can access it as desDev_xml.firstChild. This first child node has a nodeName property—macromedia_resources.

Because there is only one node at the top, from which the child nodes branch out, an XML object also forms a data structure known as a tree. (To read more about data structures, see Chapter 15, "Data Structures: Sculpting Information To Suit Your Needs.")

I prepared a file for you that shows how to access different parts of desDev_xml. Open 14_01_sample_xml_extended.fla from this book's downloadable file and do a test movie, as shown in Figure 14.1.

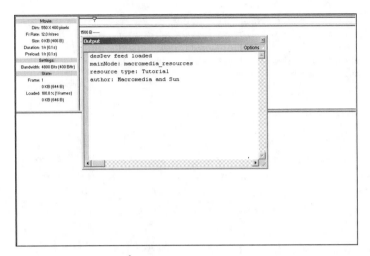

Figure 14.1 Accessing properties of an XML object.

You will see different contents traced for the values of type and author than in the snippet of the XML feed shown previously, because the news feed gets continuously updated. If you take a look at the source code, you will see that I have removed accessing the contents of the XML object from the onLoad handler, but rather pass the event on to the main Timeline—that is where you want to know about the data anyway:

```
desDev_xml.master = this;
desDev_xml.onLoad = function (success) {
  if (success) {
    this.master.desDevLoaded();
  }
  else {
    trace ("desDev load FAILED");
  }
}
```

If you don't understand why this kind of callback is used here, be sure to check out Chapter 3.

Now access the actual data in the desDevLoaded method:

```
desDevLoaded = function () {
  trace ("desDev feed loaded");

  var mainNode = this.desDev_xml.firstChild;
  trace ("mainNode: " + mainNode.nodeName);
```

continues

```
var resourceNode = mainNode.firstChild;
trace ("resource type: " + resourceNode.attributes.type);

var authorNode = resourceNode.firstChild.nextSibling;
var author = authorNode.firstChild.nodeValue;
trace ("author: " + author);
}
```

Dig through the structure of the XML object and pick up a few pieces of information—a nodeName, an attribute, and a nodeValue. If this is the first time you looked at XML from within Flash, your head might be slightly spinning right now. Take time to look at the code and the corresponding XML document to see how the structure of the text file is mapped into the XML object.

Converting XML Data to a Data Provider

In Chapter 6, "Using UI Components," you learned how to use a data provider with one or more UI components. You added data to the data provider, and saw it displayed instantly in the listbox.

Now it sure would be nice if you didn't have to enter the data every time you opened the movie, but if you could bring in external data to populate the listbox. An XML object is not a data provider though, so you need to convert the data contained in the XML object to a data provider. Open 14_02_desDev_listbox.fla and do a test movie to see how it works (see Figure 14.2).

The file is not too different from your previous versions. There is a listbox component on the stage with the instance name resources_lb, and a push button component named go_pb. The new desDevLoaded callback method looks like this:

```
desDevLoaded = function () {
    // data feed is loaded, load event passed back to this timeline
    var mainNode = this.desDev_xml.firstChild;
    var resource_array = mainNode.childNodes;
    // convert node array into a data provider
    var listBoxData = createResourceList (resource_array);
    // ... and populate the listbox:
    this.resources_lb.setDataProvider(listBoxData);
}
```

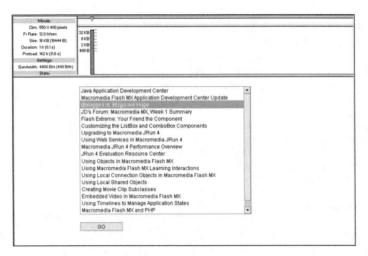

Figure 14.2 A listbox component with the headlines of the
current articles in the Macromedia Designer and Developer Center.

1. First, grab the main node of the XML object as before:

```
var mainNode = this.desDev_xml.firstChild;
```

2. Then, grab all its child nodes and keep them in resource_array:

```
var resource_array = mainNode.childNodes;
```

   An XML object provides several ways to access its data and structure.
   What you saw before is to go to a node's `firstChild`, and then from there
   to `nextSibling`. All the child nodes of a node can also be accessed with its
   `childNodes` array, which is used here.

3. Then pass `resource_array` to a `createResourceList` method and receive a
   `listBoxData` data provider in return:

```
var listBoxData = createResourceList (resource_array);
```

   We will discuss what this method does in just a minute.

4. Finally, register the data provider with the listbox on the stage:

```
this.resources_lb.setDataProvider(listBoxData);
```

The actual conversion from the XML structure to the data provider happens in the `createResourceList` method:

```
createResourceList = function (resource_array) {
  var listData = new DataProviderClass();
  var resourceCount = resource_array.length;
  var resource;
  var title, link;
  for (var i=0; i<resourceCount; i++) {
    resource = resource_array[i];
    title = resource.childNodes[0].firstChild.nodeValue;
    link = resource.childNodes[2].firstChild.nodeValue;
    listData.addItem( { label : title, data: link } );
  }
  return listData;
}
```

1. First, define `listData` as a new instance of `DataProviderClass`:

   ```
   var listData = new DataProviderClass();
   ```

2. Then, loop through the items of resource array. In each iteration of the loop you first create a shortcut to the current resource node:

   ```
   resource = resource_array[i];
   ```

3. The order of the nodes for each resource is the same. The first one is the title, the third one is the link to the article. So you just need to grab the node values found in each of these nodes' first child:

   ```
   title = resource.childNodes[0].firstChild.nodeValue;
   link = resource.childNodes[2].firstChild.nodeValue;
   ```

The actual title node doesn't have a `nodeValue`, only a `nodeName`. The value you are looking for is a step deeper, as you have seen before.

> If the order of the nodes is subject to change in the XML documents you are working with, you will have to do more work. You need to loop through the resources childNodes array, and check each node's nodeName, before grabbing the nodeValue.

4. Now create an item object with two properties, label and data, and add the item to the data provider:

```
listData.addItem( { label : title, data: link } );
```

The title you just captured functions as a label displayed by the listbox. You store the link in an additional data property so that you can later go to the article. If you were interested in capturing more data from the XML object, for example the author, you could capture it in the same way, and store it as an additional property of the data provider item.

5. The last thing left in the method is to return the newly created data provider:

```
return listData;
```

This is all the code needed to create a data provider with the data found in the XML object and display said data in the listbox.

Now you need to get the link of the currently selected item in the listbox when you press the Go button and then open a new browser window with the article:

```
this.go_pb.setClickHandler("onGo");
onGo = function (  ) {
  var titleItem = this.resources_lb.getSelectedItem();
  if ( titleItem != null) {
    var link = titleItem.data;
    if (link != null) {
      getURL (link, "_blank");
    }
  }
}
```

First, set the click handler of the Go button to onGo, and then define this handler. All it needs to do is get the currently selected item from the listbox, and use the data property in which you stored the link to open the new browser window.

This should be enough to get you started to use XML as data source for your applications. Please remember that by using a data provider to hold your data, you can use different data-aware UI components to display it or portions of it at the same time.

Miscellaneous XML Tips

The XML class has some more features I wasn't able to cover elsewhere. So here's a listing so they don't get left out:

- Like the LoadVars class, the XML class now has getBytesLoaded and getBytesTotal methods, allowing you to display the load progress.

- The XML class still has an onData handler, which gets called with the raw data received from the server. The built-in XML.onData calls parseXML to transform the raw string into an XML object before triggering onLoad. Unless you need the XML-specific methods of the XML class, I'd recommend not overwriting it just to get to the raw data, and rather using LoadVars if you need to load a different type of data structure. LoadVars is much more generic, and thus better suited for your own data structures. For example, you may want to preload several XML files, but don't want to parse them until you actually need them. In this case it would make sense to define your own onData handler that "parks" the raw XML string. When needed, you call XMLparse yourself to create the actual XML object.

- If you need to load HTML formatted data, you will need to use the CDATA tag to prevent Flash from parsing such data as XML nodes. Read more about dealing with text and HTML in Chapter 12, "Blurring the Line."

- Flash MX can read Unicode. This means you do not need to encode special characters for your language if you save the XML file as Unicode. For example, the German umlaut Ü doesn't have to be encoded as Ü—you simply type Ü.

- Windows is using a certain character range for special characters, which are officially reserved for control codes, and not used the same way on other operating systems. Although using these Windows character codes worked in Flash 5, they break in Flash MX. (An example is the bullet point.)

- The XML class also has `send` and `sendAndLoad` methods. They work very similarly to the methods with the same names in the `LoadVars` class; the main difference being that they send out XML formatted data instead. The documentation is a bit misleading—if you don't specify a window for `send`, the result is ignored. It doesn't default to `_self`. If you do specify a window, including `_self`, there will be a page refresh. The XML sending methods only support `POST`, as an XML object is unlikely to fit into the size limits for `GET`. The exceptions are again the test-movie player and the standalone player, which only send using `GET`.

- Not every backend accepts raw XML as input. Many return XML but only expect form data as input. In such a case you can use a `LoadVars` object to send out variables, and use an XML object as target for the result.

XML Drawbacks

Performance is not really an issue any more with Flash MX; you can load large files without problems, yet not everything about XML is golden:

- To work with XML data, you have to spend some time programming an interface so that you can actually use the data. Interface here means an interface to access the data programmatically, not a user interface. You need to convert the complex XML structure into simpler ones for your needs. A lot of this work has to be done again if you work on a new project with a different data source.

- There is a definitive chance for overhead. On the server, data has to be converted to XML; if it is not, the native format for storing data. In Flash, first the Flash player has to parse the text document into an XML object. Then your code has to extract the information you need from said XML object. Then you take the data in the XML object and convert it to the structure you want to work with.

- Although XML documents are human readable, they also grow in file size fairly quickly. With a majority of Internet users still using dial-up connections, this is still a valid concern. Wish for Flash to be able to read compressed XML files in the next version.

New Ways of Flash-Server Talk with Flash Remoting

Every new version of Flash since Flash 4 has introduced a new and better way of communicating with a server. When Macromedia released ColdFusion MX, an exciting new capability of Flash MX was also revealed. Flash Remoting gives Flash movies the opportunity to directly connect to the server. Data can be passed back and forth to and from the server almost as if you used a local object.

You don't need to worry about query strings any more, nor whether to use GET or POST as sending method, and you don't have dig in an XML tree to find the data you need.

Imagine this:

1. Your Flash movie connects to a server.

2. Then you choose an object on the server you want to interact with; for example the object that handles the inventory of a library.

3. You call a method of this object to receive the data you need, for example, getBooksIBorrowed().

4. After the server looks up your request, a list of borrowed books in the form of a data provider is returned to the Flash movie, along with date borrowed and due dates.

5. All you have left to do is to use that data, for example display it in a listbox component.

Sounds like wishful thinking? Dreaming? Nada. Wake up and welcome to the world of Flash Remoting. All the previous is now possible—and it's easy to do.

How Remoting Works

The fact that Flash Remoting was announced at the same time as ColdFusion MX is not coincidence. For Flash Remoting to work, the server needs to be prepared to accept a Flash Remoting connection. So let's have a look at the server side of things first. ColdFusion MX is one server middleware that is prepared to do this.

Traditional web applications work in the way that you request an HTML page from the server. You interact with a form, and eventually hit some type of a submit button. The server receives the form data, and returns you another HTML page.

The server may need to connect to other servers to fulfill your request, for example to connect to a database. There are various ways of how this is implemented, and a lot of people have spent a lot of time trying to connect different technologies.

The solution to this communication problem is called web services. Web services communicate with each other through standardized messages in XML.

"Hey, Flash can do XML, so that's where we're heading," you might think. Wrong answer. In fact, you *could* communicate with a web service by sending and receiving these XML messages. That would mean you still deal with standard XML message format called SOAP (Simple Object Access Protocol). That means work and sweat, and not the easy 5 steps above, so I really don't want to go that way here. In addition, given Flash's limited support of XML, it's not actually possible to fully support SOAP in Flash. For full SOAP compliance, a 'SOAPAction' HTTP header is required, which you can't set with Flash.

With Flash Remoting you don't need to know the details of how this works or how the message format is defined. You can just look at web services as objects that live on the server and whose methods you can call. The dirty details happen behind the scenes.

Flash Remoting consists of three parts:

- **The Flash Remoting Gateway on the server.** This enables the server to accept connections to web services from a Flash movie. It is part of ColdFusion MX and JRun 4, and Macromedia has announced to make it available for J2EE in general and for .NET.

- **The Flash Remoting Components.** This provides the APIs (application programming interface) to use with ActionScript to interact with a Flash Remoting Gateway. This is split into three main categories: Creating a connection and making calls, a debugger, and finally assistance with the returned results.

- **The Action Message Format (AMF).** AMF is the transport vehicle, or the binding element between Flash and the server. AMF is a binary format that Macromedia developed and included in the Flash 6 player. On the Flash side, you have the Flash Remoting Components to work with. On the server side, you work with the Flash Remoting Gateway. You don't have take care of the messy details in between.

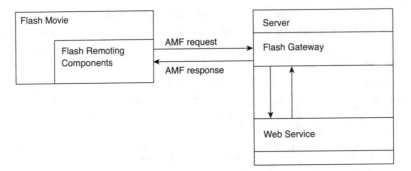

Figure 14.3 Connecting a Flash movie to a web service with Flash Remoting.

Installing the Remoting Components

You need Flash MX to develop with Flash Remoting (you've got that already), the Flash Remoting Components, and an application server with the Flash Remoting Gateway installed.

The Flash Remoting Components are available from:

`http://www.macromedia.com/software/flash/flashremoting/`

At the time of writing this, ColdFusion MX and JRun 4 had just shipped, both include the Flash Remoting Gateway. If you are interested in the server side, you can download a trial version from the following URL:

`http://www.macromedia.com/software/trial_download/`

Please note that you can use any application server for which a Gateway will be released, and you will not have to change your Flash movie to work with another back end.

To stay posted for news, updates, tutorials, and white papers about this exciting new technology, I'd recommend frequent visits to the Macromedia Designer and Developer centers at: `http://www.macromedia.com/desdev`

After you have installed the components, you can get started using them. However, unlike the Flash UI components, these components are not available through the Components panel, but are rather external .AS files. They are stored in a Configuration\Include folder below the folder where you installed Flash MX. There you will find the files in Table 14.1

You can include .AS files stored in the Configuration\Include folder directly—you don't have to specify any extra path information. This makes it much easier for several movies using the same includes. You can use this location for your own files as well, but I recommend storing them in uniquely named subfolders to avoid file-naming conflicts. However, you should *not* delete, move, or modify the Flash Remoting files, because this could stop your Flash Remoting projects from functioning.

Table 14.1 **The Files that Make Up the Flash Remoting Components**

Filename	Description
NetServices.as	The core of the Flash Remoting components. Sets up a global `NetServices` object, as well as `NetServiceProxyResponder` and `NetServiceProxy` classes.
RecordSet.as RsDataProviderClass.as	A class to hold results from database queries that will act as a data provider. Is included with NetServices.as. Discussed in more depth later in this chapter.
NetDebug.as NetDebugConfig.as NetDebugEvents.as NetDebugHelpers.as NetDebugImpl.as NetDebugLocalConnection.as NetDebugNetConnection.as	`NetDebug` class that allows you to monitor what goes in and out of Flash when you use the Remoting components. If enabled, the results are shown in the NetConnection Debugger found in the Window menu.
DataGlue.as	A class that simplifies the binding of a RecordSet or other data provider to data-aware UI components. The use of it is described later in this chapter.

The Remoting components bring their documentation with them. One part is found in the Help menu as "Welcome to Flash Remoting." From there you can get to the HTML-based documentation. The Reference panel also includes a Remoting folder with documentation of the Remoting classes once Remoting has been installed.

Using the Flash Remoting Components

With the Flash Remoting Components in place, you are just a few steps away from connecting to a web service. Here's what you need to do in Flash to get there. Please note that this won't work without a corresponding web service, which we will discuss in the following section.

1. Long story short, to use the Flash Remoting Components, you start like this:

   ```
   #include "NetServices.as"
   ```

   With this include, you get access to several objects, classes, and methods essential to Flash Remoting. Without this line you can't do Flash Remoting.

2. While developing, you want to follow it with:

   ```
   #include "NetDebug.as"
   ```

   This enables the NetConnection Debugger (found in the Window menu), which allows you to monitor what happens with your remote connection, even if your code isn't prepared for everything. Once your application is up and running, you probably want to remove this line to save file size.

3. The next steps are to set up the connection to the Flash Remoting gateway on the server:

   ```
   NetServices.setDefaultGatewayUrl("http://localhost/flashservices/gateway");
   var gateway = NetServices.createGatewayConnection();
   ```

   First you define the URL you want to connect to. In this case the application server is running on the local machine (http://localhost). "/flashservices/gateway" is actually a virtual path, not folders that actually exist on the server's file system.

   With Flash Remoting, you can't directly connect to a web service. Flash uses AMF to send out data. On the server, the gateway receives AMF messages from Flash, translates them, and forwards them to the web service. The result from the server goes back to the gateway, which converts it to AMF and sends it on its way to the Flash movie. So the purpose of the gateway is to be in between Flash and the web service and thus enabling Flash movies to connect to web services through AMF.

The gateway is running as part of the application server. It listens for any calls with a path that starts with `"/flashservices/gateway"`. It fetches those calls, and uses the rest of the information in the URL to connect to the web service.

The two preceding lines of code are what you need to do in Flash to connect to the gateway on the server. From this point on you use the returned `gateway` object to connect to web services.

> As with any Flash call to a server, the server has to be in the same domain as your Flash movie. However, that doesn't prevent your server from requesting data from a remote server and passing it on to the Flash movie.

Now you are almost ready to call a method on the server. Calling a method on the server is a bit different from calling a method within Flash. The process is asynchronous:

1. You make a call.

2. The call travels across the wire, and the server receives it.

3. The server handles the request and sends an answer back.

This could take a few seconds. In the meantime the Flash movie shouldn't freeze while waiting for the answer. Imagine if the following line of code worked:

```
var bookList = myServer.myWebService.getBookList();
```

In this scenario you call a remote method. Maybe it takes five seconds until the result is returned. In the meantime Flash would sit on this line of code, and wait until it could assign the result to `bookList`. No other code would execute in this time; the Flash movie wouldn't be able to react to any user interaction. That is certainly not a good experience.

The show must go on, therefore it is handled as follows: You make the call and specify an object to receive the result. The result is not expected to arrive instantaneously; instead you define a callback handler, which gets called when the server response arrives. When transmitting data over remote networks, there is always a chance of error. So you define not only one, but two callback handlers:

- `onResult` gets called if your request was successful.

- `onStatus` gets called if something went wrong.

This asynchronous behavior is somewhat similar to the loading process with LoadVars and XML. You make a remote request, and get notified when it is answered. The main difference is that the result can be an object of any type, not just name value pairs or an XML object.

On to the code:

```
function Result() {
  //receives data returned from a web service method
}
Result.prototype.onResult = function(result) {
  trace("onResult : " + result);
}
Result.prototype.onStatus = function(error) {
  trace("onStatus called : " + error.description);
}
var resultObj = new Result();
var service_str = "com.newriders.test.HelloWorld"

var serviceObj = gateway.getService(service_str, resultObj);
serviceObj.sayHello();
```

First, you define a result object to receive the server response, with onResult and onStatus handlers. Then you define the web service you want to connect to through the gateway, and you specify your recipient object as callback recipient. Please note the dots as the web service is specified. These dots actually represent folder separations on the server.

Finally, call the sayHello method of the web service. The process of connecting to a web service and calling its methods is often referred to as *consuming* the web service.

The result that the onResult handler receives can be of any type—a string, a number, an object, an array, or a bit. Later you will see it can even be a RecordSet.

The onError handler, on the other hand, receives an error object with the following properties: level, description, code, and details. The value for each property will vary depending on your server.

Now if you just tried to test this movie, it won't work of course, unless you have an application server on *localhost* with the Flash Remoting Gateway installed and the HelloWorld web service in place.

This example is based on Mike Chamber's tutorial "Getting Started with ColdFusion MX and Macromedia Flash Remoting" at http://www.macromedia.com/desdev/mx/coldfusion/articles/startremoting.html. His tutorial also includes the HelloWorld web service as a ColdFusion component.

Flash Remoting also offers a flatter way to define callback handlers. Instead of defining an object to receive the result of a specific call, you can define callback handlers for multiple calls in one object. To differentiate between them, you have to name them differently. The format is

```
<remoteMethodName>_result
<remoteMethodName>_status
```

However I consider this approach much less object-oriented. You could end up with one flat object containing callbacks for all server calls—and their only connection being that they are all callbacks, but don't have necessarily any other ties. It may be appropriate though if you need to call several methods of the same web service.

If you installed ColdFusion MX, and installed the samples and documentation, you can find more examples of Flash and ColdFusion integration at `http://localhost/cfdocs/exampleapps/index.cfm`.

In case you decided to install the standalone version, this link may change to `http://localhost:8500/cfdocs/exampleapps/index.cfm` or whatever port you chose ColdFusion to run on.

Detecting Network Problems

What do you do if you can't even connect to server? How do you find out what happened? When you use XML or LoadVars, Flash won't tell you if there was a network error, or if the server is down. You have to wait—and after a reasonable time you assume the server is unreachable. Flash Remoting is a bit more helpful here. The onStatus handler of the receiver object, however, will only be called if there was an actual response from the server. A network error is more of a global error that may affect any call you would attempt. So to catch the error, you define an onStatus handler for the global System object:

```
_global.System.onStatus = function(error) {
 trace("details : " + error.details);
 trace("description : " + error.description);
 trace("code : " + error.code);
 trace("level : " + error.level);
}
```

The format is exactly the same as before—it receives an error object with the same four properties.

Defining a global onStatus handler works really only for Flash Remoting, and connection attempts made through it. Unfortunately the XML and LoadVars classes do not benefit from this.

Taking Care of Database Data

Traditionally databases store data in tables with columns and rows. Each column may represent a property, such as a street name or a zip code, each row an entry into the database. When you query a database, the result is usually still in such a table.

However, the Flash Remoting components provide your Flash movie with a RecordSet class. Now when a web service you are calling returns a database query to you, Flash Remoting will automatically make it an instance of the RecordSet class. No work for you to convert anything, Flash Remoting takes care of that.

You just have to deal with the instance of RecordSet. You can think of as a RecordSet in Flash as a fancy two-dimensional array. We'll show the use some of its methods in this exercise. For a listing of all methods, take a look at the Reference panel in the Remoting category.

Let's do a little exercise. So far I haven't touched the server at all, but the whole chapter would be kind of hanging in the air without it. There is plenty of choice in what technology I could use, so I spun the bottle and it pointed to ColdFusion MX.

For the rest of this exercise I assume you downloaded and installed the trial version of ColdFusion MX on your local machine. Furthermore, I assume you installed with your web server (for example, IIS), not the standalone version. If you installed the standalone version, you will have to modify the URL used and add the port on which you decided to run the server. For example `http://localhost/flashservices/` gateway will change to `http://localhost:8500/flashservices/gateway` if you chose the default port.

Setting Up the Web Service

The first thing you need to do is set up the web service:

1. In your webroot folder, create the following sub folder structure: com\newriders\flash_mx_oop.

   com\newriders is just the reverse of newriders.com, and that is intentional. We reserved a namespace for our web service. This way we avoided naming conflict, in case someone else chose to name his or her web service the same.

▨ To learn more about namespaces, please refer to Chapter 4.

2. Now in the flash_mx_oop folder, create a file named recordset.cfc, with your text or web editor of choice. Enter the following:

```
<cfcomponent>
    <cffunction name="getEmployeeData" access="remote" returntype="query">
        <!-- CompanyInfo is a DSN name for an example DB that CFMX sets up by
        ▸default -->
        <cfquery datasource="CompanyInfo" name="result">
            select * from Employee
        </cfquery>
        <cfreturn result />
    </cffunction>
</cfcomponent>
```

This is all you need to define a simple web service with ColdFusion MX (CFMX). CFMX is a tag-based language, with which you may not be familiar. It is however not too hard to understand.

First, there is a main tag called `cfcomponent`. It doesn't need to be named—the filename is its name. Then you define a method for your web service with the `cffunction` tag. The name attribute is the name of the method. Setting access to remote is important—otherwise the method wouldn't be available to Flash Remoting. The `returntype` specifies the output format. It could also be string, array, or date. Because you want to receive a RecordSet in Flash, it needs to be set to `query`.

3. Now go inside the method with a `cfquery` tag to query a database. `CompanyInfo` is one of the demo databases installed with CFMX, so you won't have to worry about setting one up. You give it the name result and then select all columns from the employee table. Then you simply return the result.

A CFMX component could have more methods with more complex tasks, but this is all we need for now.

This is all we need to take care of on the server for this exercise. CFMX also supports Server Side ActionScript (SSAS) as well as Java. This example could have been written in either of the two. SSAS may be much more familiar to the ActionScript programmer, but it is much more limited than ColdFusion's tag language, at least in this version.

Consuming the Web Service

Hungry for more? It's time to consume your web service from Flash.

> You don't have to start from scratch—simply open 14_03_employee_recordSet.fla file from the downloadable files that are on the website associated with this book.

Take a look at the actions in the Actions layer. This should look similar to the code I described in the Hello World example. First, the Remoting Components are included, then you define a class to receive the result, and then you set up the connection to the web service, and call the `getEmployeeData` method of your RecordSet web service.

There is one significant change, and it is in the `onResult` method:

```
Result.prototype.onResult = function(employeeData_rs){
  employeeData_lb.setDataProvider(employeeData_rs);
}
```

As a result, you expect employeeData_rs and then just set its data provider for the employeeData_lb listbox on the stage (see Figure 14.4). That seems to be too easy, but it does work. Test the movie and see for yourself.

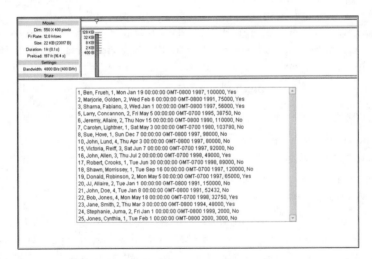

Figure 14.4　A listbox filled with employee data.

Now admittedly it doesn't look pretty, but you have the result of the database query in a listbox—and you didn't really have to break a sweat for it.

Formatting the Output

Maybe we should do a bit of extra work to have that data look a bit better.

1. First, insert the following line into the onResult method:

```
trace ("column names: " + employeeData_rs.getColumnNames());
```

2. Test the movie again and you should see the following in the Output window:

```
column names: Emp_ID,FirstName,LastName,Dept_ID,StartDate,Salary,Contract
```

Now you know what each of the values you see in the listbox actually mean.

Next, you want to display only the first and last names of each employee. With Flash Remoting comes another class to help with that: DataGlue. Its functionality is to bind data contained in a RecordSet to a UI component.

DataGlue does not only work for RecordSet, but also for other objects that act as DataProvider. Please see Chapter 6 for information about data providers.

3. Because DataGlue is not automatically included into your movie with NetServices.as, you need to add it manually as the third line of the script:

```
#include "DataGlue.as"
```

4. Now remove the line:

```
employeeData_lb.setDataProvider(employeeData_rs);
```

5. And replace it with:

```
DataGlue.bindFormatStrings (employeeData_lb, employeeData_rs,
   "#FirstName# #LastName#", "#Emp_ID#");
```

What does this do?

The first two arguments you pass to bindFormatStrings are the listbox and the RecordSet you want to connect. Your RecordSet is a table with seven columns. When you just connect it to the listbox as you did before, the listbox doesn't know what to display as label, and what to use as value when an element is clicked; therefore the result looks plain ugly.

`DataGlue` helps us to select what to use as label, and what as value for each row. Enclosed in # we can specify column names, which will be replaced with the values for each row. For the first entry, "#FirstName# #LastName#" then displays Ben Frueh. When you click on a listbox element, its value will be the unique employee ID. (See Figure 14.5.)

6. Test the movie to see the improved formatting. (In case something went wrong with editing the code, you can open 14_04_employee_glue.fla.)

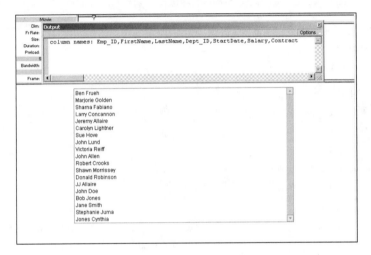

Figure 14.5 Displaying first and last names only in the listbox.

Maybe you don't want to show only the names, but also sort by the first name.

7. Enter one more line:

```
employeeData_rs.sortItemsBy("FirstName");
```

You can enter this before or after the `DataGlue` binding. The RecordSet is not copied over to the listbox but rather glued to it. If you change the data in the RecordSet, the listbox will update what you see. The listbox receives a `modelChanged` event from the RecordSet, and then it can take appropriate action to update itself. (You can find the completed glued and sorted example as 14_05_employee_sort.fla.)

The sortItemsBy may not always give you the results you expect. It compares items from a computer's perspective, and that means comparing strings with the < or > operator. A RecordSet, such as Arrays, also supports a sort function where you can define a function that does the comparison for you. However because that then happens in ActionScript, it will be slower. (See Figure 14.6.)

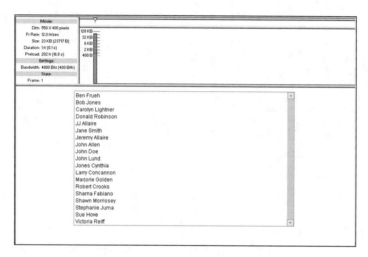

Figure 14.6 The sorted employee names.

A New Side of *Object.registerClass*

Through the course of this book, you have learned how to utilize Object.registerClass to create movieclip classes. The first argument you pass to it is the symbol ID, the second one is the class.

Have you ever wondered how the server can send a RecordSet, and Flash knows it's a RecordSet and gives you an instance of it as a result, not a plain object?

It turns out that Object.registerClass does more than link symbols to class constructors. You can associate a class with a string identifier this way. This string ends up in a global, but undocumented and internal, lookup table. This lookup table is used to associate an object with a class when Flash receives a serialized object from the outside. This applies to objects received through Flash Remoting, Shared Objects, and LocalConnection.

Enter the following code into an empty movie and do a test movie:

```
RestoreClass = function() {
}
RestoreClass.prototype.tellClass = function(){
  var sClass = "I inherited from " +
  ((this instanceof RestoreClass)? "RestoreClass" : "Object");
  return sClass;
}
Object.registerClass("RestoreClass",RestoreClass);

setData = function(){
  var so = SharedObject.getLocal("restore");
  so.data.keeper = new RestoreClass();
  so.flush();
}
getData = function(){
  var so = SharedObject.getLocal("restore");
  trace( so.data.keeper.tellClass() );
}
setData();
getData();
```

Look at the result, then remove the `Object.registerClass` line and try again. Notice the difference?

The same can be applied to receiving objects from Flash Remoting— if you take a look at NetServices.as or RecordSet.as (in the Configuration\ Include folder below your Flash MX application folder), you can see that Object.registerClass is used there to re-create NetServiceProxy and RecordSet instances received through Flash Remoting.

Kudos go to Peter Hall for figuring out the preceding example with a Shared Object.

Thoughts on Flash Remoting

With Flash Remoting you step into a whole new world. At first it seems a bit overwhelming, with a lot of new functionality. Yet after the first shock, you probably realize that all this is there to make your life easier. All the new functionality means you don't have to reinvent the wheel as often any more, and you can focus more on your actual development.

Using Flash Remoting allows you to more directly interact with application servers and databases. A lot of the programming work you have to take care of when you deal with XML data for example to convert an XML object to the data structure you need is often eliminated.

On the other hand, to use it, the Flash Remoting Gateway is required on your server. It will probably take a little while until this is widely available. However, you can make use of `RecordSet` and `DataGlue` without the Flash Remoting Gateway.

Conclusion

The communication between Flash and Server is a huge field. The scope of this chapter could only cover some aspects of it, mainly from the perspective of a Flash programmer. Flash Remoting was available as a preview release only a few weeks prior to the writing of this chapter. There is more to come—and it's probably worth writing an entire book about it. I hope this chapter gave you at least a good overview of the endless seeming possibilities, and got you started, or at least raised your appetite for more.

To follow what is yet to come I recommend again frequently checking the Macromedia DesDev (Designer and Developer) and Exchange sites:

DesDev Center: `http://www.macromedia.com/desdev`

DesDev Center for Flash: `http://www.macromedia.com/desdev/mx/flash`

Flash Exchange: `http://www.macromedia.com/exchange/flash`

15

Data Structures: Sculpting Information To Suit Your Needs

By Branden J. Hall

Help! I Lost This Chapter!

During the process of writing my sections of this book, I've been keeping my files on a little USB "keychain" hard drive that my wife Patti got me for Christmas this year. It's quite a cool little device, as it holds 64 megs of information and doesn't require any special software to work on nearly any PC or Mac that supports USB devices. The only problem with the device is what is really its greatest asset, size.

First off, let me say, I lose things. I simply forget where I put them down two seconds ago and then go running around the house like a madman trying to find an item that happened to be right on my desk under a piece of paper. It's so bad that when I'm looking for something and eventually find it, Patti asks if it was under a piece of paper this time. The smaller the item, the quicker I'm sure to misplace it.

Well, earlier this year I managed to lose the keychain. I was going nuts to say the least. I had three chapters on it, not to mention numerous figures as well as other important files. Literally for days I was digging around every chance I got trying to find it. After a few days I gave up the frantic hunt and figured I'd find it eventually (well, at least before my final deadline!).

Only a few days after that, I looked in the bag I use to carry my laptop to and from work and realized it was an awful mess. Papers were crunched up inside, bits of electronics were half hanging out, and there was more loose change and business cards in the pockets than I knew what to do with. Just dumped the thing out on the floor and guess what fell out? You guessed it, the keychain that had nearly given me a heart attack. Had I just kept my bag organized in the first place, I would have been able to find the key chain in all of two minutes rather than nearly a whole nerve-wracking week later!

Introduction

I think this little gem about my messiness illustrates nicely that organization is important. If you work within an organizational system you can easily add, remove, and find the information you need. None of this knowledge is, by any means, rocket science. In fact it probably rates pretty high the "Duh!" category, yet it's still quite rare for Flash developers to keep the data in their movies truly organized.

Part of the reason for this is the fact that ActionScript is such a loose language. Because you can basically do whatever you want, whenever you want, ActionScript simply doesn't inspire (or enforce!) organization like Java or C++ do. Another issue that exacerbates the problem is that for many people, ActionScript is one of, if not the, first programming language they have ever been exposed to.

These folks tend to start getting into trouble later because they know the programming equivalent of how to hang drywall, but are now being asked to design and build a house. Scripting, like hanging drywall, requires knowledge and experience, but building an application, just like building a house, requires more than just good scripting skills. The data structures used in a movie form its foundation and support beams. If you don't build them right the first time, your system gets stressed and your "house" of code will end up looking like a doublewide trailer after a tornado rips through town.

The best thing about ActionScript is that when it comes to data structures, you don't need to know that much to get started. The loose nature of the language actually helps here—ActionScript's built-in tools give you a real leg up compared to working with C++, for example.

Arrays—Lists of Information

The first kind of data structure that people come in contact with is the lowly array. As you probably already know by now, an array is just a list of variables where you access individual elements via the array access operator, [ ]. For example:

```
foo = new Array();
foo[0] = 2;
foo[1] = 3;
```

Creating and manipulating an array.

Arrays in ActionScript are 0-based, that is, the first element in the list is the one located at position 0. Be careful to keep an eye out for this, particularly if you usually program in ColdFusion or Director, because both of them use 1-based arrays.

Most of this information about arrays is relatively standard across a number of common languages. However, arrays in ActionScript are a bit odd; in fact, given what they can do, they wouldn't even be called arrays in most other languages.

When most other languages define an array, they must specify how big the array is—how many items it can hold at maximum. The array can then never get bigger than that size. Resizing requires creating a new, bigger array, and then copying all the data into it. In addition, arrays in most other programming languages can only consist of a single type. That is, when I create an array, I have to specify what type of data will be put in it, whether that will be integers, strings, or whatever.

> You can define the size of an array in ActionScript by passing the size in the Arrays constructor, but that doesn't force the array to stay that size. Rather, it just tells Flash how much memory to set aside at first.

Flash arrays on the other hand are much more malleable. You can change their size anytime you want (Flash handles this for you automatically), and you can put anything you want anywhere you want in the array. ActionScript arrays can really be considered the Swiss Army knife of data structures.

Sorting Arrays

All array objects in ActionScript have a handy `sort` method. This method does a standard sort on the elements of your array and rearranges them in alphabetical order. For the most part this is perfectly acceptable; however, if you are storing any numbers in your array, things won't turn out quite right because the sort always assumes the items in the list are strings. This means that an array with 2, 10, 1, and 20 in it won't sort into 1, 2, 10, 20, but instead into 1, 10, 2, 20!

Luckily, the `sort` method supports an optional method that lets you specify your own function for comparing elements in the array. This comparison function must accept two parameters and then return a negative number, 0, or a positive number. It should return a negative number if the first parameter is less than the second, 0 if the parameters are equal, and a positive number if the first parameter is greater than the second. Here's a simple comparison function that works with numbers:

```
function compareNums(a, b){
    return a - b;
}
myList = new Array(2, 1, 20, 10);
myList.sort(compareNums);
```

Using a custom comparison method.

It's important to note that if you specify a custom comparison method, it will greatly slow down the speed in which Flash can do the sorting. Just be careful with using custom comparison methods.

Natural Comparison

Another type of sort that's often desired but difficult to code is a natural comparison. *Natural comparison* compares numbers as we would; that is, it treats the numeric parts of a string separately from the rest of a string. If you had the strings foo1, foo5, foo2 and foo10 a standard sort would result in foo1, foo10, foo2, and foo5. A sort that used natural comparison would result in foo1, foo2, foo5, and foo10. Here is the full source of a natural sort that works in both ActionScript and standard JavaScript:

```
naturalCompare= function(a, b){
    // are the items equal?
    if (a == b){
        return 0;
```

```
// otherwise, let's sort!
}else{
// if needed, create a lookup table for order
   // spaces first, then numbers, then everything else in ASCII
   if (Array.$sortType == null){
      Array.$sortType = new Object();
      Array.$sortType[" "] = -2;
      Array.$sortType[1] = -1;
      Array.$sortType[2] = -1;
      Array.$sortType[3] = -1;
      Array.$sortType[4] = -1;
      Array.$sortType[5] = -1;
      Array.$sortType[6] = -1;
      Array.$sortType[7] = -1;
      Array.$sortType[8] = -1;
      Array.$sortType[9] = -1;
      Array.$sortType[0] = -1;
   }
   var charType = Array.$sortType;

   var isNum = -1;
   var isChar = null;
   var isSpace =0;

   var isLesser = -1;
   var isGreater = 1;

   var index_a = 0;
   var index_b = 0;
   var hasNumbers = false;
   var max_a = a.length;
   var max_b = b.length;
   var result = undefined;
   var buf_a, buf_b;
   var hint_a = 0;
   var hint_b = 0;
   var char_a = "";
   var char_b = "";
   var type_a, type_b;

// loop over the characters in the items until order is determined
   while (index_a < max_a && index_b < max_b && result == undefined){
      char_a = a.charAt(index_a);
      char_b = b.charAt(index_b);

      // determine the "type" of the character (space, number, other)
      type_a = Number(charType[char_a]);
      type_b =  Number(charType[char_b]);
```

continues

```
// if one or both is a string, it's easy
if (type_a == 0 || type_b == 0){
   if (type_a == 0 && type_b == 0){
      if (char_a != char_b){
         result = (char_a < char_b) ? isLesser : isGreater;
      }
   }else{
      result = (type_a < type_b) ? isLesser : isGreater;
   }


// remove any leading whitespace and 0s then chop out
// out the number until we find a non-number or the end of the item, then
compare
// the hint value of each side has to do with the size of the
// whitespace and leading 0s. This is used to resolve "ties"
}else{
   buf_a = "";
   buf_b = "";
   while (char_a == " " || char_a == "0"){
      ++hint_a;
      buf_a += char_a;
      char_a = a.charAt(++index_a);
      }
   }
   while (charType[char_a] == isNum){
      ++index_a;
      buf_a += char_a;
      char_a = a.charAt(index_a);
      hasChars = true;
   }
   index_a -= Number(hasNumbers);
   hasNumbers = false;
   while (char_b == " " || char_b == "0"){
      ++hint_b;
      buf_b += char_b;
      char_b = b.charAt(++index_b);

   }
   while (charType[char_b] == isNum){
      ++index_b;
      buf_b += char_b;
      char_b = b.charAt(index_b);
      hasNumbers = true;
   }
   index_b -= Number(hasNumbers);
   hasNumbers = false;
   buf_a = parseInt(buf_a);
```

```
            buf_b = parseInt(buf_b);
            if (buf_a != buf_b){
                result = buf_a < buf_b ? isLesser : isGreater;
            }
        }
        ++index_a;
        ++index_b;
    }

    // we found a result
    if (result != undefined){
        return result;

    // we didn't find a result, so first look to see if we finished looking
    // at both strings, if so the one with the largest "hint" is
    // is largest. Otherwise, justjust
    // consider the item that finished being checked the smaller.
    }else{
        if (index_a > max_a && index_b > max_b){
            return hint_a < hint_b ? isLesser : isGreater;
        }else{
            return index_a == max_a ? isLesser : isGreater;
        }
    }
}

myList = new Array();
myList[0] = "foo2";
myList[1] = "foo10";
myList[2] = "foo1";
myList[3] = "foo5";
myList.sort(naturalCompare);
```

Using natural comparison to sort an array.

Yes, that is a very long and quite ugly piece of code. It points out one of ActionScript's weaknesses—text parsing. Text parsing is a task that programming languages either excel at or suck at. I've never seen a language that was just "okay" with parsing text.

As for the code itself, it's not important that you understand each and every line of it because it's just meant to be used as a library. The core idea though is that two strings are sliced into their component pieces: whitespace, numbers, and characters. These chunks are then compared to each other in the appropriate fashion (numbers are compared as numbers, strings are compared as strings, and whitespace is ignored).

sortOn

There is one other way to sort an array, and that is via the sortOn method. This method of arrays allows you to sort the array based on a property that each element in the array has. For example, if you have an object in each element of an array called id, you could sort the array based on that property.

```
myList = new Array();
myList[0] = {id:5, name:"John"};
myList[1] = {id:1, name:"Pat"};
myList[2] = {id:51, name:"Chris"};
myList[3] = {id:45, name:"Jody"};
myList[4] = {id:9, name:"Bob"};
myList.sortOn("name");
```

Using sortOn to sort an array based on a property of its elements.

Multidimensional Arrays

Because ActionScript arrays can contain anything you want, it should come as no surprise that you can put arrays inside of other arrays. When you do this to each element in the array, you are creating what is known as a multidimensional array. These arrays are useful when your data needs to be located via two "addresses." A good example of this would be a Flash version of the game Battleship. Two values, the row and the column, address each square on the board.

```
myFleet = new Array();
for (i=0; i< 10; ++i){
      myFleet[i] = new Array();
}
myFleet[0][0] = "Battleship";
myFleet[0][1] = "Battleship";
myFleet[0][2] = "Battleship";
myFleet[4][2] = "PT Boat";
myFleet[5][2] = "PT Boat";
```

Creating a 2D array to store the position of elements.

Just by creating arrays within arrays, you can keep going and make three- or even four-dimensional arrays (though what you would *do* with a four-dimensional array eludes me).

Besides these comparatively amazing feats, arrays in ActionScript are even more powerful; they support methods to let you treat them like other data structures, namely stacks and queues.

Stacks

A *stack* is a relatively common and simple type of data structure that has specific rules on how data can come in and out of it. Unlike an array, you can't specify where to get or put data in a stack. Instead, you have a single method to put data in and another to get data out. The rule by which the stack determines where to put its data is often referred to as FILO (First-In-Last-Out), as shown in Figure 15.1. This may seem a bit abstract, but you use this kind of structure all the time in the real world!

Such an example of FILO data structure is a Pez candy dispenser. The first candy you put into the dispenser is in fact, the last one you actually get to eat.

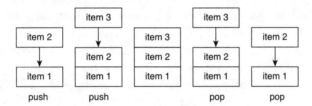

Figure 15.1 A stack data structure in action.

To use an array such as a stack, you have to use some of the built-in methods that the Array object supports:

Methods Supported by the Array Object	Description
push	Adds an element to the end of an array.
pop	Removes and returns the last element in an array.
unshift	Adds an element to the front of an array.
shift	Removes and returns the first element in an array.

By using a combination of either `push` and `pop` or `unshift` and `shift` to add and remove elements from an array, that array is now a stack. It's pretty standard for stacks to use methods named `push` and `pop`, so it's best to stick with that combination.

```
myStack = new Array();
myStack.push(4);
myStack.push(3);
myStack.push("hello");
mystack.push(true);
temp = myStack.pop();
while(myStack.length > 1){
    trace(temp);
    temp = myStack.pop()
}
```

Creating and manipulating an array as a stack.

So now that you know all the gory details, what is a stack actually good for? Well, one of the most common uses for stacks is with anything based on tracking history so that it can be backtracked later. Say you were building an application that needed an undo button: Each time the user performed an action, you would just push into your undo stack how to undo that particular action. Just by popping off the top element in the array, you could then undo the most recent action taken by the user.

Queues

A queue is similar to a stack in that there's only one way for data to get into a queue, as well as only one way for data to get out. In fact the only difference between a stack and queue is the order in which the data comes out. A queue is a FIFO structure (First-In-First-Out), as shown in Figure 15.2.

Anytime you stand in line for something you are, in fact, in a queue. The first person in line at the movie theatre is first person to get a movie ticket.

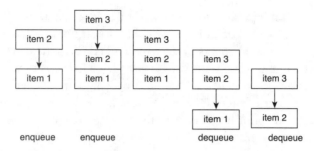

Figure 15.2 A queue data structure in action.

To use an ActionScript array as a queue, you again have to choose from a combination of `push`, `pop`, `unshift`, and `shift`. Because the goal is to put data into one end of the array, and pull data from the other, the combinations that will work are `push` and `shift` or `unshift` and `pop`. Queues created in other languages often use methods named `enqueue` and `dequeue` to add and remove items, respectively, so there's no real standard on which combination is better in Flash. The problem is that it's easy to forget which combination you are using, thereby corrupting your data. Because of this, I tend to create my own methods named `enqueue` and `dequeue` for adding to and removing from a queue, respectively.

```
Array.prototype.enqueue = Array.prototype.push;
}

Array.prototype.dequeue = Array.prototype.shift;

myQueue = new Array();
myQueue.enqueue(4);
myQueue.enqueue(3);
myQueue.enqueue("hello");
myQueue.enqueue(true);
temp = myQueue.dequeue();
while(myQueue.length > 1){
    trace(temp);
    temp = myQueue.dequeue()
}
```

*Creating and using **enqueue** and **dequeue** methods for arrays.*

Queues are useful in any situation when you need to determine who was "first in line." A good use of a queue would be for a smart preloader. Rather than loading individual elements as they were asked for, parts of your movie would instead communicate with your smart preloader object, which would place their requests in a queue. As .swfs got loaded, the preloader would pull the next element out of the queue and load it.

When you learn about heaps later in this chapter, you'll learn how to build an even better type of queue for this kind of job, a priority queue.

Using Objects as Dictionaries

Although ActionScript arrays solve a huge number of data structuring problems, there are a few problems with arrays. In an array, order and position are important. When you remove an element in the middle of an array, you are either stuck with a blank spot in the array, or you have to shuffle the items that come after the blank spot, which could cause problems if you are expecting certain items to be it certain positions in the array. In addition, because the position of an element in an array inherently doesn't have any connection to the data being held there, searching through an array to find a specific piece of data could potentially require looking at each and every element before it's found.

The solution to these issues involves again taking advantage of the loose nature of ActionScript, in particular that objects are malleable at any time. Basically, you use a standard instance of the Object class (which is normally just empty) to store information in the form of new properties. This, combined with the fact that you can use array-syntax to access properties of an object, gives you a data structure that in other languages is often referred to as a dictionary (you'll also often hear it referred to as an associative array). Creating a dictionary and putting elements in it looks like this:

```
myObj = new Object();
myObj["fname"] = "Branden";
myObj["lname"] = "Hall";
myObj["position"] = "coder";
```

Using an object as a dictionary.

This type of data structure is called a *dictionary* because like a real dictionary, you can "look up" the information you want just by knowing the name of the info. Because of this, the strings used to retrieve elements in a dictionary are referred to as *keys*. Obviously in this setup keys must be unique. If you try to set a nonunique key, the old value of that key will be destroyed. (There's another type of data structure known as a *hash* that gracefully deals with such collisions and allows both the old and new values to both stay.) Remember that, in Flash, dictionaries aren't their own real structures like arrays. Instead, dictionaries are just a result of the fact that you can modify objects at any time and use array syntax to access elements in an object (which is why they are also called associative arrays).

Sometimes you may need to loop through all the keys in a dictionary. To do this, use a `for...in` loop:

```
for (i in myObj){
    trace(i+" : "+myObj[i]);
}
```

Looping through a dictionary.

During each iteration of the loop the variable `i` is filled with a different property (key) inside of `myObj`. One thing to be careful of is to not depend on the order in which you get items out of a `for...in` loop. This order is in no way guaranteed and can change at any time. In addition, if you have messed around with the class of the object you are iterating through and perhaps added some methods to that class's prototype object, they will show up in your `for...in` loops, so be careful!

Using objects as dictionaries is handy when you need to store pieces of data inside a structure and order isn't important. The initial dictionary code you saw highlights a good use of dictionaries—storing named properties like name and position. In addition, dictionaries are good for storing data when you know there will be a lot of data added and removed, but order doesn't matter.

Advanced Data Structures

For the majority of the work you will probably do in ActionScript, the data structures you just read about should do the job. However, at times you may need something more advanced. Reasons for needing a more advanced structure include a need for greater speed, specialized data access, and special data relationships that can't be handled by normal arrays or dictionaries.

Trees

One of the first types of data structures you may need to use is a tree. Tree structures offer quick data retrieval and insertion like dictionaries, but offer more control over searching. In a tree structure, data is arranged in a hierarchical manner (see Figure 15.3). An example of a tree structure would be the XML object in Flash. Any XML object contains a single root node, and from that come child nodes, and those nodes have child nodes, and so on.

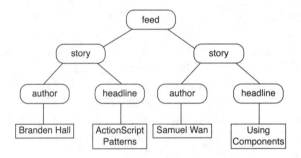

Figure 15.3   XML as a tree structure.

Flash's movieclip structure could similarly be seen as a tree structure.

Besides holding hierarchical data, trees are valuable data structures because they take advantage of the old adage "divide and conquer." Unlike an array, where finding an element could potentially require checking each and every element, in a well-balanced tree at most you will only have to check a fraction of that.

Every node in a tree has to support at least two properties; its data and a reference to another node. One of the first types of trees that computer science students learn about is a binary search tree, or BST (see Figure 15.4). Each node in a BST contains three properties; its data, a reference to the sub-tree on the left, and reference to the sub-tree on the right. When you insert data into BST, it automatically figures out where in the tree to put the data by starting at the root node and following one simple rule: If the data you are inserting is less than the current node's data, move to the left; otherwise move to the right until you find an empty spot.

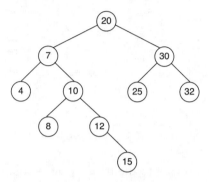

Figure 15.4 A binary search tree.

BSTs themselves have limited usefulness because, depending on the order in which you add data to it, the tree might become unbalanced and hence lose most, if not all, of its "divide and conquer" powers (see Figure 15.5).

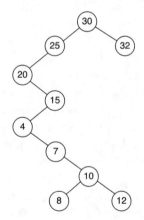

Figure 15.5 A very unbalanced BST.

As you've seen already, trees are far from limited to BSTs. In fact, an example back in Chapter 13, "Textfield Mangling," uses trees to find a particular word quickly. In that example the code had to quickly determine if the text in a textfield matched any predefined patterns to do auto-complete (see Figure 15.6). In that case, when an auto-complete pattern was defined, it was divided up letter by letter and put into a tree.

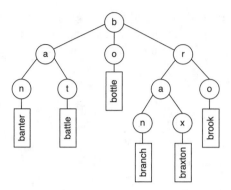

Figure 15.6 A tree used to hold words for auto-complete.

Now, just by scanning down into the tree, the auto-complete function quickly finds whether there were any words that matched the current text in the textfield.

The trees I've mentioned so far are quite simple in nature, but keep in mind that there are numerous other more complex tree types out there: red–black trees, b-trees, minimum spanning trees, and so on. In fact, most 3D first-person shooter games store their level data in a special type of tree known as a binary space partition tree.

Heaps

A *heap* is a special type of tree where there are only a couple of rules. The first rule is that each parent node always has to have two children, or its only child must be the last node in the tree. The second rule is that a parent node must be larger (or smaller as long as it's consistent) than the children. The third and final rule is that the tree must be "complete" at all times. A "complete" tree is one where there are no "holes" in the tree and new nodes fill in at its bottom level starting on the left (see Figure 15.7).

These rules may seem a bit arbitrary, but they give heaps a particular property that makes them very useful: you can store them in a regular old array! The way this works is a simple equation. For any element i in the array, its left child can be figured out by rounding down the result of (i-1)/2 and its right child may be found by rounding down the result of (i-2)/2.

Heap represented by a tree

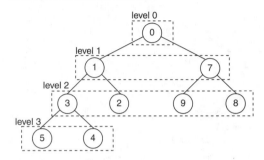

Same heap as an array

level 0	level 1		level 2				level 3	
0	1	7	3	2	9	8	5	4

Figure 15.7 A heap represented as a tree and as an array.

Heaps are handy structures, and in fact most operating systems use them heavily for memory management. In our examples, though, a heap is most useful when it is used as the base of another type of data structure known as a priority queue.

A priority queue acts similarly to the normal queue you learned about earlier. That is, at its base it's a first-in-first-out structure. Each item in a priority queue happens to have an additional property: its priority. This priority overrides the normal rules of a queue, and no matter what item comes out of the priority, queue is always the one with the highest priority. If two items have the same priority, then the normal "seniority" rules of a queue apply.

Priority queues are great structures to have in Flash because they let you built complex and intelligent preloader systems quite easily. Think about it a bit; with a priority queue, you can queue up which external assets to load up in a standardized order. Then if the user jumps to a section that doesn't yet have its assets loaded, you can easily reprioritize parts of the queue as needed so that it starts loading the proper asset immediately as well as increasing the priority of elements that are related to the current section.

Here is an implementation of a priority queue in ActionScript:

```
// constructor
_global.PQueue = function() {
   this.heap = new Array();
   this.map = new Object();
   this.idInc = 0;
}

// insert items into the queue
PQueue.prototype.insert = function(obj, priority) {
   if (priority == null) {
      priority = Number.MAX_VALUE;
   }
   var pos = this.heap.length;
   var temp = new Object();
   var id = this.idInc++;
   temp.priority = priority;
   temp.data = obj;
   temp.id = id;
   temp.pos = pos;
   this.map[id] = temp;
   this.heap[pos] = temp;
   this.$filterUp(pos);
   return id;
}

// get the value of the top priority w/o removing it
PQueue.prototype.getTop = function(){
   return this.heap[0].priority;
}

// remove, and return, the top element in the heap
PQueue.prototype.removeTop = function() {
   if (this.heap.length>0) {
      var result = this.heap[0].data;
      delete this.map[this.heap[0].id];
      delete this.heap[0];
      this.heap[0] = this.heap[this.heap.length-1];
      this.heap[0].pos = 0;
      this.heap.splice(this.heap.length-1, 1);
      this.$filterDown(0);
      return result;
   } else {
      return false;
   }
}

// reprioritize an element
PQueue.prototype.setPriority = function(id, value) {
   var element = this.map[id];
```

```
      var pos = element.pos;
      var oldPriority = element.priority;
      element.priority = value;
      if (oldPriority>element.priority) {
         this.$filterUp(pos);
      } else {
         this.$filterDown(pos);
      }
   }


// return the priority of an element
PQueue.prototype.getPriority = function(id) {
   return this.map[id].priority;
}


// determine if the queue is empty
PQueue.prototype.isEmpty = function() {
   return (this.heap.length == 0);
}


// get priority of top element
PQueue.prototype.getTopPriority = function() {
   return this.heap[0].priority;
}


// check to see if an ID is in the queue
PQueue.prototype.isQueued = function(id) {
   return (this.map[id] != null);
}


// remove an object from the queue
PQUeue.prototype.remove = function(id) {
   if (this.isQueued(id)) {
      var index = this.map[id].pos;
      delete this.map[id];
      delete this.heap[index];
      this.heap[index] = this.heap[this.heap.length-1];
      this.heap[0].pos = 0;
      this.heap.splice(this.heap.length-1, 1);
      return true;
   } else {
      return false;
   }
}
//-----------------------------------------------------------
// Private "helper" methods
//-----------------------------------------------------------
PQueue.prototype.$filterUp = function(index) {
   var i = index;
   while(i>0 && this.heap[int((i-1)/2)].priority > this.heap[i].priority){
```

continues

```
      var parent = Math.floor((i-1)/2);
      var temp = this.heap[i];
      this.heap[i] = this.heap[parent];
      this.heap[parent] = temp;
      this.heap[i].pos = i;
      this.heap[parent].pos = parent;
      i = parent;

  }
}

PQueue.prototype.$filterDown = function(index) {
  var i = index;
  var left, right, k;
  if (i < (this.heap.length-1)/2){
    left = 2 * i + 1;
    right = 2 * i + 2;
    if (right >= this.heap.length){
      k = left;
      right = left;
    }else{
      if (this.heap[left].priority < this.heap[right].priority){
        k = left;
      }else{
        if (this.heap[left].priority == this.heap[right].priority){
          if (this.heap[left].id < this.heap[right].id){
            k = left;
          }else{
            k = right;
          }
        }else{
          k = right;
        }
      }
    }
    if (this.heap[i].priority > this.heap[k].priority){
      var temp = this.heap[i];
      this.heap[i] = this.heap[k];
      this.heap[k] = temp;
      this.heap[i].pos = i;
      this.heap[k].pos = k;
      this.$filterDown(k);
    }else{
```

```
        if (this.heap[i].priority == this.heap[k].priority){
            if (this.heap[i].id > this.heap[k].id){

                var temp = this.heap[i];
                this.heap[i] = this.heap[k];
                this.heap[k] = temp;
                this.heap[i].pos = i;
                this.heap[k].pos = k;
                this.$filterDown(k);
            }
        }
    }
    }
}
```

That probably seems like a lot of code, but the most important parts to understand are the insert, setPriority, and removeTop methods. Also, understand that filterUp and filterDown are what handle the enforcement of the heap "rules" and hence re-organize the heap as needed whenever items are added or removed from it.

```
// insert items into the queue
PQueue.prototype.insert = function(obj, priority) {
    if (priority == null) {
        priority = Number.MAX_VALUE;
    }
    var pos = this.heap.length;
    var temp = new Object();
    var id = this.idInc++;
    temp.priority = priority;
    temp.data = obj;
    temp.id = id;
    temp.pos = pos;
    this.map[id] = temp;
    this.heap[pos] = temp;
    this.$filterUp(pos);
    return id;
}
```

The *insert* method.

The `insert` method takes two parameters; the first is the object to insert into the queue and the second is its priority. If no priority is given, it's set to positive infinity (this is because it's actually smaller priorities that are more "important" in this implementation). When the `insert` method is finished it returns back an id. You can use this id to access the data in the queue later.

```
// reprioritize an element
PQueue.prototype.setPriority = function(id, value) {
    var element = this.map[id];
    var pos = element.pos;
    var oldPriority = element.priority;
    element.priority = value;
    if (oldPriority>element.priority) {
        this.$filterUp(pos);
    } else {
        this.$filterDown(pos);
    }
}
```

The `setPriority` method.

The most common use of this id is with the `setPriority` method. This method accepts two arguments: the id of the item to update and that item's new priority.

```
// remove, and return, the top element in the heap
PQueue.prototype.removeTop = function() {
    if (this.heap.length>0) {
        var result = this.heap[0].data;
        delete this.map[this.heap[0].id];
        delete this.heap[0];
        this.heap[0] = this.heap[this.heap.length-1];
        this.heap[0].pos = 0;
        this.heap.splice(this.heap.length-1, 1);
        this.$filterDown(0);
        return result;
    } else {
        return false;
    }
}
```

The `removeTop` method.

The removeTop method does not accept any arguments and simply returns the topmost element in the queue (which is always the element with the lowest priority value, or if there are multiple items sharing that priority, the one that's been in the queue longer). If you get this chapter's files from the web site (http://www.wheelmaker.org) there is an example of a pQueue in action.

Graphs

The last type of data structure you're going to learn about in this chapter is the graph data structure. A graph is used to store data about how objects are connected. The elements that make up a graph are nodes and vertices (also known as edges). The vertices explain how the various nodes are connected. In addition to explaining the link, a vertex can also have a weight, which signifies the "distance" between the two nodes. Obviously this doesn't have to signify actual physical distance, but that is a common use for weights.

Graphs come in two main flavors: directed and nondirected. In a directed graph you might be able go from node A to node B, but you might not be able to go back from node B to node A. That is, each vertex only explains a single direction of travel. In a nondirected graph all vertices are bi-directional. (see Figure 15.8).

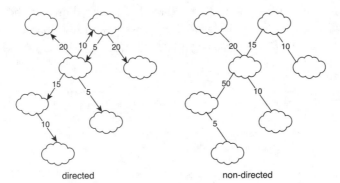

directed   non-directed

Figure 15.8 Directed and nondirected graphs.

Graphs are traditionally implemented in two-dimensional data structure. If such a structure were to be drawn out, it would look like this:

	Washington	**Baltimore**	**New York**
Washington	0	50	250
Baltimore	50	0	200
New York	250	200	0

The rows represent where you are coming from and the columns where you are going. The values in the grid are the weights for that connection; in this case that's the number of miles between the nodes. You may have spotted that the array is just a reflection of itself across that line of 0s. This shows that this graph is in fact of the nondirected variety.

Graphs are great data structures to have anytime you need to represent the spatial relationship between items. My personal favorite use of a graph is a project I had to do while I was in college. I had to use a graph to power a program that would play the Six Degrees to Kevin Bacon Game™ (http://www.endlessgames.com). If you haven't heard of it, this game makes you try to figure out how to go from any actor or actress to Kevin Bacon in six or less steps. Each step consists of linking the actor to another actor via a movie they were in together. For example, if you wanted to link Julia Roberts to Kevin Bacon, you could link them directly, because they were both in the movie *Flatliners*. Or you could take a longer route and link Julia Roberts via Cher (they were in *Pret-a-Porter* together), who was in *Mayor of Sunset Strip* with Kevin Bacon.

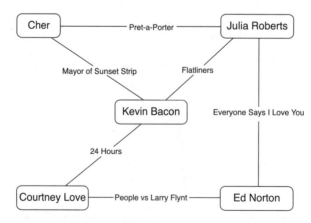

Figure 15.9   The "Kevin Bacon Game"™ as a graph.

In this case the nodes are all the actors, and the vertices are the movies in which they co-starred. To complete this project I had to implement a well-known algorithm for finding the shortest path between any two items in a graph known as Dijkstra's algorithm. Dijkstra's algorithm is of note because when it's done it tells you the shortest path between each source node and every other node!

Here is an implementation of a graph prototype object. The `findPaths` method uses Dijkstra's algorithm to find and return the distance and paths from any one node to all the others:

```
#include "PQueue.as"

// constructor
_global.Graph = function(nonDirected) {
   this.nonDirected = nonDirected;
   this.nodes = new Object();
}

// adds a new node to the graph
Graph.prototype.addNode = function(name, info) {
   if (this.nodes[name] == null) {
      this.nodes[name] = new Object();
      this.nodes[name].info = info;
      this.nodes[name].vertices = new Object();
      this.nodes[name].vertices[name] = new Object();
      this.nodes[name].vertices[name].weight = 0;
      return true;
   } else {
      return false;
   }
}

// removes a node from the graph
Graph.prototype.removeNode = function(name) {
   delete this.nodes[name];
   for (var i in this.nodes) {
      delete this.nodes[i].vertices[name];
   }
}

// adds a vertex to the graph
Graph.prototype.addVertex = function(node_a, node_b, weight, info) {
   if (weight == null) {
      var weight = 1;
   }
   this.nodes[node_a].vertices[node_b] = new Object();
   this.nodes[node_a].vertices[node_b].weight = weight;
   this.nodes[node_a].vertices[node_b].info = info;
   if (this.nonDirected) {
```

continues

```
      this.nodes[node_b].vertices[node_a] = this.nodes[node_a].vertices[node_b];
    }
}

// removes a vertex from the graph
Graph.prototype.removeVertex = function(node_a, node_b) {
    delete this.nodes[node_a].vertices[node_b];
    if (this.nonDirected) {
        delete this.nodes[node_b].vertices[node_a];
    }
}

// get the info stored in a particular node
Graph.prototype.getNode = function(node) {
    return this.nodes[node].info;
}

// get the info stored in a particular vertex
Graph.prototype.getVertex = function(node_a, node_b) {
    return this.nodes[node_a].vertices[node_b].info;
}

// find all of the paths between the source node and all
// other nodes in the graph
// return both the distances and the path
Graph.prototype.findPaths = function(source) {
    var settled = new Object();
    var pq = new PQueue();
    var estimates = new Object();
    var path = new Object();
    var p;
    var dist;
    var curr;
    var oldDist, newDist;
    for (p in this.nodes) {
        estimates[p] = pq.insert(p, Number.MAX_VALUE);
        path[p] = null;
    }
    pq.setPriority(estimates[source], 0);
    while (!pq.isEmpty()) {
        dist = pq.getTop();
        curr = pq.removeTop();
        settled[curr] = dist;
        for (p in this.nodes[curr].vertices) {
            oldDist = pq.getPriority(estimates[p]);
            newDist = dist+this.nodes[curr].vertices[p].weight;
            if (newDist<oldDist) {
```

```
            pq.setPriority(estimates[p], newDist);
            path[p] = curr;
        }
      }
   }
   return {distances:settled, path:path};
}
```

A graph data structure implementation.

You'll see that the first line of the code is to include Pqueue.as, which is the priority queue code given earlier. Using a graph created from this object is easy. You use addNode to create nodes, addVertex to create vertices and findPaths to find all the paths from a source node. When you create a graph, you can specify that you want it to be a nondirected graph, and it will handle that option for you as well.

```
map = new Graph();
map.addNode("atlanta");
map.addNode("new york");
map.addNode("detroit");
map.addNode("san francisco");
map.addNode("london");
map.addNode("paris");
map.addNode("lisbon");

map.addVertex("atlanta", "new york", 900);
map.addVertex("new york", "detroit", 600);
map.addVertex("san francisco", "atlanta", 2500);
map.addVertex("new york", "london", 3000);
map.addVertex("new york", "paris", 4000);
map.addVertex("paris", "lisbon", 750);
map.addVertex("detroit", "atlanta", 700);
map.addVertex("paris", "atlanta", 3500);

origin = "san francisco";
result = map.findPaths(origin);

for (var i in result.path){
   stops = new Array();
   current = i;
   stops.unshift(current);
   while (result.path[current] != null){
```

continues

```
            current = result.path[current];
        stops.unshift(current);
    }
    if (stops.length > 1){
        trace(origin+"  —> "+i);
        trace("--------------------------------");
        trace(result.distances[i]+" miles");
        trace("route: "+stops.toString());
        trace(" ");
    }
}
```

Creating and manipulating a **Graph** *object.*

One thing to note is that the findPaths method returns an object that has two properties, distances and path. The distances property is just an object containing a key for each node the origin can reach with the value being the distance from the origin to that node. The path property is also an object where the keys are the nodes that are reachable from the origin; however the data stored for each one of these keys is a bit tricky—it's the name of the node that you have to travel from in order to go from the origin to the current node in the least distance. Essentially you are backtracking through the path.

Conclusion

In this chapter you've scraped the surface of data structures, and you can see that it's a large field of study. Now that you have a better understanding of data structures, I highly recommend you learn more about them on your own. The more ways you know how to structure your data, the easier you will find it to figure out the tough programming challenges you are presented with. Remember, oftentimes the solution to a problem is easy to find once your information is organized.

16

Useful Code and Handy Ideas

By Branden J. Hall

Knot a Problem

I spent a large part of my time as a kid in the Boy Scouts. Most of my summers were spent earning merit badges, learning first aid, and so on. One of the big skills to learn, at least in my troop, was knot tying. I don't know how long I spent learning to tie bowlines, sheet bends, monkey's fists, and hitches. At the time, I just sort of did it without thinking about it. I mean, I was a Boy Scout, so I learned to tie knots.

Fast forward now to Christmas 2001…my wife Patti and I decided that it would be nice to get a Christmas tree for the first time together. So it was my job one Saturday in mid-December to go out and buy the tree. I finally found a place relatively nearby and found a tree that was nice and would actually fit in the living room of our little Cape Cod house. Unfortunately though, we also happen to have a small car, and the tree wouldn't fit inside of it. I had to do the old strap-it-to-the-roof-with-twine bit.

For some reason, at the exact moment I was tying the beast to the roof of the car, I remembered how to tie a taut-line hitch, a knot that you can tighten up without worrying about it loosening on you. In just a couple of minutes I had the tree tight on the roof, and in a few more I was home and it was resting on our front porch waiting for me to fit it into the stand.

It's wonderful when you have the right knowledge at just the right time!

Introduction

Just like when I was learning knots, you tend not to know the value of knowledge when you are learning it. It's only with experience using that knowledge that you see it for its true power.

This chapter is all about that kind of information—the good stuff that people usually just pick up along the way and only later realize its value. These are some of the gems of ActionScript and often, programming in general.

This chapter is going to bounce all over the place— recursion, optimization, physics—you name it, so hold on for the ride!

Recursion

Recursion is one of those topics that you can learn in 10 minutes but not fully understand for months. Even then you may still not use it to its full potential for years. It's one of those simple ideas that is more powerful than it ever seems.

The whole idea behind recursion is that by dividing a problem into smaller and smaller pieces it's easier to solve; the old divide and conquer gag. A recursive function does this by calling itself with different parameters until the problem is solved.

The classic textbook example of recursion is finding the factorial of a number (which honestly, is actually a really bad use of recursion, because it is easily solved using iterative or simple loop-based methods). In case you don't know, the factorial of a number is the result of multiplying a number by each of the numbers less than itself. For example, the factorial of 3 (which is represented by 3!) is the result of 3 * 2 * 1, and equals 6.

To solve this problem with recursion, take a look at the problem and see how to break it down. What's the factorial of N? N * (N-1)!? Okay, then what's the factorial of N-1? N-1 * (N-2)!, and so on?

You keep passing the buck until N equals 1, and at that point you know that the rules say that the factorial of 1 is 1 and the recursion ends.

```
function factorial(n){
    if (n == 1){
        return 1;
    }else{
        return n * factorial(n-1);
    }
}
```

A simple recursive function.

Figure 16.1 shows a map of what happens if you call this function asking for the factorial of 3.

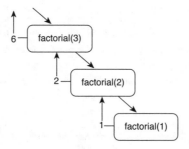

Figure 16.1 Recursively solving for the factorial of 3.

I'm sure you agree that recursion is a pretty neat idea. It can come in really handy in certain situations; the problem is figuring out what those situations are.

The types of problems that lend themselves to recursive solutions are those that are self-similar. That is, you can break down the parts of the problem into smaller versions of the over-all problem. One example of this is tree traversal (see Chapter 15, "Data Structures: Sculpting Information To Suit Your Needs," for more information on tree structures). Say you had a tree where each node had references for two other nodes, left and right, as well as value. If you wanted to do any kind of traversal of the tree, you could easily do so with a recursive function. For example, here's a function that, given a node at which to start, finds the sum of all the nodes beneath it:

```
function sumNodes (node){
    var sum = 0;
    if (node != null){
        sum += node.value;
        sum += sumNodes(node.left);
        sum += sumNodes(node.right);
    }
    return sum;
}
```

A recursive function to find the sum of a tree of values.

One thing that's important to note about this function is that it declares sum as a local variable via var. If var isn't there, the function doesn't work properly because each call to sumNodes would share a single copy of that variable. Be sure you make any variables you use inside a recursive function local to that function, otherwise your code will break.

Another important point to notice in this code and in the code for the factorial function is that there is always a way out. That is, there's always a way for the function to be called and *not* call itself. In the preceding case when the node passed to sumNodes doesn't exist, the function exits. If you don't have such a condition in a recursive function you'll end up with an infinite loop and the Flash player will stop running your code. Be very conscious of this fact and be sure you test any recursive function you write to make sure it never gets stuck in such a loop.

For more information, see Chapter 11, "Debugging: Annoying Bugs and Where to Find Them."

Anytime you have a tree structure, recursion is going to come in handy. For example, there's a built-in object in ActionScript that's based around tree structures, XML!

In fact, with a small recursive function you can take an XML object and print its resulting XML document to the Output window.

```
function printXML(node, ws) {
    // first see if this is normal node or a text node
    // if it is a normal node, it has a nodeName property
    if (node.nodeName != null) {
        var str = "<" + node.nodeName;
        var i, prop;
        // loop through the attributes of the node
        for (prop in node.attributes) {
            str += " " + prop + "='" + node.attributes[prop] + "'";
        }
        var child = node.firstChild;
        // see if this node has any child nodes
        if (child) {
            trace(ws + str + ">");
            // loop through the child nodes
            while (child) {
                printXML(child, ws + "    ");
                child = child.nextSibling;
            }
            trace(ws + "</" + node.nodeName + ">");
        } else {
            trace(ws + str + "/>");
        }
    } else {
        trace(ws + node.nodeValue);
    }
}
```

A recursive XML printer.

One of the coolest things about this function is that it even manages to print the XML with proper indenting. It does this by passing around a special variable, ws, to represent the white space that should be printed before a node's information. Every time printXML is called it adds a set amount of white space, so hence each "level" in the XML has been "tabbed in" the proper amount.

```
var xmlData = new XML();
xmlData.ignoreWhite = true;
xmlData.onLoad = function(success) {
    if (success) {
        printXML(this.firstChild);
    } else {
        trace("Error loading XML.");
    }
};
xmlData.load("SomeXMLDoc.xml");
```

Code that calls the recursive printer.

Again, recursion is one of those things you just have to play with to fully "get," so start playing. (Just be careful if you are using it in production work—one infinite loop in a production piece can ruin your day!)

Physics

After playing with ActionScript for a bit, almost everyone seems to want to try to create realistic motion with ActionScript. There's just something appealing about creating really nice motion all with code.

Simple Motion

One of the most common types of motion you see is simple code-driven easing using a type of math known as Zeno's paradox. The idea is that you know your position and you know the position of the goal. During each frame the target moves halfway between itself and the goal. The result is a nice, but easy to program, easing motion.

```
ball_mc.goal_x = 100;
ball_mc.goal_y = 100;
ball_mc.easing = .5;
ball_mc.onEnterFrame = function(){
    this._x += (this.goal_x - this._x) * this.easing;
    this._y += (this.goal_y - this._y) * this.easing;'
}
```

Basic easing with ActionScript.

The easing variable can be any number between 0 and 1. The closer to 1 the variable is, the faster it will go.

You can take this concept a bit further. Track the speed of the object in each frame and allow the `ball_mc` to keep some of its speed from the previous frame; you can actually create elastic type motion:

```
ball_mc.goal_x = 100;
ball_mc.goal_y = 100;
ball_mc.damping = .8;
ball_mc.easing = .5;
ball_mc.speed_x = 0;
ball_mc.speed_y = 0;
ball_mc.onEnterFrame = function(){
    this.speed_x = this.speed_x*this.damping+(this.goal_x-this._x)*this.easing;
    this.speed_y = this.speed_y*this.damping+(this.goal_y-this._y)*this.easing;
    this._x += this.speed_x;
    this._y += this.speed_y;
}
```

Elastic "bouncy" motion.

Notice that the only real differences in this code are that you keep track of the speed each frame, and part of that speed is a percentage of the last frame's speed.

The damping variable limits how much elasticity the object has. As this value approaches 1, there will be more and more "bounciness."

Zero-Energy Systems

After you have a handle on elasticity, you can do some interesting things with it. One of my personal favorite tricks is what I refer to as zero-energy systems. The idea is that if you have a series of five movieclips, you can make them grow and shrink on rollover in an elastic fashion, but the actual space they take up all together never changes, only their relative sizes (see Figure 16.2).

This is done in three steps. First, the code that handles the "bounciness" of boxes; making sure they always try to return to their base size.

The second step is the code that keeps the boxes all proper distance from each other. This code just aligns the clips next to each other by measuring the previous clip's position and size.

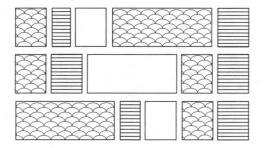

Figure 16.2 The relative size of the movieclips changes but not their total size.

Finally, there's the code attached to each clip that gives it a "boost," making it grow larger on rollover. The secret to making the whole system of movieclips never grow as a whole is to cancel out the "boost" added to the one movieclip with an equal amount "anti-boost" added to every *other* clip in the system. So, if there are five clips in the system and I add a boost of 20 to one of them, I then need to add an anti-boost of −5 to the four other clips. (20 − 5 − 5 − 5 − 5 = 0)

In this example, it's assumed that there are five movieclips on the stage named box0_mc, box1_mc, box2_mc, box3_mc, and box4_mc.

```
baseSize = 50;
damping = .6;
easing = .5;

boxes = new Array(box0_mc, box1_mc, box2_mc, box3_mc, box4_mc);
max = boxes.length;
for (i=0; i<max; ++i){
    box = boxes[i];
    box.speed = 0;
    box.num = i;
    box.max = max;
    box.boost = 40;
    box.antiboost = -box.boost / (max -1)
    box.onRollOver = function(){
        this.onEnterFrame = function(){
            for (i = 0; i< this.max; ++i){
                if (i == this.num){
                    this.speed += this.boost;
                }else{
                    this._parent.boxes[i].speed += this.antiboost;
                }
```

continues

```
            }
          }
        }
        box.onDragOver = box.onRollOver;

        box.onRollOut = function(){
            this.onEnterFrame = undefined;
        }
        box.onDragOut = box.onRollOut;
        box.trackAsMenu = true;
    }

    onEnterFrame = function(){
        var box;
        for (var i=0; i<max; ++i){
            box = boxes[i];
            box.speed = box.speed*damping + (baseSize - box._width) *easing;
            box._width += box.speed;
            if (i > 0){
                box._x = boxes[i-1]._x + boxes[i-1]._width + 5;
            }
        }
    }
```

A basic zero-energy system.

You can take this same idea and apply it to two dimensions to create "bouncy" grids as well! You can see a "classic" implementation of this at `http://yugop.com/ver2/works/typospace3.html`.

Equation-Based Movement

One of the advantages of all the methods for moving clips around shown so far is that, while the clip is moving, you can modify the "goal" and the clip will adjust. The problem with this though is that you have no direct control over how long the object will take to get to the goal. One nice way around this is to avoid dealing with tracking speed at all and instead base the movement on a mathematical equation.

One way to create equation-based motion is by using two variable equations where when the x is 0, the y is 0, and when the x is 1, the y is 1. See Figure 16.3 for some equations that will do the job nicely.

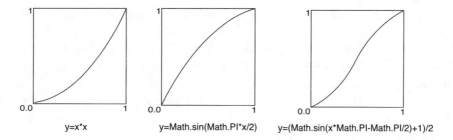

Figure 16.3 Equations for movement.

For ease of use later, stick these equations into their own methods in the `Math` object:

```
Math.easeType0 = function(t){
    return t * t;
}

Math.easeType1 = function(t){
    return Math.sin(Math.PI*t/2);
}

Math.easeType2 = function(t){
    return (Math.sin(t*Math.PI-Math.PI/2)+1)/2;
}
```

Code for movement equations.

If you look at these curves you can "see" how they will affect a movieclip's speed by understanding that the speed of the object at any given point in its animation is driven by the slope (angle) of the line at that point. If it's a slight angle the object will be moving slowly, while a steep angle will make it move quickly.

The actual code for creating the movement from these equations isn't much, but in order to handle it easier, the code is contained within a `Flair` object. (See Chapter 3, "Event Wrangling: When To Do What," for more information about the Flair design pattern). When an object is animated with this code, you tell the object where its goal is, how many frames it should take to get there, and which of the three methods above it should use to handle the easing of the object.

```
if (MovieClipFlair == null){
    _global.MovieClipFlair = new Object();
}

MovieClipFlair.MoveFlair = new Object();

MovieClipFlair.MoveFlair.snapOn = function(obj){
    // create a new "place" for this flair
    obj.$moveFlair = new Object();
    obj.$moveFlair.obj = obj;
    obj.$moveFlair.move = this.move;

}

MovieClipFlair.MoveFlair.snapOff = function(){
    // just remove this object
    delete this;
}

MovieClipFlair.MoveFlair.move = function(goal_x, goal_y, frames, meth){
    this.goal_x = goal_x;
    this.goal_y = goal_y;
    this.start_x = this.obj._x;
    this.start_y = this.obj._y;
    this.meth = meth;
    // t goes from 0 to 1 so step is how much it should increment each frame
    this.step = 1/frames;
    this.t = this.step;
    this.dist_x = goal_x - this.obj._x;
    this.dist_y = goal_y - this.obj._y;

    // the code that actually moves the object
    this.obj.onEnterFrame = function(){
        // if t > 1, exit…
        if (this.$moveFlair.t > 1){
            this._x = this.$moveFlair.goal_x;
            this._y = this.$moveFlair.goal_y;
            this.onEnterFrame = undefined;
        // otherwise adjust the position based on the easing method
        }else{
            var value = this.$moveFlair.meth(this.$moveFlair.t);
```

```
            this.$moveFlair.t += this.$moveFlair.step
            this._x = this.$moveFlair.start_x + this.$moveFlair.dist_x* value;
            this._y = this.$moveFlair.start_y + this.$moveFlair.dist_y * value;
        }
    }
}
```

A `Flair` *object to do equation based movement.*

After you have this code in a movie, you apply it like this (assuming your clip is named `foo_mc`):

```
MovieClipFlair.MoveFlair.snapOn(foo_mc);
foo_mc.$moveFlair.move(400, 450, 20, Math.easeType2);
```

Moving foo_mc to 400, 450 over 20 frames.

As you can see, the first two arguments of `move` are the goal x and y. The third argument is how many frames you would like it to take and the final argument is a reference to the easing equation you'd like to use.

This is just one way to control movement with equations; there are numerous other methods. Robert Penner has developed a particularly nice one (`http://www.robertpenner.com`), make sure you check it out.

Math Tricks

It's often the case that all you need in order to make a program work is a tiny math equation. You know that you could sit down and easily work it out on paper, but making the same thing work in ActionScript is often a royal pain. The following is a collection of the most common ActionScript related math problems and their solutions.

Pick a Number...

One question you see from time to time on the various Flash boards and mailing lists is how to pick between either 1 or −1 randomly. Most solutions you see for this are multiline monsters, so here are a couple of choices that take up but one line of ActionScript:

```
n = 1 - Math.round(Math.random()) * 2;
```

or

```
n = Math.random() < .5 ? 1 : -1;
```

Shuffle

Another question you'll see pop up occasionally is how to create a non-repeating but random array of values. The only thing you need to do is to think of how you shuffle a deck of cards. You randomly choose two cards from the deck and then swap their positions in the deck. You do that enough and you have a shuffled deck!

```
Array.prototype.shuffle = function(times){
    var max = this.length;
    var a, b, temp;
    while (times--){
        a = Math.floor(Math.random() * max);
        b = Math.floor(Math.random() * max);
        temp = this[a];
        this[a] = this[b];
        this[b] = temp;
    }
}
```

*Shuffle method of for **Array** objects.*

Now you only have to specify how many swaps you want to do when you call this method!

Radians <-> Degrees

Parts of ActionScript use radians (such as `Math.sin` and `Math.cos`) and other parts use degrees (`mc._rotation`). If you need to convert between the two, here's how:

```
D = r * 180 / Math.PI;
```

Converting from radians to degrees.

```
R = d * Math.PI / 180;
```

Converting from degrees to radians.

One additional issue you may run into is that you'll sometimes get angles that are negative or over 360. There is a really easy way to fix such angles though:

```
angle = ((angle %= 360 ) < 0) ? angle + 360 : angle;
```

I often wrap this code into a custom add-on to the Math object like this:

```
Math.fixAngle = function(angle){
    return ((angle %= 360 ) < 0) ? angle + 360 : angle;
}
```

This code looks a bit goofy, but it does work perfectly fine. First, the ? and : signs make up what is known as the tertiary operator, which is just a fancy way of doing an if...else statement. The code before the ? is the condition, the code after the ? is the code to execute if the condition is true, and the code after the : is the code to execute if the condition is false.

As you can see, the condition is ((angle %= 360) < 0). This first bit sets angle equal to itself modulus 360 (angle %= 360 could be expanded to angle = angle % 360). Modulus calculates the remainder from even division. For example, if angle was 365 then angle could divide into 360 once with a remainder of 5, hence the result of angle % 360 would be 5. This quickly brings angle into the range of −359 to 359.

If the resulting angle is less than 0, then 360 is added to it, otherwise if the angle is positive it is returned.

Find the Angle

Back in the days of Flash 4, you had to do all sorts of nasty scripting to figure out the angle between two points; now it's much easier and in fact only takes one method.

The Math.atan2 method accepts two arguments, the change in y and the change in x. It then returns the resulting angle in radians. So say you have two points, x1/y1 and x2/y2 and you want to find the angle from x1/y1 to x2/y2:

```
angle = Math.atan2(y2 - y1 , x2 - x1);
```

Finding the angle between two points.

Then, if needed, just use the preceding equations to convert to degrees. Just be careful if you are going to use this to affect the angle of a movieclip on the stage because 0 degrees in terms of atan2 points up, while in relation to movieclips it points to the right. You can adjust for this by subtracting 90 from the angle you get out of atan2 (after you convert to degrees of course).

Using All the Stage

One extremely neat new object in Flash MX is the Stage object. It gives you full control over the main stage, including scaling mode and alignment. You can use this to do all sorts of things, but one of the most valuable is to create a movie that can automatically modify its layout if the user resizes the browser in which the .swf movie is living.

This technique is based around you having the embed options for the movie set to display the .swf at 100% for both dimensions (percent, not pixels). After you know your publish settings are set up correctly (that option is in the HTML tab of the Publish Settings window) hop into your ActionScript panel and add this to the main Timeline:

```
Stage.scaleMode = "noscale";
Stage.align = "LT";
Stage.addListener(this);
onResize = function() {
    ...
}
```

Using the whole stage by capturing when it's resized.

Optimization Techniques

One common complaint about ActionScript is that it is slow, and in all fairness, compared to compiled languages such as C++, it really is slow. However, a lot of the perceived slowness of Flash can be either optimized or hidden away with not all that much work on your part! In fact, with the exception of heavy computational work, any major slow down in your movies is usually a sign of a major design flaw—either in the algorithms you use or your data structures.

Use Local Variables

When at all possible, use var to create local variables within a function. This allows Flash to look up the value of that variable much quicker. Just be sure that you don't have a var statement within a loop, this just wastes CPU time! Declare the variable as local outside the loop and then just access it directly within the loop.

Optimizing Loops

It's a pretty standard axiom of programming that your program is going to spend 90% of the time in only 10% of the code. Most of that fraction of code is, you guessed it, loops! You can get some serious speed improvements just by optimizing the main loops in your movie.

The biggest improvement you can make is to *not* calculate anything in the loop that you don't have to. For example, if I was looping through an array named list, I could do this:

```
for (i=0; i<list.length; ++i){
  ...
}
```

However, this would make the loop calculate the length of the list each turn! Do this instead:

```
var max = list.length;
for (i=0; i<max; ++i){
  ...
}
```

The same holds true for any kind of operation within a loop; if you can take it outside of the loop, do so!

Also, if you need to run a loop that can start at a positive integer and ends on 0, here's the most efficient loop you can have:

```
max = list.length;
while (max--){
  ...
}
```

An efficient way to loop from a positive integer down to 0.

Shortcut Variables

Sometimes you will end up with a big long nasty reference like this:

```
this._parent.info[foo].clip[myName];
```

If you are referring to that same variable more than once though, you are making Flash do more work than it has to. Each time you run that string to ActionScript, it has to do a lot of work to spit back the resulting object. Why not just calculate it once and store the result in a temporary "shortcut" variable?

```
tempPortrait = this._parent.family[genus].species[dog].portrait;
```

Conclusion

The tips, tricks, and algorithms discussed in this chapter should go a long way in helping you solve a lot of the everyday problems you encounter while developing ActionScript. However, this is far from an exhaustive list of such valuable nuggets of ActionScript knowledge. For a growing list of this info and any updates to the sample code, be sure you check out this book's web site at http://www.wheelmaker.org/.

Index

Solutions from experts you know and trust.

www.informit.com

New Riders has partnered with **InformIT.com** to bring technical information to your desktop. Drawing on New Riders authors and reviewers to provide additional information on topics you're interested in, **InformIT.com** has free, in-depth information you won't find anywhere else.

- **Master the skills you need, when you need them**
- **Call on resources from some of the best minds in the industry**
- **Get answers when you need them, using InformIT's comprehensive library or live experts online**
- **Go above and beyond what you find in New Riders books, extending your knowledge**

As an **InformIT** partner, **New Riders** has shared the wisdom and knowledge of our authors with you online. Visit **InformIT.com** to see what you're missing.

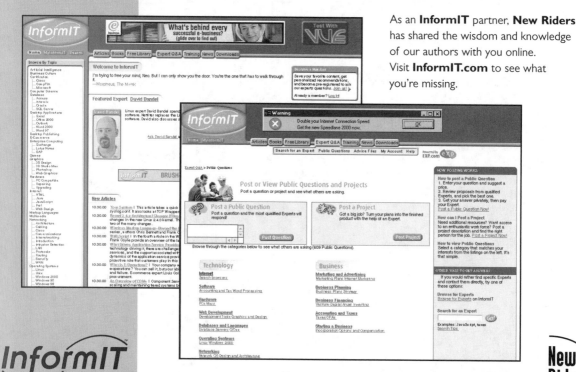

H O W   T O   C O N T A C T   U S

VISIT OUR WEB SITE

W W W . N E W R I D E R S . C O M

On our Web site you'll find information about our other books, authors, tables of contents, indexes, and book errata. You will also find information about book registration and how to purchase our books.

EMAIL US

Contact us at this address: **nrfeedback@newriders.com**

- If you have comments or questions about this book
- To report errors that you have found in this book
- If you have a book proposal to submit or are interested in writing for New Riders
- If you would like to have an author kit sent to you
- If you are an expert in a computer topic or technology and are interested in being a technical editor who reviews manuscripts for technical accuracy

- To find a distributor in your area, please contact our international department at this address. **nrmedia@newriders.com**

- For instructors from educational institutions who want to preview New Riders books for classroom use. Email should include your name, title, school, department, address, phone number, office days/hours, text in use, and enrollment, along with your request for desk/examination copies and/or additional information.
- For members of the media who are interested in reviewing copies of New Riders books. Send your name, mailing address, and email address, along with the name of the publication or Web site you work for.

BULK PURCHASES/CORPORATE SALES

The publisher offers discounts on this book when ordered in quantity for bulk purchases and special sales. For sales within the U.S., please contact: Corporate and Government Sales (800) 382-3419 or **corpsales@pearsontechgroup.com**. Outside of the U.S., please contact: International Sales (317) 581-3793 or **international@pearsontechgroup.com**.

WRITE TO US

New Riders Publishing
201 W. 103rd St.
Indianapolis, IN 46290-1097

CALL US

Toll-free (800) 571-5840 + 9 + 7477
If outside U.S. (317) 581-3500. Ask for New Riders.

FAX US

(317) 581-4663

Publishing the Voices that Matter

OUR AUTHORS

PRESS ROOM

| web development | design | photoshop | new media | 3-D | server technologies |

EDUCATORS

ABOUT US

CONTACT US

You already know that New Riders brings you the **Voices that Matter**.

But what does that mean? It means that New Riders brings you the

Voices that challenge your assumptions, take your talents to the next

level, or simply help you better understand the complex technical world

we're all navigating.

Visit **www.newriders.com** to find:

- ▸ 10% discount and free shipping on all purchases
- ▸ Never before published chapters
- ▸ Sample chapters and excerpts
- ▸ Author bios and interviews
- ▸ Contests and enter-to-wins
- ▸ Up-to-date industry event information
- ▸ Book reviews
- ▸ Special offers from our friends and partners
- ▸ Info on how to join our User Group program
- ▸ Ways to have your Voice heard

New Riders

WWW.NEWRIDERS.COM

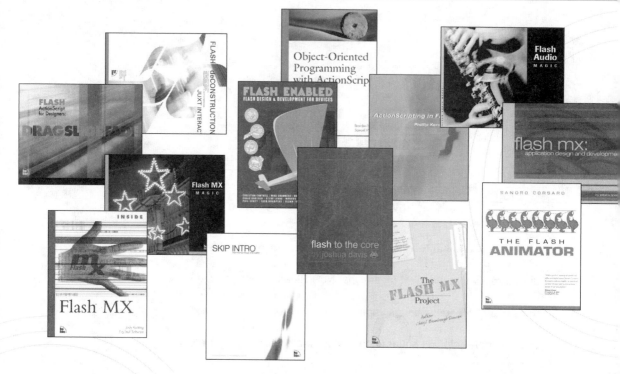